Yale French Studies

NUMBER 127

Animots:
Postanimality in
French Thought

SPECIAL EDITORS: MATTHEW SENIOR, DAVID L. CLARK, AND CARLA FRECCERO

Yale French Studies

Matthew Senior, David L. Clark, and Carla Freccero,
  Special editors for this issue
Alyson Waters, *Managing editor*
Editorial board: Alice Kaplan (Chair), R. Howard
  Bloch, Ian Curtis, Edwin Duval, Elizabeth Hebbard,
  Thomas Kavanagh, Christopher L. Miller, Maurice
  Samuels, Christopher Semk, Yue Zhuo
Editorial assistant: Laura B. Jensen
Editorial office: 82-90 Wall Street, Room 308
Mailing address: P.O. Box 208251, New Haven,
  Connecticut 06520-8251
Sales and subscription office:
Yale University Press, P.O. Box 209040
Hew Haven, Connecticut 06520-0940

Designed by James J. Johnson and set in Trump
  Medieval Roman by Newgen North America.
  Printed in the United States of America by Sheridan
  Books, Ann Arbor, Michigan.

ISSN 044-0078
ISBN for this issue 978-0-300-20665-4

MATTHEW SENIOR, DAVID L. CLARK,
AND CARLA FRECCERO

Editors' Preface: *Ecce animot*: Postanimality from Cave to Screen

In "The Animal That Therefore I Am" (1999), Jacques Derrida coined the portmanteau word *animot* as a challenge and an alternative to *l'animal*, the collective singular noun habitually used to group all animal species together into a single homogeneous category opposable to Man. In contrast to this general singular, the phonetically plural *animot* signifies, "a heterogeneous multiplicity of the living," which cannot be separated from the human by a single indivisible line.[1] Encountering the diversified mass of the *animot*, the human is confronted with multiple forms of life, highly differentiated among themselves, separated from each other and from human animals by complex, layered borders that are at once "intimate" and "abyssal." An outspoken critic of continualism in biology, Derrida declares his intention to "complicate," "thicken," "delinearize," "fold," and "divide" such boundaries, thus opening up for exploration an intermediary, hybrid realm between nature and culture.[2]

A banal incident from daily life gives rise to the *animot*: On the way to the shower, Derrida encounters his cat. Standing naked before the animal, he feels a vague, inexplicable sense of shame, an *animalséance*, although, clearly, the cat must be totally indifferent to human prudishness and fastidiousness. The gaze of the cat reveals, nonetheless, a penetrating yet obscure intelligence. The philosopher feels he is in the presence of a "seer," "a visionary," an "extralucid blind person." The cat is "innocent," "cruel," "good and evil,"

---

1. Jacques Derrida, "The Animal That Therefore I Am (More to Follow)" in *The Animal That Therefore I Am*, ed. Marie-Louise Mallet, trans. David Will (New York: Fordham University Press, 2008), 31.
2. Ibid., 29.

YFS 127, *"Animots": Postanimality in French Thought*, ed. Senior, Clark, and Freccero, © 2015 by Yale University.

"uninterpretable," "unreadable," "entirely other."[3] This totally other perspective, from before the dawn of human guilt and consciousness, inspires Derrida to take his stand, autobiographically, before the animal: "*Ecce animot*, that is the announcement of which I am (following) something like the trace, assuming the title of an autobiographical animal, in the form of a risky, fabulous, or chimerical response to the question: 'But as for me, who am I (following)?'"[4]

In addition to signifying a plurality and an alterity that defy human understanding, *animot* makes explicit the fact that the being of the animal always passes through the medium of words. The neologism suggests, very broadly, that the animal, the figural, and the discursive have something important and generative in common. The encounter with the animal produces language from the human side, but also signs, traces, and *responses* from the animal side. *Animot* thus means granting a kind of language to animals and developing subtle, poetic expressions that capture the proximity yet separateness of humans and animals, arising in moments when animal movements, paths, and sounds intersect with human displacements and language. Derrida argues, at various points throughout this essay, that such moments of figurative working-through of the relationship between humans and animals are productive of the meaning of "living," "speaking," "dying," "being," and "world."[5] Man's "becoming subject," "emergence out of nature," "sociality," and "access to knowledge and technics" are all embedded in myths and metaphors related to animals.[6] All of these key words in Western philosophy are thus, in an important sense, *animots*, created in the presence of animals and susceptible to the kind of deconstruction and revision that occur when Derrida examines the aporias of nakedness, shame, and human disability under the gaze of a cat.

The publication of "The Animal That Therefore I Am" in 1999, as part of the proceedings of the 1997 Cerisy Conference devoted to "The Autobiographical Animal" was a moment of synthesis and new departures for Derrida and for animal studies in France. There had been a long tradition of reflection on the human-animal relationship in modern French thought, dating back to Alexandre Kojève's lec-

3. Ibid., 6.
4. Ibid., 48.
5. Ibid., 10.
6. Ibid., 45.

tures on Hegel in the 1930s and the antihumanist tradition these lectures inspired. The publication of Élisabeth de Fontenay's *Le silence
des bêtes* in 1998, followed by Derrida's three essays on animality and
two volumes of *The Beast and the Sovereign*, suggest, however, that
the animal question had reached a critical juncture, for theoretical as
well as historical reasons.

Two crises in the 1980s and 1990s contributed to the urgency
with which these works were written and received by a wider public. The bovine spongiform encephalopathy epidemic of 1986–96 and
the cloning of Dolly the sheep in 1996 had profound reverberations
in France and Great Britain. A new threshold seemed to be crossed
with these two crises, raising the specter, simultaneously, of a lethal
epidemic and the end of natural reproduction in both animals and
humans. Psychologically, "mad cow disease," as it was called, and
cloning were last straws, apocalyptic events, states of exception, that
led to the dismantling of the traditional concepts of the human and
the animal. *La maladie de la vache folle* revived ancient associations
between contagion, animality, and madness, but the vernacular name
for this terrifying disease also hinted that it was human madness and
hubris that had produced the epidemic, and that an entirely new way
of looking at animals was called for if future ecological catastrophes
were to be avoided. In truth, Foucault had uncannily anticipated this
sobering nexus of death-dealing pathogens and life-generating technology in the closing remarks of his lectures at the *Collège de France*
(1975–1976), where he leaves his audience with the prospect of what
he calls the "excess of biopower" that threatens the future of human life. This dangerous supplement, he points out, "appears when
it becomes technologically and politically possible for man not only
to manage life but to make it proliferate, to create living matter, to
build the monster, and ultimately, to build viruses that cannot be
controlled and that are universally destructive."[7] The postanimal
means something terrifying for Foucault, a future in which biopower
morphs from making live and letting die into its dark simulacrum,
making life that makes death. In France, the critical response to the
animal-human crises of 1980s and 1990s was widespread and nuanced, resulting in the production of a rigorous and diverse body of

7. Michel Foucault, *"Society Must Be Defended": Lectures at the Collège de
France*, trans. David Macey (New York: Picador, 2003), 254.

theoretical and political work that created, effectively, a new lingua franca of bio-politics and animal studies, despite the claim by some that critical theory has contributed little to the "the way we think about nonhuman animals."[8] The production of a Continental discourse of animal studies, and more specifically a French tradition, was the result of several philosophical heritages and lines of inquiry.

One such line of thought is the tradition of radical anthropology reaching back to Marcel Mauss and George Bataille and continuing in the work of Michel Foucault, Gilles Deleuze, and Jean Baudrillard. A consistent anti- or alter-humanist current runs through the work of these thinkers, as the practices of sacrifice, symbolic exchange, and play reveal an inner core of animality in the human. Two passages from Bataille and Foucault give the measure of this animal otherness. The first example, discussed in this volume by Yue Zhuo, occurs in Bataille's commentary on a hunting scene painted on the walls of the Lascaux cave (see Figure 1). Visible on the walls of the cave are two animals, "on one side, a rhinoceros, on the other, a bison; between them, falling or supine, is a bird-headed man; below him, a bird poised on an upright stick . . . The infuriated bison's hair literally stands straight on end, it lashes its tail, intestines spill in thick ropes from a gash in its belly."[9] In Bataille's reading of this painting, the bird-headed man lying between the bison and the rhinoceros is in a religious trance, sharing in the death of the bison he has killed, assimilating the "unimpaired dignity" of the animals.

Another example of animal alterity can be found in Michel Foucault's *History of Madness*, published in 1961, in commentary on the paintings of Renaissance artists Hieronymous Bosch, Stefan Lochner,

8. In his preface to *Animal Philosophy: Ethics and Identity: Essential Readings in Continental Thought*, ed. Matthew Calarco and Peter Atterton (New York: Continuum, 2004), xii, Peter Singer questions "the philosophical traditions of Continental Europe, . . . such thinkers as Heidegger, Foucault, Levinas, and Deleuze" for having "failed to grapple with the issue of how we treat animals." The philosophers on Singer's list vary considerably in their views of the relationship between humans and nonhuman animals. Many contemporary French thinkers, including Derrida, Élisabeth de Fontenay, Vinciane Despret, Dominique Lestel, Florence Burgat, and others have argued specifically for the ethical treatment of animals. The list of authors included in Jean-Baptiste Jeangène Vimer's *Anthologie d'éthique animale: Apologies des bêtes* (Paris: PUF, 2011) includes many familiar names in the Continental tradition, among whom Theodor Adorno, Claude Lévi-Strauss, Marguerite Yourcenar, Milan Kundera, Jürgen Habermas, de Fontenay, Derrida, and Peter Sloterdijk.

9. Georges Bataille, *Lascaux; or, The Birth of Art: Prehistoric Painting*, trans. Austryn Wainhouse (Lausanne: Skira, 1955), 110.

and Matthias Grünewald. In these works, holy men are often tempted and persecuted by nightmarish animals, "screech owls with toad-like bodies mingle with the naked bodies of the damned . . . winged insects, cat-headed butterflies and sphinxes with mayfly wingcases, and birds with handed wings that instil panic . . ."[10] As in Bataille and Derrida, the animal gaze imposes an unsettling vision on the human recipient of such looking: "In an astonishing reversal, it was mankind that began to feel itself to be the object of the animal's gaze, as the animals took control and showed man his inner truth."[11]

The legacy of Foucault's sense of the animal nature of man is carried forward in Fontenay's *Le silence des bêtes*, whose title was inspired by the "archeology of silence" in *The History of Madness*. Foucault paid particular attention to the seventeenth century, when madness and reason were still in dialogue, even as reason began to impose silence on madness. Fontenay's encyclopedic volume of over 1,000 pages is a similar attempt to constitute an archeology of the silencing of animals who had had a voice in Greek and Biblical myths, and who had shared "consanguity" with humans through sacrifice, only to be silenced and cut off from humanity by the cumulative effects of Christianity, metaphysics, and technology.

Fontenay was a professor of philosophy at the Université Paris I Panthéon-Sorbonne; her work is representative of the scholarship of academic philosophers and historians, such as Robert Delort, Eric Baratay, and Michel Pastoureau.[12] In Fontenay's discipline of philosophy, two contributors to the present volume have distinguished themselves: Florence Burgat, who wrote her doctoral thesis under Fontenay, published *Animal, mon prochain* in 1997, one of the first philosophical works in France to use the concepts and terminology of the Continental tradition to advance arguments for the ethical treatment of animals.[13] Jean-Luc Guichet published *Rousseau, l'animal et*

10. Foucault *History of Madness*, trans. Jonathan Murphy and Jean Khalfa (New York: Routledge, 2006), 19.

11. Ibid., translation slightly modified.

12. Notable books by French historians include: Robert Delort, *Les animaux ou une histoire* (Paris: Seuil, 1993); Eric Baraty, *Zoos: Histoire des jardins zoologiques en occident (XVIe-XXe)* (Paris: La Découverte, 1998), *Le point de vue animal: Une autre version de l'histoire* (Paris: Seuil, 2012), *Bêtes de somme: Des animaux au service de l'homme* (Paris: Seuil, 2011); Michel Pastoureau, *L'ours: Histoire d'un roi déchu* (Paris: Seuil, 2007).

13. See Florence Burgat, *Animal, mon prochain* (Paris: Odile Jacob, 1997); *Liberté et inquiétude de la vie animale* (Paris: Klimé, 2006); *Une autre existence: La condition*

l'homme in 2006 and organized an annual seminar, between 2004–
2010, on Animality and Anthropology from the Enlightenment to
the Present at the Collège International de Philosophie, founded in
1983 by François Châtelet, Derrida, Jean-Pierre Faye, and Dominique
Lecourt. The seminar resulted in the publication of numerous works
on René Descartes, Jean-Jacques Rousseau, Denis Diderot, Georges-
Luis Leclerc (Comte de Buffon), Etienne Bonnot de Condillac and
others.[14]

Another branch of French animal studies grew out of the critiques
of science by Bruno Latour and Isabelle Stenghers. Latour published
Laboratory Life: The Social Construction of Scientific Facts (1979),
followed by *We Have Never Been Modern* (1991), and *Reassembling
the Social: An Introduction to Actor–Network Theory* (2005). Stenghers has collaborated with Latour throughout her career, publishing *La
nouvelle alliance: Metamorphose de la science* in 1979 and several
volumes of *Cosmopolitiques*. Latour and Stenghers influenced the
work of Donna Haraway and Vinciane Despret; their work is characterized by close investigations of the real conditions of animals in
laboratory and agricultural settings and an analysis of the biases that
creep into scientific experimentation as a result of prejudices on the
part of experimenters as well as the material conditions and protocols
scientists use to conduct their experiments and collect data.[15]

Frantz Fanon's explorations of race and animality, Achille
Mbembe's *De la postcolonie*, and Etienne Balibar's commentaries on
the animalization of the worker and the subaltern represent another
tradition of French thought related to animals that is opening new
fields of investigation, a compelling example of which would be the
collective volume *Zoos humains*, edited by Nicolas Bancel, Pascal
Blanchard, Gilles Boëtsch, Éric Deroo, and Sandrine Lemaire, which

---

animale (Paris: Klimé, 2012); and *Ahimsa: Violence et non-violence envers les animaux en Inde* (Paris: Maison des sciences de l'homme, 2014).

14. See Jean-Luc Guichet, *Rousseau, l'animal et l'homme* (Paris: Cerf, 2006);
Usages politiques de l'animalité (Paris: L'Harmattan, 2008); *Douleur animale, douleur
humaine* (Paris: Quae, 2010); *L'animal des Lumières*, special edition of *Dix-huitième
siècle*, 2010; *De l'animal-machine à l'âme des machines* (Paris: Publications de la Sorbonne, 2010); and *Problématiques animales: Théorie de la connaissance, Anthropologie, Éthique et Droit* (Paris: PUF, 2011).

15. See Vinciane Despret, *Quand le loup habitera avec l'agneau* (Paris: Les
empêcheurs de penser en rond, 2002); *Bêtes et hommes* (Paris: Gallimard, 2007); *Penser
comme un rat* (Paris: Quae, 2009); and *Que diraient les animaux si on leur posait les
bonnes questions* (Paris: La découverte, 2012).

analyzes the display of native peoples from Africa, the Pacific and other areas in colonial exhibitions held at the turn of the century in Paris, Berlin, and London.[16]

Deleuze, Derrida, and Jacques Lacan have inspired highly original work in visual animal studies as well. Beginning in 1993, with *Picturing the Beast: Animals, Identity, and Representation,* Steve Baker has published three pathbreaking works on animals in art. Akira Mizuta Lippit published *Electric Animal: Toward a Rhetoric of Wildlife* in 2000, and Jonathan Burt published the first complete study of animals in film, *Animals in Film,* in 2002. Raymond Bellour's *Le corps du cinema* (2009), referencing Deleuze, Lippit, and Burt, argues that cinema is comparable to hypnosis and communicates most essentially through the emotions, repeatedly using the animal body to achieve its hypnotic and emotive effects.[17] Another strikingly original French philosopher of the visual, Jean-Christophe Bailly, has published several important works related to the animal, most notably *Le versant animal,* in 2007.[18] Considering the role animals play in painting, photography, and film, in conveying movements, meanings, and truths that humans cannot express or discover otherwise, one could say that there is a distinct dimension of the visual that one could call *photoanimalité,* or *ciné-malité.*

POSTHUMANISM AND POSTANIMALITY

The idea that the phenomenon of man is of relatively recent date and may come to an end soon, if it has not already done so, is widespread.

16. Frantz Fanon, *Les damnés de la terre* (Paris: Maspéro, 1961); Etienne Balibar and Immanuel Wallerstein, *Race, nation, classe: Les identités ambiguës* (Paris: La Découverte, 1988); Achille Mbembe, *De la postcolonie: Essai sur l'imagination politique dans l'Afrique contemporaine* (Paris: Karthala, 2000).

17. On animals in contemporary art, see Steve Baker, *Picturing the Beast: Animals, Identity, and Representation* (Cahmpaign IL: University of Illinois Press, 1993); *The Postmodern Animal* (London: Reaktion Books, 2000); *Artist Animal* (Minneapolis: University of Minnesota Press, 2013). On animals in film, see Akira Mizuta Lippit, *Electric Animal: Toward a Rhetoric of Wildlife* (Minneapolis: Univeristy of Minnesota Press, 2000); Jonathan Burt, *Animals in Film* (London: Reaktion Books, 2002); Raymond Bellour, *Le corps du cinema* (Paris: P.O.L., 2009); and Anat Pick, *Creaturely Poetics: Animality and Vulnerability in Literature and Film* (New York, Columbia University Press, 2011).

18. Major works by Jean-Christophe Bailly include *Le versant animal* (Paris: Bayard, 2007), *La véridiction sur Philippe Lacoue-Labarthe* (Paris: Christian Bourgois, 2011), *Le parti pris des animaux* (Paris: Christian Bourgois, 2013), and *Le dépaysement : Voyages en France* (Paris: Seuil, 2012).

Some view the posthuman as an indictment of humanism and progress, following centuries of war, colonialism, genocide, and the destruction of the environment at the very time when man was reaching his maturity, according to Enlightenment ideology. Others think
a bright technological future may await posthumans, as they take up
residence in artificial bodies and minds and escape the confines of the
solar system. We propose the idea of the *postanimal* as a corollary and
accompanying phenomenon to the rise and fall of man. The "post"
of the postanimal preserves the interrogative force and irremissible
open-endedness of the question that Derrida is compelled to venture
before the deranging gaze of the animal other: "What does 'to be after'
mean?"[19] In the face of the radical precedence of the singular animal,
every answer to that question will come and will have come both too
early and too late. By postanimal we principally mean three things:
(1) The human comes after, is derived from, and follows the animal,
not only as evolution tells this story, but in non-linear and recursive
modes that unsettle the narrative form itself. This is suggested by
Derrida's pun on the double meaning of "je suis" in the title of his
essay, "L'animal que donc je suis," meaning both "the animal I am"
and "the animal I am following." (2) The traditional concept of the
animal, like that of the human, is obsolete, ideological, and oppressive. Postanimals could be those freed from the conceptual and bodily
restraints of metaphysics and technology. (3) The apocalyptic version
of the postanimal would be the *last* animal, such as can be found in
Cormac McCarthy's recent novel *The Road* (2006), which chronicles
the long struggle and disappearance of two last men (a father and his
young son) after a nuclear holocaust. McCarthy concludes his novel
with an elegy to an extinct species, the brook trout, on whose backs
once could be seen "maps and mazes. Of a thing which could not be
put back. Not be made right again. In the deep glens where they lived
all things were older than man and they hummed of mystery."[20]

FROM CAVE WALL TO SCREEN

Another glimpse of "things older than man that hummed of mystery"
is offered by the recently discovered animal paintings in the Chauvet
Cave, dating back over 30,000 years. If McCarthy's extinct brook trout
sets a somber and tragic mood for thinking the postanimal, perhaps

19. *The Animal That Therefore I Am*, 55.
20. Cormac McCarthy, *The Road* (New York: Vintage Books, 2007), 286.

Figure 1. Animal Painting, ca. 32,000–30,000 BCE. Chauvet Cave. Photo: Art Resource, NY.

the Chauvet animals may offer hopes and dreams, as alluded to by the title of Werner Herzog's moving documentary of the discovery, *Cave of Forgotten Dreams*. According to Jean Clottes, the leader of the research team that explored the cave, over four hundred images of animals are painted on the walls of the cave, but only six "indisputably" human figures. Five of these figures are schematic "pubic triangles," and the sixth is described by Clottes as "a woman's body seen from the front, reduced to the pubic triangle and the legs, associated with a strange composite creature, a bison-man."[21]

   In the Chauvet Cave, before the earliest humans created integral images of their own bodies, they painted and etched animal figures and faces onto cave walls, juxtaposed with a single, partial image of a female body. From the beginning – in the beginning – it would seem that the human came after the animal and represented herself (it is the case to say so here) as a fragmented body – a spectator, a hunter, a worshipper of moving herds of animals, which the Chauvet artists captured in multiple, overlapping images that have a proto-cinematic

21. Jean Clottes, *Chauvet Cave: The Art of Earliest Times*, trans. Paul Bahn (Salt Lke City: University of Utah Press, 2003), 195. The interpretation of this "Paleolithic Venus" is also discussed in depth in Werner Herzog's *Cave of Forgotten Dreams* (2010).

quality to them. The cave artists also used the bulges and contours of the rock to create depth, inspiring the filmmaker Werner Herzog to use 3-D cameras for the first time in his work, as though the most experimental, marginal technology were necessary to capture the haunting, enigmatic work of the first human artists.

Our volume begins with similar animal and human images, found in the Lascaux Cave in Dordogne, dating back an estimated 17,300 years, the focus of a radical rethinking of art, anthropology, and religion on the part of Georges Bataille. The discovery of this "virgin territory unscathed by World Wars and past human tragedies," as Yue Zhuo writes, revealed the obscure moment in prehistory when *homo sapiens* succeeded or followed homo *faber*, who himself had followed the higher apes. The "knowledge" that defined *homo sapiens* was a poetic knowledge of the lost animal nature of man. The first step forward into fully realized humanity was a stepping backward; the Lascaux men sought to reverse and negate the technical accomplishments of *homo faber* and return to proximity with "divine animals." "What was divine was the unknown, the sudden apparition of the animal like a bolt of lightning in the darkness, not as an object, but as a violent force suddenly rising above a flat world, facing death, beyond definition, beyond comprehension."[22]

The named and painted "critters" of medieval bestiaries, as Sarah Kay calls them in her essay in this volume, following Haraway, reveal a similar desire on the part of their authors to situate man in the company of animals. In total indifference to our modern taxonomic and morphological schemes, Kay writes, the first Latin bestiaries joined together indiscriminately "chapters on stones, plants, birds, fish, and mythical creatures like the siren, as well as on quadrupeds, reptiles, and insects." Later vernacular bestiaries such as Pierre de Beauvais' *Livre d'amour* contained definitions of the nature of man; however, according to Kay, in distinction to Giorgio Agamben's anthropological machine, "the man who figures in a vernacular bestiary is not a speech-capable animal, but a subcategory of beast." The medieval bestiary is a *zoological* machine.

The first manifestations of Renaissance humanism reveal continuities with the medieval zoological machine. In Pico della Mirandola's *Oration on the Dignity of Man* (1487), God grants to Adam the freedom to assemble whatever animal parts he chooses and "trace for

22. Yue Zhuo, "Alongside the Animals: Bataille's 'Lascaux Project,'" 30.

himself the lineaments of his own nature."[23] With Descartes, however, such Renaissance "self-humaning" takes the form of a radical exclusion of animality from the core of the self. As Derrida remarks about the *Meditations*, "Descartes proposes abstracting from his 'I am,' if I can put it this way, everything that recalls life."[24] Matthew Senior argues that Derrida continues the practice of self-humaning, but in radically anti-Cartesian fashion, searching for the definition of his own humanness in the presence of his cat, finding it meaningful and necessary to record his emotional *responses*, his *animalséance* before his cat. Guichet argues that twentieth and twenty-first century attempts such as Derrida's to erase metaphysical barriers between humans and animals can be traced to Enlightenment philosophers such as Rousseau, Diderot, and Condillac. In a sense, poststructuralism and deconstruction complete the work of these thinkers. With the coming of the Industrial Age, however, despite a newly discovered theoretical proximity between humans and animals, real animals began to disappear from humans lives: "Actual proximity has declined and the density and variety of animal presence in the immediate space of our surroundings has evaporated (household pets being an exception that does not invalidate this general trend). . . . As for the practical treatment of animals, it has never been more 'dehumanized' and ethically indefensible than it is today, because man has replaced cruelty with a ghostly form of existence." With this "ghostly" existence, we see for the first time one of the apocalyptic forms of post-animality. The animal is not extinct, but it has been dehumanized, or, in Guichet's words, "de-animalized."

Jean-Christophe Bailly is also preoccupied with animalian disappearance (he suggests that the term "beasts" might more effectively capture the affective specificities—"cries, smells, fear"—that characterize what we take to be the distance and difference between us), addressing the relationship between animals and humans by rejecting the fable of beastly talking (always, as he notes, allegorical) and approaching animal worlds instead from the point of view of those silent activities that we both do and do not share, specifically flying and sleeping. The question is how to approach the immediacy of living things, how to sense, experience, admire, observe but not clinically

---

23. Giovanni Pico della Mirandola, *Oration on the Dignity of Man*, trans. Robert Caponigri (Washington: Regnery, 1956), 7.
24. Derrida, "But as for me," in *The Animal That Therefore I Am*, 71.

something like the *umwelt* that late nineteenth-, early twentieth-century biologist and behaviorist Jacob Johann von Uexküll imagined belonging to the tick and the other animals who share our environment but not our lifeworld.[25] Bailly argues for something like a non-anthropocentric semiotics that would allow for the interpenetration of human-beast perception and that would, ultimately, open up the human to an understanding of the myriad worlds that are in existence in and around "our" world. At the same time, he argues, through an extended and lyrical description of a lynx, the "beast" remains, to us and for us, "an almost pure 'extimacy'" moving fleetingly between, outside, across the poetry—the *animots*—with which we try to capture her.

Bénédicte Boisseron, Carla Freccero, and Vinciane Despret all grapple with questions of response, respons(e)-ability, and accountability in the human "address" to animal being and what that address might have to do with animals themselves. Each tackles the question of the "material-semiotic" status of "the" animal: animal being's simultaneously representational, that is meaningful, and material presence in human lives, work, and writing. For Boisseron, Derrida's "cat" episode in *The Animal That Therefore I Am* (in its "original" instantiation as a Cerisy lecture in 1997) works as an allegory of the "A-cat-emic," the academic philosopher standing before the concentrated gaze of another, of others, seeing himself being seen, giving himself to be seen. She sets up a kind of call-and-response between Derrida's lecture and J. M. Coetzee's *The Lives of Animals*, showing how *mise-en-abyme*, indirection, and ventriloquism perform the author's question about whether the animal concerns him (*le regarde*) and his anguish at an inability to do justice to the question (of the animal, of the animal's *regard*). But Boisseron's essay also begins "after" Derrida to examine the "following" that the "post" of postanimal and postcoloniality represents. She reminds us that Jean-Paul Sartre had also been concerned with a certain gaze regarding a certain other, and that both Derrida and Sartre experience a shock, a dis-ease, a *malséance*, both *animalséance* and *noirséance*, at the experience of having already been seen and, perhaps, of not being of concern to the other—in Sartre's case, *le Nègre*—whose gaze the philosopher has so

---

25. Jacob Johann von Uexküll, *Forays into the Worlds of Animals and Humans: With a Theory of Meaning*, trans. Joseph D. O'Neill (Minneapolis: U of Minnesota Press, 2010).

recently become aware of. In a lovely brief excursus into postcolonial and Négritude deployments of the animal-human hybrid Caliban, Boisseron brings critical race theory, postcolonial studies, and animal studies into conversation on the question of that animated *animot* and the ethics of *regarder*.

Freccero's essay, "A Race of Wolves," seeks trans-historically to account for the material-semiotic dimension of animal being by examining wolves and humans as historical agents in their own right, while tracking the meaningful and embodied material and representational relationships between them. It considers the long genealogy of the relationship between humans and wolves—the former intent upon the genocide of the latter—as it finds figuration in medieval, early modern, modern, and postmodern texts. In Derrida's seminar on *The Beast and the Sovereign*, the wolf figures prominently as "wild" double of the sovereign. Both represent exceptions insofar as they are a law unto themselves, the one on the outside of the polis, the other mirroring him as the "tyrant" within. From Hobbes's famous deployment of Plautus's phrase, *"homo homini lupus"* onward, the wolf has been asked to stand in for something particularly "savage" about *man*kind, what Freccero calls, after Derrida, "carnivorous virility."[26] The wolf-human merger—most famously and, in recent US culture, affirmingly—also carries with it atavistic fantasies about racial difference that continue to impress modernity with their spectral effects. Freccero, in analyzing some of these cultural fantasies of species, race, and sexuality as they are figured textually, argues that while representation may not suffice to address and respond to animal being, it may enable alternatives to—and even undo—some of the lethal effects that representational work has performed.

Despret, invoking the terms of concern, question, response and respons-ability in a wholly different register—she is a philosopher of science, a psychologist, and an ethologist—explores the material world of human-animal relationships in the shared "laboratory" environment of the workaday world. She asks, "Do animals work?," not only providing some surprising responses to this question but also demonstrating how the effort to answer it occasions a reframing of its terms. For Despret, the question counts—the address to the animal is not allegorical, although it does involve representation.

---

26. See Freccero, "Carnivorous Virility, or Becoming-Dog," *Social Text* 106, 29/1, 177–95. Special Issue: *Interspecies*, ed. Julie Livingston and Jasbir Puar (2011).

Instead, Despret shows us, through the "experiments" (in the sense of experience as well) of sociologist and "zootechnicienne" Jocelyn Porcher, who works in the field of animal husbandry, that the Derridean supposition—"and say the animal responded?"—returns, in her case, with a resounding affirmation. In the course of her observations about breeders and animals working together—in the context of industrial and non-industrial food production—Despret matter of factly challenges her readers to rethink work itself—in part by bringing nonhumans into the illustrious history and theory of work by Marx and others—as a modality of fulfillment whose breakdown reveals what is beautiful, worthwhile, and relationship-building about it: when the cows do their work properly, she says, the whole machinery of production is rendered invisible. It is in the cows' resistance, their non-cooperation, that the failure of "work" to fulfill its purpose is revealed. Despret thus wonders less, and without anguish, about what business the philosopher/writer has in being concerned with, or being looked at by, the animal, and encourages us instead to learn a language, acquire a vocabulary, for asking good questions (and listening to the responses), so that all animals (human or otherwise) can indeed respond.

Florence Burgat examines the fate of animals in the work of two philosophers of existence: Sartre and Emmanuel Levinas. For Sartre, animals live merely at the level of the in-itself (*en-soi*); as Burgat writes, "outside of nature without being part of culture, they [animals] float in a pitiful in-between that exiles them twice over." Sartre is indifferent to animal suffering, writing with enthusiasm about the "wonders of the corrida" in letters to Simone de Beauvoir. In *The Family Idiot*, a more nuanced but still bleak account of animal consciousness appears. A domestic dog hears humans speaking about him without understanding what is said. The unhappy animal is "penetrated" by human language: "This dog passed from discomfort to rage, feeling at his expense the strange reciprocal mystification which is the relationship between man and animal."

The ethics of the face in Levinas would seem to offer a move beyond Sartrean contempt for animals, the possibility of a new ethical stance towards animals. In a 1988 interview, Levinas was pressed on the question of the animal face; he hedged, declaring himself to be against "useless" animal suffering, while still stridently affirming human exceptionalism. For Burgat, Levinas's intransigence stems from the non-phenomenal character of the human face. She writes: "The face is not the perceived face. Its transcendence does not result from its expressivity. The face is what exceeds the idea of the Other in me, what exceeds the plastic image the Other leaves in me."

In her contribution, Anat Pick tarries with a memorable wartime scene at the beginning of René Clément's 1952 neorealist film, *Les jeux interdits (Forbidden Games)*. A girl cradles the body of a little terrier who has been grievously injured in an air attack by German forces in the Battle of France. As the dog breathes its last, its body twitches involuntarily. Why is that detail so strangely affecting? As Pick suggests, this encounter between human and animal is more than calculatingly sentimentalizing, although it is certainly that too. It is also marks the place where the film is, as it were, beside itself, ambivalently taking on an evanescent and expressive creatureliness that is beyond anthropocentrism. Where cinema exposes itself to exposure, rendering itself unexpectedly vulnerable to the *partage* of animal vulnerability, it makes glancing contact with the liminal differences between human and nonhuman life, as between life and thought, fictional space and actuality, the indexical mark and the figure of the animal in the cultural imaginary. After Bailly, Pick describes that moment of betweenness as "pensivity," a cinematic mood that is neither simply human nor nonhuman.

To bring out the significance of the uncanny appearance of the animal body on film, Pick turns to a consideration of an animal encounter on the margins of archival footage of Nazi executions of Jewish men in Liepāja, Latvia in the summer of 1941. David L. Clark also examines this *film maudit*, whose horror lies partly in the depraved indifference of the assembled Latvian and German spectators for whom the public and photographed executions are a kind of beach-side social gathering. As the executioners' guns go off, a small terrier jumps briefly into the foreground, startled by retort of the rifles. Clark considers the layered meanings of the dog's advent on the scene of a murder. On the one hand, the fact that local Latvians, for whom the Jewish victims are neighbors, bring a family pet to the slayings puts to us that the SS make homicide part of the everyday of the new world order. On the other hand, in the absence of responsible human witnesses, the monstration of the dog's trembling body bears inadvertent witness to the murders. The affecting presence of the surprised animal unsettles the very idea of the testamentary, which Clark argues

is inhuman even as it is called upon to attest to the humanity of the human. The "insentient" body of the animal witness makes legible what is insentient about witnessing.

Several essays collected in this volume address the question of the vexed "comparison," "equivalence," or "analogy" between the Nazi extermination of the Jews and the killing of animals. As Pick notes elsewhere, "in post-Holocaust rhetoric, . . . human and animal, humanity and inhumanity continue to circle each other in contagious proximity."[27] More work certainly needs to be done analyzing what the figure of "comparison" both accomplishes *and* obscures, not least because of the figure's inherent and irresolvable ambiguity as a figure for figurality itself. Worry about putatively dehumanizing analogies may symptomatize an anxiety about the inhumanness of the figural turns that make those analogies possible. The history of the figure of human and animal equivalency also matters. In a 1949 lecture that he delivered in Bremen, and talking as if the catastrophe were safely behind him, Martin Heidegger claimed that the "motorized food industry" was "in essence the same as the production of corpses in gas chambers and extermination camps."[28] For French thought, outrage about the unseemliness of forming anything looking like an equivalence between the extermination of the European Jews and the killing of industrial farm animals arguably begins here. About Heidegger's remark Levinas is unequivocal: it is "beyond commentary," he says, and perhaps understandably so.[29] The P.O.W. camp in which Levinas was interned and where he was, as he says, "stripped" of his "human skin," was only forty miles from where Heidegger would make his lofty pronouncement after the war.[30] Bergen-Belsen was a few miles further away. Yet in a short autobiographical reverie about an animal encounter, Levinas experiments with bringing the thought of the two catastrophes into contiguity. In this way, he overwrites Heidegger, not by dismissing the "comparison" as grotesquely unbecoming, but by insisting that the "comparison"—if it is a "comparison"—needs to

27. *Creaturely Poetics: Animality and Vulnerability in Literature and Film* (New York: Columbia University Press, 2011), 25.

28. Martin Heidegger, *Bremen and Freiburg Lectures: Insight Into That Which Is and Basic Principles of Thinking*, trans. Andrew J. Mitchell (Bloomington: Indiana University Press, 2012), 27.

29. "As if Consenting to Horror," trans. Paula Wissing, *Critical Inquiry* 15 (Winter 1989): 487.

30. "The Name of a Dog, or Natural Rights," *Difficult Freedom: Essays on Judaism*, trans. Seán Hand (Baltimore: Johns Hopkins University Press, 1990), 153.

be made in a certain way. As Fontenay argues in "The Slaughterhouse or a Common Fate," it is possible to think the dreadful and dreaded comparison as otherwise than irresponsible. Indeed, as she points out, there is a salutary history of writers for whom there is nothing less than an *obligation* to consider Nazi violence against the Jews in the context of violence against animals, and vice versa. She evokes moments in the work of Primo Levi and Vasily Grossman, among others, in which the kinship of unregarded suffering that joins human and nonhuman animals makes its awful presence felt. In each case, a desire to insist on this bleak affinity can be traced back to childhood experiences involving the violation of animal life. Early animal encounters form an immemorial resource from which these writers draw the courage to speak of precarious life, not from some lofty perch, as Heidegger did, but from the bloody floor of the slaughterhouse of history. The Holocaust doesn't make comparisons between the killing of the Jews and of animals impossible; quite to the contrary, it activates the responsibility to bear witness to atrocity in all of its hideous forms. The worry, of course, is that speaking of the lives and deaths of animals in the same breath as the Jews who perished in the Holocaust not only degrades the lives and deaths of the Jewish victims but risks reproducing the murderously animalizing vision of the Nazis. In "Return to Sacrifice," Fontenay reverses the angle and worries aloud about the ways in which Derrida's work cheapens the lives of animals. She acknowledges the critical power of Derrida's argument that the denegation of murder, how its disavowal in plain sight, as it were, not only makes the non-criminal putting to death of others possible; it also links the institution of the subject as virilely carnivorous, i.e. as the one who accepts sacrifice and eats flesh. Imagining a differently instituted subject is difficult, Derrida suggests, because relationality remains consumptive, implicitly or explicitly a matter of ingesting and metabolizing the other. But Fontenay suggests that by generalizing the sacrificial structure, Derrida risks obliterating the singularity of the animal other that he so frankly affirms.

And yet this is the insight, in a very different critical and far more pragmatic tradition, that Haraway, Despret, and others affirm: putting to death, killing and being killed, are mortal realities. The issue for Haraway, then, is not to make the other "killable," that is, not to confer upon a being the property of being able to be killed as a constituent of its (his or hers would be better) identity, whether that identity goes by any one of a number of human and nonhuman names (and we are reminded of this especially now in the US when to be human does not at all serve as a guarantee of non-killability). Derrida too suggests that the sacrificial logic of Western carnophallogocentrism is neither inevitable nor universal; what the animation of the word of the animal might show us, then, is how to forge a subjectivity otherwise, how, finally, to achieve a posthumanism—or a postanimality—that would obviate the necessity for a culture, a socius, and a subjectivity fundamentally premised on such sacrifice.

YUE ZHUO

Alongside the Animals:
Bataille's "Lascaux Project"

Although Georges Bataille's interest in prehistoric art dates back to as early as the beginning of the 1930s, his writings and lectures on Lascaux and other cave paintings only emerged in a straightforward manner during the last nine or ten years of his life, roughly from 1952 to1961. By the time of his death in 1962, Bataille was known for having authored an accomplished art book, *La peinture préhistorique. Lascaux, ou, la naissance de l'art (Lascaux; or, The Birth of Art: Prehistoric Painting)*. Published by Editions Skira in 1955 as the first volume of an impressive series called "The Great Centuries of Painting," both in French and in English, it was also the first book to illustrate the painted rocks of Lascaux with color photographs. Because of the detailed description of the cavern and the meticulous study he devoted to some of the mural images, Bataille was quickly considered an impromptu specialist on the newly discovered cave.[1] Over the last half-century, this work has been cited, often alongside the discoveries of Henri Breuil (also known as Abbé Breuil), the famous French archaeologist and authority on cave art, as a valuable source that has contributed to the study of Paleolithic paintings and engravings.

Less known is a group of texts Bataille wrote on the same subject before and after the publication of the book, half of which remained unpublished during his lifetime, and some of which he integrated into two of his last anthropological-philosophical treatises: *L'érotisme* (*Eroticism*) and *Les larmes d'Éros* (*The Tears of Eros*). In 1979, Denis Hollier constituted a "dossier of Lascaux" in volume IX of Bataille's

---

1. Lascaux was discovered in September 1940. Bataille first visited it in the spring of 1954.

YFS 127, *"Animots": Postanimality in French Thought*, ed. Senior, Clark, and Freccero, © 2015 by Yale University.

Œuvres complètes by listing chronologically the author's dispersed writings on cave paintings and prehistoric culture,[2] and published the previously inaccessible pieces as a supplement[3] to the main book, which he also annotated and reprinted in the same volume. Thanks to the careful editorial work of Stuart Kendall and the remarkable translation by him and Michelle Kendall, all of these pieces are now available to the Anglophone reader. *The Cradle of Humanity: Prehistoric Art and Culture*, published by Zone Books in 2005, compiles in a single volume all of Bataille's shorter writings on cave culture that had not been previously translated into English.[4]

We have thus in front of us a book, and a constellation of about ten loosely connected article-length pieces dealing with the same subject. The question is, does this group of texts constitute a "Lascaux project"? In a way, these writings resemble the moving frescos[5] inside the cavern itself. Outspread, wavering, and at the same time intertwined, they attempt to grasp the same origin from different angles. This origin is not simply of art; it is of the birth of mankind as a whole. Bataille viewed Lascaux as the first true majestic sign of the appearance of art, but the "birth" he wanted to examine points to an opaque phase in human evolution during which the "human beast" transformed into the "keener, shrewder and less encumbered

2. See Georges Bataille, *Œuvres complètes* (Paris, Gallimard, 1970–1988) (henceforth *OC*), IX, 419–20. The "dossier" includes eleven elements: a film project (1952); two lectures (one given at the Société d'Agriculture, Sciences, Belles-lettres et Arts d'Orléans in December 1952, and one on January 18, 1955); three previously published articles ("Le passage de l'animal à l'homme et la naissance de l'art" [1953], "Au rendezvous de Lascaux, l'homme civilisé se retrouve homme de désir" [1953], and "La religion préhistorique" [1959]); two hitherto unpublished articles ("La Vénus de Lespugue" [1958] and "Le berceau de l'humanité: La vallée de la Vézère" [1959]); two segments of writing that were integrated into *L'érotisme* (1957, [chapter VII, "le meurtre et le sacrifice"]) and *Les larmes d'Éros* (1961, [Part I, "Le commencement"]), finally, the book on Lascaux (1955).

3. See "Dossier de Lascaux," *OC*, IX, 317–76.

4. See Bataille, *The Cradle of Humanity: Prehistoric Art and Culture* (New York: Zone Books, 2009 [2005]), ed. Stuart Kendall, trans. Michelle Kendall and Stuart Kendall (hereafter *Cradle of Humanity*).

5. According to A.S., the editor who helped to photograph for the book on Lascaux, the paintings inside the cavern "mysteriously shift and change" when they are viewed, due to the uneven surface of the rock wall and to the difference in perspective. See the editor's "Presentation" in Bataille, *Lascaux; or, The Birth of Art: Prehistoric Painting*, trans. Austryn Wainhouse (Lausanne: Skira, 1955) (henceforth *Lascaux*, or the *Lascaux* book), 5; *OC*, IX, 421.

being that we have become."[6] Anthropologists have dated this crucial step in human prehistory to a period they call the Middle-Upper Paleolithic Transition,[7] and have respectively used the terms *Homo neanderthalensis* and *Homo sapiens* to designate the two types of "man": the first rudimental, an anthropoid-like creature that had a less-developed mental structure, capable of making tools, but not yet capable of "symbolic behavior," and the second more sophisticated, anatomically resembling modern humans, who used advanced portal artifacts, carried out elaborate burial practices, and left traces of representational "art": cave paintings and engravings.

According to Bataille, Lascaux symbolizes the "cradle" of humanity because it embodies this transitional period during which the Neanderthal man (*homo faber*) transformed slowly into what he now calls the "Lascaux men," the first creators of "art." These "first men" were *sapiens*, however, for a different reason: they had with them a secret knowledge, a knowledge that was lost in the development of man as a modern being. Bataille makes the strong argument that the work of art is inseparable from the birth of *homo sapiens*, that is, indissociable from what he calls "religion," or "at least the religious mood or attitude."[8] Lascaux, the emblem of the ages during which the passage from animal to man completes itself, should therefore not be understood merely as a historical site where archaeologists and Paleolithic art historians go to carry out "scientific" studies. For Bataille, it is above all a fantasized time/space where art, play, and religion join each other in a single backward movement toward the recovery of a lost intimacy with animals and with nature, this "regressive" *élan* being a defiance of the principles that govern the modern world: work, reason, utility, and increasingly, in modern times, violence and war.

In the following pages, I will push Steven Ungar's idea of "Phantom Lascaux" further to argue that Bataille's rendition of Lascaux is

6. *Lascaux*, 20; *OC*, IX, 22. I have modified here the original English translation of ". . . the subtler, keener, unfettered individual we are" to better convey the highly polysemous French expression of "l'être délié."

7. In the European Paleolithic chronology, the incoming of *Homo sapiens* occurs in the beginning of the Upper Paleolithic. The "Transition" refers to a period (45, 000 and 35,000 years ago) between the Middle Paleolithic the Upper Paleolithic, during which the Aurignacian culture of the *Homo sapiens* overlapped with the Châtelperronian culture of the *Homo neanderthalensis*. *Homo sapiens* gradually "took over" the Neanderthals, who went extinct around 35,000 years ago.

8. *Lascaux*, 7; *OC*, IX, 9–10.

22   *Yale French Studies*

not only atemporal and fictional,[9] but also utopic and phantasmatic. His meditations on cave paintings do not deviate, as Ungar suggests, from art to other "social sciences";[10] instead, prehistory allows him to fantasize a point outside history that sidesteps the divisions established by modern disciplines, a utopian space where the earliest men's relation to death, eroticism, religion, interdiction, and transgression is seen as tangled, poetic, and mysterious, and art as an ultimate expression resulting from this sensitive distress and confusion. Far from being a conscious "project," Bataille's writings on Lascaux can be best viewed as a *point of arrival* that converges many of his postwar preoccupations, which began with *Théorie de la religion* (*Theory of Religion*) and remained ongoing until the end of his life. At the center of these reflections is the question of animality and its close rapport with the sacred, or what man has lost in becoming the species he has become.

Lascaux appears to Bataille primarily as a wonder, a huge hole in the ground found accidentally, through which deep time is revealed, and human beings of modern times are invited to experience the most distant past. Discovered by four teenagers living in the village of Montignac (on the banks of the Vézère river in southwestern France) on 12 September 1940, the prehistoric cave that contains nearly 2,000 painted figures dating back some 17,000 years was like a fertile ground suddenly resurfacing from beneath a wasteland, a virgin territory unscathed by two World Wars and past human tragedies. Bataille describes his visit to the cave as being marked by strong emotions: the figures depicted on the rocks, most of them large animals, often overlaying one on top of another and appearing in motion, evoke a feeling of "burning presence" of primeval time and of "brotherhood" (*l'amitié*), entirely different from museum visits during which one would look at the petrified remains of prehistoric men or neat rows of their stone instruments through glass cases.[11] This breathtaking

9. In his well-known article, "Phantom Lascaux: Origin of the Work of Art," Steven Ungar has pointed out the ahistorical and phantasmatic nature of Bataille's Lascaux "inquiry": "Bataille violates the historical nature of his project". . . . "Lascaux provides a master narrative of life and death forces that is staged rather than simply illustrated or drawn. This staging – rather than any temporal determination of origin – inaugurates a human order set apart from the profane world of work." See Steven Ungar, "Phantom Lascaux: Origin of the Work of Art," *Yale French Studies* 78, *On Bataille* (1990): 246–62, 250, 258.
    10. Ibid., 247, 249.
    11. *Lascaux*, 12; *OC*, IX, 13.

tangibility of the ancient yields quickly to a feeling of perplexity and powerlessness: "We know next to nothing of the men who left behind only these elusive shadows": neither the date of their existence, nor their group organizations, nor the place these animals occupied in their beliefs or rites.[12] Yet these paintings move us deeply precisely because they are indecipherable, their charm and meaning to be found in their *apparition*, their entanglement, and their "continual, lively negation of the durable object."[13] These paintings, as Bataille explains, can in no way be considered as "art objects," since the Lascaux man did not know what "art" was: "[he] would not have known how to go about such a thing and furthermore, it would appear, had no desire to try."[14]

Why prehistoric men penetrated the deep limestone caves of France and Spain to make these images in total darkness, for whom they painted these figures and what these imageries meant for those who viewed them, is of course a much debated area in archaeology and the study of Paleolithic art. Bataille bases much of his readings on Breuil's hypothesis of sympathetic magic, according to which the depicted species would either multiply in number to become prey themselves, or give hunters power over their prey. He may also have been influenced by an earlier article by Salomon Reinach, "L'art et la magie" ("Art and Magic"), in which the classical archaeologist claims the best way to understand the burgeoning of Upper Paleolithic art is by examining the lifestyles of existing hunting populations, through ethnographic "analogies."[15] One striking aspect of the parietal paintings that particularly catches Bataille's attention is what Breuil describes as the prevalence of "animal disguise": "In the wall art of the dark caverns in which hunting magic holds the greatest place," the Abbé writes, "the human figure is always rare though not absent. . . . Most of these figures are masked, or if one prefers, provided with non-human attributes."[16] Images of man on the cave walls appear almost always with an animal head, whether it is a mammoth, a bird,

12. Ibid.

13. *Cradle of Humanity*,78; *OC*, XII, 274–75.

14. *Lascaux*, 11; *OC*, IX, 11.

15. "L'art et la magie: à propos des peintures et des gravures de l'Age du Renne" (1903) is reprinted in Salomon Reinach's *Cultes, mythes, religions* (Paris: E. Leroux, 1905), 125–36, 132 for our quotation. Bataille read the book in 1931. See "Emprunts de Georges Bataille à la BN" (1922–1950), *OC*, XII, p. 571–72.

16. Abbé H. Breuil, *Four Hundred Centuries of Cave Art* (Montignac : Centre d'études et de documentation préhistorique, 1952), trans. Mary E. Boyle, 24.

a bison, or a stag. While Breuil interprets these semi-human figures mainly as hunters in disguise, or imitations of spiritual and mythical beings during magic rites, Bataille reads in them a stronger statement that translates the "first men's wish to 'negate' human life."[17] Cave men, according to him, did not feel they were clearly separated from animals. They portrayed the "share of the animal that remained within [them], and disguised the humanity that distinguished [them] from animals."[18]

In Bataille's view, prehistoric men maintained with animals a poetic bond that is definitely lost in modern times: they treated the latter as their fellow creatures, desired them, moved alongside them, felt sympathy for them; but these positive feelings never excluded their desire to kill. It is this paradoxical rapport that Bataille finds most fascinating: "'Primitive' hunters feel no contempt for what they kill. They grant their prey a soul like their own as well as an intellect and feelings that do not differ from their own. They ask their prey to forgive them for killing them, and sometimes they cry for it, in a touching mixture of distracted sincerity and simple playacting."[19] Modern men, on the other hand, have a distanced relation with animals. We might love them, even co-exist with them, but we would never go as far as to consider them as fellow creatures, because animals are after all things, whereas "we precisely are not."[20] Humanity has thus forgotten that first intimacy prehistoric men shared with animals, that complex yet subtle fusion they created together. Humanity was born from this "poetic animality," but it was born from it "by founding its superiority on the forgetting of this [very] poetic animality and on a contempt for animals—deprived of the poetry of the wild, reduced to the level of things, enslaved, slaughtered, butchered."[21]

Lascaux represents therefore an opposite pole of modernity and of the hierarchical relation man now entertains with animals. It becomes a phantasmatic space in which a "return" is seen as possible, to a lyrical state that I would call an "animal utopia." In such a fantasy, animals are not yet objects and man is not yet entirely man. Indistinct, they coexist closely through their similar gestures and activities. The Dordogne cave "sets us free," Bataille writes, it "asks us to

17. *Cradle of Humanity*, 65; *OC*, XII, 265.
18. *Cradle of Humanity*, 61; *OC*, XII, 263.
19. *Cradle of Humanity*, 74–75; *OC* XII, 271–272.
20. *Cradle of Humanity*, 75; *OC* XII, 272.
21. *Cradle of Humanity*, 76; *OC* XII, 273.

no longer deny *what we are.*"[22] Deep in space and in time, the hallu-
cinatory paintings on the walls of Lascaux incite a backward passage
that Maurice Blanchot terms the "second moment of transgression."
If in the first moment man "transgresses nature" by standing up, by
rising up against the animal in himself, by working and by becoming
gradually something "unnatural," in the second instant he questions
this separation now established between himself and his origin, and
"transgresses" his own humanness by aiming at a "return" to the
"first immensity" of nature, to the state of indifferentiation he had
once known.[23]

Blanchot's outlining of "two moments of essential transgression"
is but a response to Bataille's own imagination of Lascaux as a theatrical stage, where an ancient play of "the birth of man" takes place
outside time. The coming of humanity, Bataille announces, was a
"drama in two acts": after a long and vague period of "incubation," a
second episode presents itself as a moment more "spectacular" and
more "essential."[24] The first act points to an indefinite time during
which man rises up, makes tools out of things, steps back from nature and learns to handle destruction and death, its main character
being *Homo faber,* the Neanderthal. The second act coincides with
the birth of art, of religion, and of eroticism. A more skilled man
masters the fabrication of tools and initiates himself to the realm of
"work." He discovers at the same time the sacred in the animal world
and learns to surmount death by play, feast, and transgression of in-
terdictions. This is the coming of the *Homo sapiens,* the "first men"
who used "blind unthinking" and "intimate signs" to express their
emotions and to "oppose" them to the reality of everyday utilitarian
activity.[25]

Bataille's compulsive interpretation of an enigmatic painting from
the "Well" (or "Shaft") section of Lascaux can be seen as a highpoint
of carrying out the "impossible" return that Blanchot delineates earlier.[26] Known as "The Shaft of the Dead Man," or "Man in the Well,"
this much-debated image is considered as one of the most significant
of the earliest known figurations of the human being (See Figure 1).

22. *Cradle of Humanity,* 85; *OC,* XII, 292.
23. Maurice Blanchot, *L'amitié* (Paris: Gallimard, 1971), 14–15.
24. *Cradle of Humanity,* 145; *OC,* IX, 355.
25. *Lascaux,* 11–12; *OC,* IX, 12–13.
26. "Impossible" in the sense that one is aware that such a backward movement is
illusory and phantasmatic. See Blanchot, *L'amitié,* 15.

Figure 1. Hunting Scene ("Well Scene"), ca. 15,000–10,000 BCE. Lascaux Cave. Photo: Art Resource, NY.

Unable to grasp its full meaning, Bataille comments on it repeatedly, in his lecture at the Société d'Agricultures, Sciences, Belles-lettres et Arts d'Orléans, in *L'érotisme*, in his articles "La religion préhistorique" ("The Prehistoric Religion") and "Le berceau de l'humanité" ("The Cradle of Humanity") and finally, in *Les larmes d'Éros*. But it is in the *Lascaux* book that he gives the most detailed description of the painting:

> . . . A narrow platform brings one opposite a rock shelf [. . .] bearing images, on one side, of a rhinoceros, and, on the other, of a bison; between them, falling or supine, is a bird-headed man; below him, a bird poised on an upright stick (. . .). The infuriated bison's hair literally stands straight on end, it lashes its tail, intestines spill in thick ropes from a gash in its belly. A spear is painted diagonally across the beast's flank, passing over the place where the wound has been inflicted. The man is naked and ithyphallic: drawn in a puerile fashion, he is shown as though just felled by the bison's two projecting horns; the man's arms are flung wide and his four-fingered hands are open.[27]

27. *Lascaux*, 110; *OC*, IX, 59–50.

In his initial comments on the image, Bataille hesitated essentially between Breuil's interpretation of the scene as a hunting accident and the German archaeologist Horst Kirchner's reading of it as a religious sacrifice. According to the latter, the man "fallen on his back" is not a dying hunter but rather a shaman entering into a moment of ecstatic trance.[28] In later writings such as *L'érotisme*, "Le berceau de l'humanité" and *Les larmes d'Éros*, Bataille invalidates his earlier "borrowed" analyses and admits he had refrained from giving a more "personal reading" of the painting.[29] What is this "personal reading"? And how does it tie into his continuous reflections on death and religion?

The exegesis of the scene, most fully developed in "Le berceau de l'humanité," can be summarized by two expressions Bataille uses here and there: "the murder and expiation," and "man clad in the glory of the beast" (*l'homme paré du prestige de la bête*).[30] They convey, on the one hand, the idea of sympathy and of intimate "friendship" with animals, and on the other, the birth of spirituality through contact with animals as they "appear so as to die" (*apparaissent pour mourir*).[31] By painting the animals that they killed, Lascaux men envisioned something other than their daily desires: what they wanted to depict was the haunting question of death. In the "Well" painting, the quasi-dead state of the man is represented as closely linked to the imminent death of the bison, because although it was he who killed the animal, he felt sympathy for it as if he had lost a loved one. "It was necessary to mourn the victim, to honor it like a god. Because death transformed the victim, it had the supernatural prestige inherent in the beyond."[32] The murder of the animal thus "required expiation from its author": "he who gives death enters into death" himself.[33] The bird's head, portrayed both as an integral part of the

28. *Lascaux*, 139–140; *OC*, IX, 94–95.

29. See *OC*, X, 77, note; *Cradle of Humanity*, 171; *OC*, IX, 374. For a fuller discussion of Bataille's self-corrected readings of "The Shaft of the Dead Man," see Milo Sweedler, "Bataille et le premier homme," in *Écrivains de la préhistoire*, ed. André Benhaïm and Michel Lantelme (Toulouse-Le Mirail: Presses Universitaires du Mirail, 2004), 107–110.

30. In *L'érotisme*, Bataille writes, "the subject of this famous painting . . . will be the murder and the expiation." See *OC*, X, 77. In *Lascaux*, "L'homme paré du prestige de la bête" is a subtitle under the title of a chapter called "The Representation of Man." See *Lascaux*, 115, *OC*, IX, 62.

31. *Cradle of Humanity*, 167; *OC*, IX, 371.

32. Ibid.

33. *Cradle of Humanity*, 171; *OC*, IX, 375.

man and outside him (poised on the stick), symbolizes the "shaman's voyage into the beyond, into the kingdom of death."[34] It is through the bird's presence that the man overcomes death; it is with the spiritual promise it brings that he manages to confront the painful dying of the bison, by lying down alongside it as an equal.

The key element that defines the transition from the Neanderthal-*faber* stage to the human *sapiens* stage, as Bataille affirms now more openly, involves a semi-conscious "overcoming of death" through the recognition of the sovereign value of animals:

> Nothing proves that the religious thought of the Mousterian era exceeded the terror of death, but the religious thought of the Upper Paleolithic acceded to a more expansive form of religion that founded the sentiment of the divinity of the animal, of the divine nature of animality. In other words, if the animal world was divine, it was so projected into the unreal domain of death: religious thought has always engaged in the contemplation of a world *entirely other* from that of human life. It is always a question of this terrified feeling that death inspires in man. But the animal is, in every sense, on a par with death. The animal is the being that the hunter only saw in order to kill. In the killing of the divine animal, the hunter overcame the terror of death.[35]

Aware of the fact that his depiction of the association between animality, death, and the sacred is somewhat elusive, Bataille adds that prehistoric men's "play of contradictory feelings" would be the key to understanding the hidden meaning of the cave paintings of animals.[36]

In order to explain the functioning of the unfathomable cave minds, Bataille resorts indeed to a contemporary ethnographic work by the French anthropologist Eveline Lot-Falck, who, in her *Rites de chasse chez les peuples sibériens* (*Hunting Rituals Among Siberian Peoples*, 1955), gives an explanation as to why the Siberians consider the animal they hunt not only an equal, but "superior":

> The hunter . . . regards the animal as at least his own equal. Like himself, the animal hunts to procure its food, has, he believes, a life like his own, and the same sort of social organization. Man's superiority appears only in the sphere of techniques. . . . In the sphere of magic, he will grant the animal a prowess no less considerable than

34. *Cradle of Humanity*, 172; OC, IX, 375.
35. *Cradle of Humanity*, 165–66; OC, IX, 370.
36. *Cradle of Humanity*, 166–67; OC, IX, 370–371.

his own. On the other hand, the animal outdoes man in several characteristics: it is better in its physical strength, in agility, in its keen senses of hearing and smell, qualities a hunter appreciates. He will allot an even higher value to the spiritual powers he associates with these physical qualities. . . . The animal is in more direct contact with the divinity, it is closer than man to the forces of nature.[37]

This passage and other fragments Bataille quotes from the same book show that the hunter's relation to the prey is imbued with ambiguities. First, their horizontal, non-hierarchical, and "intimate" coexistence is only temporary, for it is quickly followed by the violence of capturing and mastication. Between the two stages, between play and violence, there is no time to enter into what Alexandre Kojève calls, in his *Introduction to the Reading of Hegel*, the master-slave dialectic or the anthropogenetic "desire for recognition."[38] Animals appear "so as to die," which is why they are "on a par with death." Second, the hunter enters into a contract with the prey that is both "friendly" and "hypocritical." According to Lot-Falck, in order to be killed, the animal must first "consent to die"; therefore, the hunter must "keep on the best possible terms" with his prey, to the point of seducing it.[39] Bataille adds that the hunter, precisely because he "knows" that his action is subject to useful ends (he hunts in order to eat), recognizes paradoxically the "unimpaired dignity" and the "sovereign value" of the animal, whose power surpasses his own, because the animal is "without calculation."[40] Elsewhere, Bataille further suggests that the hunter, faced with the animal, feels the dangerous

37. Cited in *Lascaux*, 125–26, *OC*, IX, 75. For a different version of the same passage cited in "La religion préhistorique," see *Cradle of Humanity*, 131, and *OC*, XII, 503–504. For *Les rites de chasse chez les peuples sibériens*, see Stuart Kendall's excellent note in *Cradle of Humanity* (207), in which he discusses the relation between Lot-Falck's work and the unfinished research of Anatole Lewiszky on shamanism. It is worth restating that Lewiszky was a Russian émigré and a friend of Bataille's during the period of the Collège de Sociologie. He was shot in 1942 for his Resistance activities. Bataille's reference to hunting activities, in my opinion, can by no means be considered trivial.

38. See Alexandre Kojève, *Introduction to the Reading of Hegel* (New York: Basic Books, Inc., 1969), trans. James H. Nichols, Jr., 6–9, 224–25. The "desire for recognition" is a human desire that requires the "other" to recognize one's own desire (or value). It differs from animal desire in that, instead of annihilating instantly the "other" as a thing, it must "win out" the animal part in itself and enters into a confrontational relation with the "other" through a "fight to the death for pure prestige." I will come back to this point in my conclusion.

39. Cited in *Lascaux*, 126; *OC*, IX, 76.

40. *Lascaux*, 126, 128; *OC*, IX, 76, 78.

forces of nature and his imminent separation from this first order. This causes a feeling of malediction and anxiety, which prompts him, in a reverse move, to attribute the magic power to the animal during sacrificial rites in order to compensate for his own alienation.[41]

The "first men," to come back to our cave, in Bataille's view, were more sophisticated than we are because they were already "conscious," in the sense of having an equivocal feeling that does not belong to the order of language, of their "crime" and their "loss." Their need for survival coexisted with a strong desire for returning to immanence and for reversing the technical world they had created. Art and religion are born out of this "negative" effort. The world of religion is "developed through the negation, sometimes through a destructive effort, of this world of understanding (*connaissance*) and of work," and art is "primarily, and remains primarily play."[42] The word "religion," however, did not mean much to the Lascaux men, for although they endowed the animal with supernatural power, they did not know what "divine" power was. What was divine was the unknown: the sudden apparition of the animal like a bolt of lightning in the darkness, not as an object, but as a violent force suddenly rising above a flat world, facing death, beyond definition, beyond comprehension. Bataille considers "this equivocal, indefinable meaning" the final definition of religion: "we must (. . .) renounce this attempt to define it (religion), but in accepting this ignorance, in refusing to define religion, paradoxically and profoundly, we are religious."[43] Art, for him, translates the first confusing words (*balbutiement*) of this religious feeling: "*Sapiens'* contribution is art, not knowledge."[44]

Occupying an important place in his writings on Lascaux and prehistoric culture, Bataille's imagination of primitive men's "friendship" with animals should be inscribed into his continuous reflections on the sacred, especially those of the postwar period, which establish a close link with animality. In *Théorie de la religion*, written in 1948 and published posthumously in 1973, he already presented the animal realm as a world of intimacy and immanence that does

41. *Cradle of Humanity*, 166–67; *OC*, IX, 370–371.
42. See *Cradle of Humanity*, 138; *OC*, XII, 511, and *Lascaux*, 27, *OC*, IX, 28. I modified here the English translation of *"jeu"* as both "game" and "play" to simply "play."
43. *Cradle of Humanity*, 135; *OC*, XII, 508.
44. *Lascaux*, 35; *OC*, IX, 38, translation modified.

not require human representation: "every animal is *in the world like water in water*," unaware of the relation of subordination that connects an object to a man.[45] Bataille calls his animal utopia a "poetic fallacy," because it is guided by an absence of vision, or an "empty intoxication" of the power of the unknown: "This is a simple truth, [that] animal life, halfway distant from our consciousness, presents us with a more disconcerting enigma. In picturing the universe without man, a universe in which only the animal's gaze would open to things, . . . we can only call up a vision in which we *see nothing. . . .*"[46] Only poetry can describe what shifts into the unknowable, only poetic capacity can "substitute a vague fulguration for the nothing of ignorance."[47] Lascaux provides the very condition for such a "poetic fallacy of animality." Between their existence and their extinction, prehistoric men transcribed the gaze of animals and left the traces of their daily world in the thick darkness of the caverns. Remembering the original terror and distress, they kept the animal instincts alive and the nakedness of nature intact, creating a power that neither came directly from the consciousness of man nor was addressed to it.

Bataille's writings on prehistory, in an even larger context, can be considered as a final stage of a tenacious effort to pursue what he calls the "blind spot" of the "total" system of Hegel (of Spirit and Absolute Knowledge), especially its anthropologized version presented by Kojève in his famous lectures on *The Phenomenology of Spirit*, edited and published by Raymond Queneau in 1947 under the title of *Introduction à la lecture de Hegel*. Shortly before his death, Bataille wrote to Kojève, his long-time friend, that he had wanted to pursue "some kind of parallel" to the latter's book, but it would bear on "arbitrary" subjects that would address what Hegel had left out or neglected: prehistory, the present time, the future.[48] Some of these "arbitrary" subjects, such as the origin of religion, eroticism, the sovereign power of art and poetry, joined the prehistoric imagination in his writings on cave paintings. This is not the place to pursue Kojève's reading of Hegel and Bataille's "parallel" that attempts to overtake

45. Bataille, *Theory of Religion* (New York: Zone Books, 1992), trans. Robert Hurley, 18–19; *OC*, VII, 291–92.

46. *Theory of Religion*, 21; *OC*, VII, 293.

47. *Theory of Religion*, 22; *OC*, VII, 294.

48. Bataille, *Choix de lettres*, 1917–1942 (Paris: Gallimard, 1997), ed. Michel Surya, 573.

it. But I would like to suggest two hypotheses that would further integrate the "Lascaux project" into Bataille's larger philosophical and
ethical reflections. First, Lascaux as a monumental prehistoric site
discovered in the early stages of the World War II arises as a utopian space standing *outside* history, allowing Bataille to envision a
nascent state of man similar to the existence of animals, that is, prior
to the understanding of the Master and Slave dialectic and indifferent to what Kojève calls the "fight to the death for 'recognition.'"[49] In
such an embryonic state of civilization, man's activities are seen as
free and equal; men were ignorant of wars and slavery, which grew
later out of work and social divisions.[50] Second, the "poetic fallacy of
animality" that Bataille pursues in these writings can be considered
a direct response to Kojève's caricature of the Intellectual and the
Poet as an unhappy consciousness fleeing social responsibilities. The
"only difference between an Intellectual and a Bestiary," Kojève contends, is that "the first describes himself, cheerfully reveals himself."
The Poet creates a fictional world for himself and "reduces himself
to it," in the end "he exhausts himself, and vanishes utterly in his
own nothingness."[51] Bataille's fantasy of Lascaux pushes this negative image of the Poet to the extreme; not only does he identify with
animals, but he also follows them into their disappearance. A work of
art, Bataille replies to Kojève in his famous "Letter to X, Lecture on
Hegel . . . ," "answers by evading, to the extent that it gives a lasting
answer, it answers no specific situation."[52] Art assumes the function
of sacrifice and of expenditure that refuses the positivity of meaning,
and there is no better art than the paintings of Lascaux to convey that
feeling acutely:

> A vain search, true though; nothing will ever enable us really to relive
> this past, irretrievably sunk in the night. And vain in the sense that

49. Kojève has stated explicitly: "[I]n his nascent state, man is never simply man.
He is always, necessarily, and essentially, either Master or Slave." See *Introduction to
the Reading of Hegel*, 8; see also note 39, supra.
50. Bataille, *The Tears of Eros* (San Francisco: City Lights Books, 1989), trans. Peter
Connor, 58, 143; *OC*, X, 595, 620.
51. See Bataille, *The College of Sociology* (1937–1939) (Minneapolis: University
of Minnesota Press, 1988), ed. Denis Hollier, trans. Betsy Wing, 89. See also Kojève,
Introduction à la lecture de Hegel (Paris: Gallimard, 1947), 152 (I refer to the French
edition here because this section, "Courses of 1936–1937," is not included in the English translation).
52. *The College of Sociology*, ibid., 91

human desire is never satisfied, since it is forever a straining toward a fugitive goal. But the quest, at least, is possible, and we must recognize whither we strain. Little would it matter what those dead ancestors bequeathed to posterity were it not that we hoped to make them, if for only one fleeting instant, live again in ourselves.[53]

53. *Lascaux*, 50; *OC*, IX, 43.

SARAH KAY

Before the *Animot*: *Bêtise* and the Zoological Machine in Medieval Latin and French Bestiaries

Derrida's bid to overwrite the French plural *animaux* with the singular neologism *animot* is meant as a reproach to speakers' tendency to
create and maintain a homogeneous category of "animals in general."[1]
His pun on the plural ending –*maux* (wrongs) and the singular noun
mot (word) identifies the power of speech, denied to other animals,
as a source of the injustices inflicted on them. Obviously Derrida is
right to insist that vocabulary has categorical and hence ethical implications. Just as obviously, the French word *animaux* (like English
animals) has fluctuating meanings today (does it encompass birds,
fish, and insects? does it include human beings or not?) and an even
more contested history. This paper argues that what Derrida reproves
as an indiscriminate gesture also warrants being seen as the outcome
of centuries of conflicting discriminations over the range and significance of the "a-word." The corollary of this process, I contend, are
shifts in what we might call the "b-word"—*bêtise*, which for Derrida
means the simultaneous definition and denigration of human beings
in terms of their perceived similarity with beasts,[2] but which operates differently in different periods, as we will see.

Critical animal studies have documented the vanity of historical
efforts to shore up the category "human." Agamben devotes a chapter of *L'aperto* to this endeavor, which he dubs the "anthropological machine." The human, he argues, results from an arbitrary, pro-
visional and always unsatisfactory decision about the limits of that

1. Jacques Derrida, *L'animal que donc je suis. L'animal autobiographique*, ed.
Marie-Louise Mallet (Paris: Galilée, 1999), notably 65, 73.
2. Derrida, *L'animal*, 65, "Stupidity [*bêtise*] and bestiality [. . .] of which beasts
are by definition exempt [. . .]. Why, one wonders, should the distinctively human be
shored up in the last resort by features termed *bêtise* or bestiality?" (My trans.)

YFS 127, *"Animots": Postanimality in French Thought*, ed. Senior, Clark, and Freccero,
© 2015 by Yale University.

which can be adjudged different from (other) animals.[3] Critical preoccupation with identifying "the human" implies that recognizing
"the animal" is easier, and masks a complementary effort at conceptualization which could be termed the "zoological machine." We are
often reminded that Adam's naming the animals was a sign of human
dominion over them, but naming particular creatures—even under
the nerve-wracking conditions of God's watchful stare—is a different
order of task from that of devising a name for all critters together, or
conceiving in what that totality consists. It has taken someone as
inventive as Donna Haraway to elevate the humble word "critter" to
this philosophical task.[4]

This article traces how medieval bestiaries set up and run a zoological machine. Bestiaries derive from an early (probably second-
century) Greek work known after its imputed author as *Physiologus*;
it offers Christian homiletic readings of the "natures" of elements of
the natural world, and includes plants and stones alongside a variety of sentient and imaginary beings. Composed mainly in the elev-
enth and twelfth centuries, and copied mainly through the twelfth
and thirteenth, European Latin bestiaries progressively accrete material from sources other than *Physiologus*, the most important being
Book XII, *De animalibus*, of Isidore of Seville's enormously influen-
tial encyclopedia *Etymologiae* (early seventh century). Despite their
zoocentric titles—in Latin *Liber animalium* or *Liber bestiarum* (book
of animals/beasts), vernacular *Bestiaire*—bestiaries continue to contain chapters on stones, plants, birds, fish, and mythical creatures
like the siren, as well as on quadrupeds, reptiles, and insects. Typically each short chapter comprises two parts of which the first names
its subject and describes its appearance and behavior (often in ways
that seem quite fanciful), and the second adduces its spiritual meaning. The panther, for instance, is said to be a gentle, multicolored animal which sleeps for three days after eating, then roars; the sweetness
of its breath attracts all the other creatures to it except for the dragon
that fears it; it signifies Christ with his infinite qualities who, following his death and resurrection, drew all humanity to him, but was
dreaded by the Devil. As this example suggests, the teaching offered

3. Giorgio Agamben, *L'aperto. L'uomo e l'animale* (Torino: Bollati Boringhieri,
2002), chap. 9.

4. Donna J. Haraway, *Where Species Meet* (Minneapolis: University of Minnesota
Press, 2008), 5 and *passim*.

in bestiary chapters is fairly basic, closer to the parish catechism than to university theology.

I discuss two Latin bestiaries and four of six surviving French ones. The early so-called B-Isidore version, which compiles a Latin version of the *Physiologus* with Isidore (henceforth B-Is), is represented by the early thirteenth-century manuscript British Library Royal 2. C. XII;[5] the most widely copied bestiary, the so-called Second-family bestiary (henceforth SF), is consulted from British Library manuscript Additional 11283 of ca. 1180.[6] B-Is is the source of most vernacular bestiaries in French or Anglo-Norman, which were composed between ca. 1120 and ca. 1260.[7] In their approach to taxonomy and encyclopedism, however, the *langue d'oïl* authors share common ground with the SF compiler. I focus on the Anglo-Norman verse bestiaries by Philippe de Thaun (ca. 1121–35), Gervaise (ca. 1200), and Guillaume le Clerc (1210 or 1211), and on the last in date of the continental French prose ones, the so-called "long version" of the bestiary by Pierre de Beauvais (ca. 1246–60), abbreviating textual references to PT, G, GC, and LV respectively.[8] I examine them first as lists of individual entities and their names, and then as early essays in classification, before asking how they integrate human beings in that taxonomy.

"IL N'Y A PAS D'ANIMAL AU MOYEN AGE"

The medieval Latin word *animal* is rare outside learned works, where it tends to encompass the human (Laurie Shannon makes the same point for Shakespeare's English).[9] This inclusiveness stems from an-

5. In *Bestiari Medievali*, ed. Luigina Morini (Turin: Einaudi, 1996), 5–102.

6. Willene B. Clark, *A Medieval Book of Beasts. The Second-family Tradition. Commentary – Arts – Text and Translation* (Woodbridge: Boydell, 2006).

7. Florence McCulloch, *Medieval Latin and French Bestiaries* (Chapel Hill, NC: University of North Carolina Press, revised ed., 1962), 45. She excepts Gervaise's *Bestiaire* which derives from the *Dicta Chrysostomi* (55–6).

8. The *Bestiaires* of Philippe de Thaun and Gervaise are cited from Morini, ed., *Bestiari medievali*, 103–285 and 289–361 respectively; Guillaume le Clerc's *Bestiaire* is cited from Robert Reinsch, *Le Bestiaire. Das Thierbuch des Normannischen Dichters Guillaume le Clerc* (Leipzig: Reisland, 1892) and the "Long version" from *Le Bestiaire. Version longue attribuée à Pierre de Beauvais*, ed. Craig Baker (Paris: Honoré Champion, 2011).

9. Pierre-Olivier Dittmar, "Il n'y a pas d'animal au Moyen Age" (paper presented at the International Medieval Society Conference, Paris, June 2012; I thank the author for sharing his work); Laurie Shannon, "The Eight Animals in Shakespeare; or, Before the Human," *PMLA* 124:2 (2009): 472–79.

tique ontology and psychology, according to which the corporeal is either animate or inanimate, and within the animate everything capable of locomotion and sentience is reckoned to be "animal" whereas animate life that neither moves nor feels is vegetative; animal life is then subdivided between rational (speech-capable) and non-rational forms, hence the classical definition "man is a rational animal."[10] Outside this philosophical usage, Pierre-Olivier Dittmar contends, medieval thought opposes a pre-lapsarian account, in which Adam's naming of individual animate species reiterates the order of their creation and confirms human privilege with respect to them, and a post-lapsarian one, in which the relations between humans and other animate species are thrown into turmoil: medium-sized animals, which are also domestic or herd animals (*pecus*), maintain the submission to human beings of Eden; large wild animals (*bestiae*) and many small ones now represent a danger to them; and sin-prone men (*homines*) are threatened from within by their new proximity to animality at large.[11] Just as Foucault could hold that, before the early modern period, "man" does not exist,[12] so we can say that there is no such being as "the animal" in the Middle Ages.

Bestiaries retain traces of this opposition between pre- and postlapsarian conceptualizations of the natural world, but they are more interested in the Edenic act of naming particular creatures than in generalizing about them. The structure of a typical B-Is redaction bears no relation to biological categories. The thirty-seven chapters of Royal 2. C. XII run lion, antelope, firestones (*terobolem*), swordfish (*serra*), *caladrius*, pelican, screech owl (*nicticorax*), eagle, phoenix, hoopoe, ant, siren and centaur, hedgehog, ibis, fox, unicorn (*monoceros*), beaver, hyena, water-serpent (*hydrus*) and crocodile, roe deer (*caprea*), wild ass (*onager*), ape, coot (*fulica*), panther, great fish (*aspidocelo*), partridge, weasel and asp, ostrich, turtledove, stag, salamander,

10. As in treatises on the soul (*De anima*) by Aristotle, Avicenna, Albertus Magnus, and Aquinas.

11. An opposition pioneered by Augustine and adopted by Isidore; see Pierre-Olivier Dittmar, "Le seigneur des animaux. Les animalités paradisiaques des années 1300," in *Micrologus. Adam Premier Homme*, ed. A. Paravicini Bagliani (Florence: Sismel, forthcoming).

12. Michel Foucault, *Les mots et les choses* (Paris: Gallimard, 1966), 398, "Taking a relatively narrow chronological range and a restricted geographical focus—European culture since the sixteenth century—we can be sure that, within it, Man is a recent invention." (My trans.)

dove, peredixion tree, elephant, the prophet Amos, diamond, and pearl. Ron Baxter contends that the aim of this organization is to illustrate Christian tenets, not to inform about natural entities. According to him the opening chapters, lion to swordfish, represent Christ's divinity, those from *caladrius* to eagle his rejection by the Jews, and so on, to the final group, diamond to pearl, which symbolize the incarnation.[13] But this explanation only succeeds in making the order of tenets as arbitrary as that of the chapters; the relation of the allegoreses to the creatures also frequently seems entirely random.

Although, as we will see, SF and some vernacular texts adopt an order seemingly motivated more by species than by allegory, they nevertheless continue the *Physiologus* tradition of presenting above all a list of creatures; the material added from Isidore's *Etymologies* only accentuates this effect by drawing attention to the listed names. Of the onager, B-Is begins formulaically "Est animal quod dicitur *onager*" (§21, There is an animal called *onager*), explaining that the name means "wild ass," from the Greek words *on* (ass) and *agrian* (wild). In some cases the name provides the key to the animal's nature. Of the ant, B-Is writes, "The ant (*formica*) is so called because it carries (*ferat*) grains of wheat (*micas farris*)" (§11). Philippe de Thaun resourcefully translates, "About the ant,/ Isidore further says in his text /and explains /why it is named "*furmi*": /because it is strong (*fort*) and carries a grain (*mie*), /that is what it means" (PT, 1031–6). The ant's name epitomizes its industrious behavior which in turn sustains its moralizations. The additional entries in SF contribute some new etymologies, such as sheep (*oves*, §33) from sacrifice (*oblatio*). Although the etymologizing impulse slackens in vernacular authors after Philippe, their bestiaries continue to take the form of listed names, with Latin (and sometimes Greek) forms appearing alongside French.

GOD'S WORDBOOKS

Christopher Lucken argues that bestiaries are "God's hieroglyphs" in that they unite depiction with meaning.[14] The Egyptian reference makes sense for *Physiologus*, composed in Alexandria, but a more pertinent one for European bestiaries is the medieval wordbook. Written

13. Ron Baxter, *Bestiaries and their users in the Middle Ages* (Thrupp & London: Sutton Publishing/ Courtauld Institute, 1998), 34–37.

14. Christopher Lucken, "Les hiéroglyphes de Dieu. La *demonstrance* des bestiaires au regard de la *senefiance* des animaux." *Compar(a)ison* 1 (1994): 33–70.

by prominent masters, wordbooks were tools of vocabulary-building
of a kind fundamental to medieval (indeed, any) education; critters
occupy whole sections of at least two widely-diffused examples.[15] In
their discursive sparseness, their uniting of name and nature, and their
layout, bestiaries can be seen as moralized and illustrated wordbooks
that teach the lexicon of the natural world. The difference between
critters which readers might actually know (foxes, weasels, beavers,
monkeys, screech owls, coots, eagles . . .), ones they were less likely
to have seen (elephants, lions, antelopes, crocodiles . . .) and those
they could not have (caladrius, siren, centaur, unicorn . . .) pales into
insignificance beside the pedagogical value of learning their names
together with a sense of what they are like. As Rita Copeland puts
it, "In the most concrete and fundamental way, language itself constitutes its own reality in the scene of instruction."[16] This emphasis
on the critter-as-word shares linguistic terrain with the *animot* but
remains resolutely tied to the specific.

The oldest vernacular bestiary represents itself as the translation
of a *livre de grammaire* (PT, 4, 1958). The phrase is usually understood as meaning "a book in Latin," but likely also means "a Latin
schoolbook," one designed (as wordbooks were) for use in a grammar (or elementary) school, where the privileged syntactic category
in teaching Latin grammar was the noun or name. Remnants of Latin
adhere to Philippe's text in extensive rubrics where the Latin forms
of critters' names are preserved; since the chapters typically begin by
supplying that name in the vernacular, the result is not unlike a bi-
lingual, encyclopedic dictionary. The format of his chapters, which is
modeled on but renders more formulaic that of B-Is, is also pedagogical in the way it alternates between the enigma of a critter's potential
"great significance" and its exposition, as if piquing and then satis-
fying the student's curiosity. That the Latin SF redaction was used
as a textbook for schoolchildren is the main conclusion drawn by
Willene B. Clark. Clinching evidence is her discovery, in fourteen SF

15. Tony Hunt, *Teaching and Learning Latin in 13th-century England*, 3 vols.
(Woodbridge: D. S. Brewer, 1991), especially Alexander Neckam's *De nominibus uten-
silium* §§65, 71–72 (I: 182, 184) and its French glosses (II: 68, 72, 83, 84–85, 87, 88,
91–92, 98, 101–102, 111, 113, 122), and John of Garland's *Dictionarius* §§ 70–74 (I:
201–202) and its French glosses (II: 140–42, 152). There are also medieval word-lists
involving critter; one with Anglo-Norman glosses described by Hunt, *Teaching and
Learning*, I: 22–26, shares common ground with bestiaries.
16. Rita Copeland, "Naming, Knowing, and the Object of Language in Alexander
Neckam's Grammar Curriculum," *Journal of Medieval Latin* 20 (2010): 50.

manuscripts, of glosses and annotations consistent with those found in other contemporary schoolbooks.[17] She also notes that SF bestiaries are often found as single, relatively portable books, suitable for use in the classroom.[18] Vernacular bestiaries, however, are more often compiled in miscellanies; and while they may be placed alongside other pious-didactic works, they also keep company with vernacular encyclopedic texts, most commonly the *Image du monde*.[19] Indeed, the sections of encyclopedias that deal with the wildlife of exotic realms overlap substantially with vernacular bestiary texts, though without the moralizations.[20] Such kinship underlines the bestiaries' function of teaching readers to recognize and name aspects of the world around them.

A large part of the appeal of bestiaries as books is that, like modern children's literature, they almost always use pictures to draw readers in and to help them remember the names they illustrate. Many illustrations are simple portraits of the critter concerned, framed and placed at the head of the relevant chapter, and often clearly linked by a rubric to the name at issue (stones and plants are less frequently illustrated). Sometimes, and typically in SF manuscripts, the picture represents the critter in action, performing its nature (see Figure 1).[21] In a few copies, pictures are squeezed into the text near the relevant noun, like in a Larousse *illustré* (see Figure 2). Only in a minority of (mainly early) manuscripts is the picture geared more to the moralization than the critter, and placed half-way through the chapter or at its end.[22] The convention of placing the image at the head of the

17. Clark, *Medieval Book of Beasts*, chap. 8, especially 103–105.

18. Clark, *Medieval Book of Beasts*, 85–91, 103.

19. Anglo-Norman copies of GC tend to juxtapose the bestiary with sermons and religious texts; see Betty Hill, "A Manuscript from Nuneaton: Cambridge Fitzwilliam Museum MS McLean [sic] 123," *Transactions of the Cambridge Bibliographical Society* 12:3 (2002): 191–205. Continental copies where GC is compiled with the *Image du monde* include BnF fr. 2168, fr. 14964, fr. 1444, and fr. 24428; fr. 2168 additionally contains a French text of the *Elucidarium*; in Fitzwilliam J 20, another continental manuscript, GC is compiled alongside excerpts of Brunetto's *Tresor*. LV is also found together with the *Image du monde* in Montpellier, Bibliothèque interuniversitaire, Section de médecine, H.437, and Arsenal, 3516.

20. "*L'image du monde*, une encyclopédie du XIIIᵉ siècle," Chantal Connochie-Bourgne (Ph.D. diss., Université de Paris-Sorbonne, 1999), 2307–596 (*bestes* of India), 2857–900 (*poissons* of India), 3151–350 (*bestes* of Europe and Africa).

21. Clark, *Medieval Book of Beasts*, 62–64.

22. Images are placed just before the moralizations in PT manuscript Copenhagen, Kongelige Bibliotek, Gl. kgl. S. 3466 8°, and were intended to be in British Library Cotton Nero A. v, though they were never executed. Images in Brussels, Bibliothèque

chapter becomes more established over time; it is the norm in SF manuscripts.[23]

A typical Latin SF page layout is illustrated in Figure 1: that of London, British Library Harley 3244, a relatively large (27 × 16, 19.5 × 11 cm) and handsome compilation of mainly devotional Latin texts copied in England ca. 1240.[24] Fo. 41r contains the end of the chapter on the hyena (§12), that on the *bonnacon* (§13, one of the chapters introduced by the SF compiler), and that on the ape (§14). According to the text, the *bonnacon* cannot defend itself with its horns, since they curve backward, instead repelling potential assailants with a scorching fart "three acres long"; no spiritual teaching accompanies this memorable claim. In the tinted drawing all the critters are labeled in addition to the rubric identifying the chapter's subject. The chapter following depicts the mother ape, said to love one but hate the other of her twin offspring. When pursued by a hunter, she first tries to save them both, instinctively clasping to her the preferred child while the other clings to her back. The picture captures this moment, the mother looking lovingly at the child in her arms. But as the hunt intensifies she is obliged to run on all fours so the ill-favored child is able to ride safely, while the favorite is dropped, an outcome that earns her the description "perverse." The rubric identifies the ape by name and the chapter opens with the (pseudo-)etymology *simia* < *similis* – the ape is so called because of its (deceptive) likeness to man. Both images, then, capture the nature attributed to the animal by lore, and in both cases that nature is yoked to its name by the layout of the page.

London, BL Additional 28260, fo. 90r of which is reproduced in Figure 2, is at the opposite end of production quality from Harley 3244. This small format (12.2 x 10, 11 x 7 cm) French manuscript of the late thirteenth century is the sole witness of Gervaise's Anglo-Norman verse *Bestiaire*. Fo. 90r contains the closing lines of the chapter on the centaur; then the chapters on the hyena and the ape; and the start of the chapter on the elephant (G, vv. 343–385). Its only decoration are the enlarged red initials marking the beginnings of chapters and (in

---

Royale, MS 10066–77, are located mainly at the end of chapters and divided between two registers, "beast" and "gloss"; see Baxter, *Bestiaries and their users*, 62–72.

23. Clark, *Medieval Book of Beasts*, 55.

24. Clark, *Medieval Book of Beasts*, 232–34, describes the bestiary in this manuscript and dates it to the 1240s; it has been digitized, see http://www.bl.uk/manuscripts/Viewer.aspx?ref=harley_ms_3244_f036r .

Figure 1. London, British Library Harley 3244 (ca. 1340), fo. 41r. Second-family Latin bestiary, chapters on the hyena, bonnacon, and ape. © British Library Board.

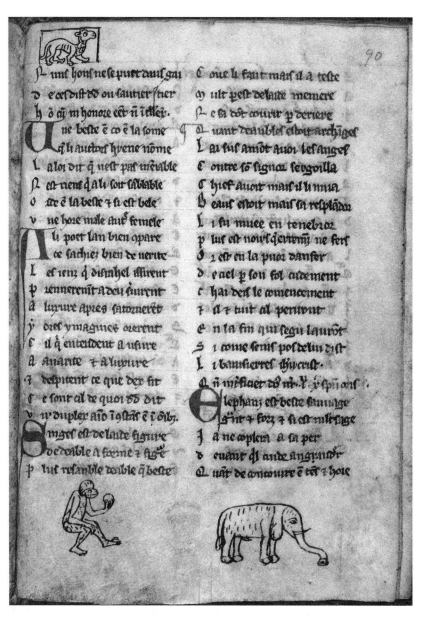

Figure 2. London, British Library Additional 28260 (late thirteenth century), fo. 90r. Gervaise's Anglo-Norman verse *Bestiaire*, chapters on the hyena, ape, and elephant. © British Library Board.

the case of the hyena), the start of the allegoresis; and the simple line drawings in ink, placed as close as possible to the start of the relevant chapter: the hyena (top margin), the ape (bottom margin, left), and elephant (bottom margin, right). A verse of Scripture, quoted in Latin, is placed between each of the chapters on this page. Although not highlighted visually, it has the effect of making each critter appear part of a sermon. As also in the Harley text, the hyena is said to be a filthy *beste* capable of changing sex; it represents the Jews and, more broadly, usurers, the avaricious, and the lustful. The ape, in a simpler chapter than Harley, is said to look more like a demon than a *beste*. And the elephant, as is traditional, represents the chaste sexuality of Adam and Eve before the fall. Each image is placed very close to the lines declaring its name and is a simple portrait except for that of the ape, shown holding and studying an object in imitation of human behavior; this nature reflects the etymology of its name even though Gervaise does not cite it.

Whatever format is preferred, bestiaries are not just descriptive and moralized wordbooks but also illustrated ones. With their seeming union of word and world, these critters graphically promote the creative multiplicity of Adam's names on a different axis from the *animot*.

TERMINOLOGY, TAXONOMY, AND THE RISE OF THE BEAST

Bestiaries do not, however, lack all interest in generalization. They reflect various potential classifications of critters, among which the word *bestia* (vernacular *beste*) becomes gradually more inclusive, eventually incorporating even human beings in its compass.

The oldest Latin text considered here, that preserved in Royal 2. C. XII, is titled "liber de natura quondam animalium, et lapidum" (book about the nature of *animals* and stones), implying that all its chapters except those on stones have a common focus on the *animal*. Given their wide range of subjects (including one chapter devoted to a man, the prophet Amos), *animal* here is presumably used in the learned sense referring to all living, sentient beings. Individual chapters, however, tell a different story, since within them *animal* is used only to introduce critters that live on land, usually in the phrase "Est animal, quod dicitur [*monoceros, castor, hiena, hydrus, panthera, elephas* ...]" (There is an animal that is called [*unicorn, beaver, hy-*

ena, hydrus, panther, elephant . . .]]. Birds are introduced in the same way but with *volatile* (flying creature) in lieu of *animal* (except for the ostrich, which is an *animal*); the swordfish and great fish are each a *belua* (monster, §§4, 25). The salamander is introduced by "Est reptile quoddam quod graece dicitur *salamander*" (§31, there is a crawling creature called *salamander* in Greek). The ant is compared with other living beings incapable of speech (*irrationalibus animalibus*) and also with weak crawling critters (*infirmis reptilibilus*); the conjunction of "living being" with "crawling thing" recalls the "reptile animae viventis" of Gen. I:20. As in all bestiaries, the text opens with the lion, its first chapter being rubricated "De natura leonis, bestiarum seu animalium regis" (of the nature of the lion, king of beasts or, of animals). But the meaning of *bestia* is at once defined, following Isidore, as a distinct subdivision of *animal*: "The word *bestiae* applies properly to lions, pards, foxes, tigers, wolves and the like, bears and so on, which menace with either their mouths or their claws, excepting serpents. They are called beasts because they menace with violence."[25] *Bestiae*, then, are carnivorous animals, or rather, carnivorous quadrupeds, snakes being excluded. This manuscript's categories approximate to the fourfold morphological-ecological division of Genesis I:21–30, between land animals, birds of the air, creatures that live in water, and creeping things indeterminate between water and land. Its relation to biblical terminology is less exact, however, since while it reprises the Vulgate's terms *bestia*, *reptile*, and *volatile*, it diverges by using *belua* ("monster") where Genesis has *ceta* "whale"/ *pisces* "fish."

The three biggest changes relative to the B-Is redaction that are introduced almost a century later in the Second Family are the expansion and re-ordering of chapters, the inclusion of a chapter on Adam naming the animals (§32), and the introduction of two long chapters on man (§§121–2). The first two changes impact on the bestiary as a zoological machine that strives to conceptualize animals as such. The third, the inclusion of human beings, points to the nature of medieval *bêtise* and will be addressed in the last section of this paper.

In the new organization, §§1–27 are about large wild quadrupeds, §28–30 address the dog, §33–45 concern domestic animals or livestock (herd and draft animals), §§46–50 group together small wild land animals (mouse, weasel, mole, hedgehog, ant), §§51–89 are mainly

25. Clark, *Medieval Book of Beasts*, 120.

about birds (though they include among flying creatures the siren, bat, and bee), §§90–109 focus on snakes (though including the crocodile, lizard, and salamander), §§110–111 are on worms (including the spider, purportedly a kind of aerial worm), §§112–119 on fishes (including the crocodile again, and dolphins and whales), §120 on trees, §§121–122 are the new chapters on the anatomy and ages of man, and the final chapter (§123) is on firestones. Although typically bestiary manuscripts are segmented by rubrics, BL Additional 11283 has only four, which mark the onset of some of its major categories: *De naturis avium* (of the natures of birds), *De vermibus* (of worms, though in fact the worm is introduced as an *animal* in §110), *Incipit de piscibus* (here begins a section on fishes), and *De etatibus hominum* (the ages of man). After the rubric introducing the natures of birds the text reads: "there is but one name for birds (*unum nomen avium*) but the genus is diverse (*genus diversum*)." The SF redaction is more than three times as long as the modest, 37-chapter B-Is, and its change of scale is matched by one of conception as it moves the bestiary text away from a chaotic enumeration of critters given sense by divine meaning toward a list of named species organized in something approximating morphological-ecological categories.

The new chapter about Adam's naming of the animals, absent in B-Is, is lifted from the opening of Book XII of the *Etymologiae*, and somewhat incongruously removed to §32 of the Second Family text, where it belatedly reflects on categories of critter. Here is a modified version of Clark's English translation, with the original Latin terminology in parentheses:

> Those which, although they are similar to herd animals (*pecoribus*), yet are not under human care, such as hinds, fallow deer, wild asses, and so forth, are called quadrupeds (*quadrupedia*) because they walk on four feet, but neither are they wild beasts (*bestiae*), such as lions, not animals yoked (*iumenta*) so that they can help man. We call everything that lacks a human voice and form a herd animal (*pecus*), although the name of herd animals is properly applied to those animals (*animalibus*) that are fit to eat, such as sheep and pigs, or to those suited to the use of men, such as horses and cattle (*boves*); furthermore, there is a difference between herd animals (*pecora*) and livestock (*pecudes*). Now the ancients, in referring to all animals (*animalium*), generally called them herd animals (*pecora*). Livestock (*pecudes*), however, include only those animals (*animalia*) which are eaten, as if to say "you may eat" (*pecu – edes*); moreover, every animal (*animal*)

is generally called a herd animal (*pecus*), from feeding (*pascendo*). Wherefore the beasts of burden (*iumenta*) took their names from the fact that they aid (*iuvent*) our labor, either by transporting a load with their assistance, or by plowing. [. . .] Whence they are called beasts of burden (*iumenta*), from the fact that the assist (*iuvent*) men, for they are animals of great strength. And likewise they are called work animals (*armenta*) either because they are suited to carrying arms (*armis*), that is, in war, or because we use them in arms. Others understand work animals (*armenta*) to mean only oxen, from plowing (*arando*) or because they are armed (*armata*) with horns. Yet there is a difference between work animals (*armenta*) and flocks (*greges*), for there are work-herds (*armenta*) of horses and cattle, but flocks (*greges*) of goats and sheep. (cf. Clark, *Medieval Book of Beasts*, 150–51)

Here the bestiary most explicitly acknowledges the post-lapsarian division, underlined by Dittmar, between wild critters (*bestiae*) and critters which remain in the service of man (*pecus*), though this latter heading allows many distinctions and some confusion. *Pecus*, it emerges, is broadly equivalent to *animal*, although *animal*, here at least, is also a synonym of *quadrupedis*. The passage also advises that *animans* is an acceptable variant of *animal*, and seemingly extends the term to all sentient and mobile beings ("Latine autem animalia sive animantia dicta, quae animantur vita et moventur spiritu," 150; "in Latin they are called *animals* or *animate creatures* because they are animated by life and moved by breath").

The passage strikes above all as an example where material has been compiled without being fully integrated. Oddly displaced from its initial position in Isidore, it has scant influence on the rest of the SF text. Its division between wild and herd or draft animals, for instance, is undercut by the text inserting domestic animals between two groups of wild ones seemingly distinguished by size, although size is nowhere made an explicit criterion of classification. And its elaborate vocabulary for domestic and draft animals does not extend outside these lines: the generic term used in individual chapters is *animal* or *animans*. When the SF text retains critters found in B-Is, it presents them in the same way as the earlier text. Thus in SF the opening sentence for the beaver remains "Est animal, quod dicitur castor" (There is an animal called the beaver, §10, cf. ed. B-Is §17), and so on. Despite the presence of *pisces*, the term *belua* (monster) continues to be used of the great fish and swordfish, and is extended rather surprisingly to the hyena (§12). However, when SF introduces new critters, it often presents them instead as *bestia*: the lynx (§7), leucrota (§21), manticora (§23), parandrus (§24), eale (§26, "yale"), and whale (§114: "balenae autem sunt immensae magnitudinis bestiae," "whales are beasts of immense size"). This expansion in the range of the term *bestia* corresponds with the tendency increasingly to designate the whole text as *Liber bestiarum*.

This Latin promotion of the word *bestia* is matched and outstripped in the French texts. Vernacular bestiarists never use the term *animal* and deploy the word *beste* ever more widely. They omit Isidore's definition of *bestia* as a carnivorous quadruped, and designate all the critters referred to in Latin as *animal* as *beste* including the ant-lion (PT, 1095) and ostrich (PT, 1246), though the latter is more often a *oisel* ("bird"; G, 950; GC, 2591; LV §§29, 52). In tandem with SF's covert introduction of a criterion of size, the shadowy concept of the "small beast" emerges: Philippe de Thaun terms the weasel and salamander *besteste* (PT, 1216, 1305); Gervaise and Guillaume both call the weasel a *petite beste* (G, 1237; GC, 2427), and the LV introduces *bestelete* to refer to the cricket (§14), though it continues to use *beste* in reference to both the ant and the spider (§§28, 33). Serpents, strictly distinguished from *bestiae* by Isidore, can also be *bestes* in the vernacular: see the asp (G, 1131–76; LV, §13), the viper (LV, §6), the basilisk (LV, §34), and a species of snake called the *tyris* (LV, §36); the preponderance of these examples in LV, the last bestiary in date, confirms the onward march of the term *beste* in French since *serpent* is more common in the earlier texts. Creatures designated *belua* in Latin bestiaries are also now *bestes*: serra (PT, 1681; GC, 399; LV, §3), *cetus* (PT, 1915), and *lacoine* (LV, §51), though Gervaise refers to the *sereine* as "de mer .i. peril" (G, 305, a peril of the sea) and Guillaume to the *cetus* as "une grant merveille de mer," (GC, 2240, a great marvel of the sea), phrases presumably meant to translate *belua*. New chapters introduced by LV such as the harpy (LV, §16) and the *muscalliet* (§71) also call their subjects *bestes*.

Thus the most general words for critter in Latin, *animal /animans* and *pecus*, have no vernacular equivalent. All critters that live on land, and some that live in water, however large or small, are henceforth some kind of *beste*; even the concept of *reptile*, insofar as it occurs, is represented by *beste rampans* ("crawling beast"), like the dragon (GC, 2223) and salamander (LV, §56). Airborn critters alone are distinct: *bestes* are broadly distinguished from *oisel* by all vernacular bestiarists (cf. Gervaise's programmatic "*bestes* have diverse appearance / and meaning, / and so do birds," G, 51–3); that said, the word *poissons* is found sporadically (G, 1180, 1188; GC, 2247,[26] 2293; LV, §64). The texts of Philippe de Thaun and Gervaise reflect this broad-brush division of critters between birds and beasts. Philippe de Thaun's chapters, in fact, fall into three groups, beasts, birds, and stones, while Gervaise has two main sections, *bestes* and *oisel*. Both bestiaries seemingly transgress their own taxonomy at a number of points, however, which suggests that what today are accepted as "natural" categories were far from obvious then.[27] On the other hand, Guillaume le Clerc and the LV compiler both retain a chapter order whose seemingly random relation to the natural world is closer to B-Is than to SF. The term *beste* becomes increasingly elastic as the genre advances and vernacular authors seem to feel no need for intermediate terms like the Latin *quadrupedis* or *pecus*.

The success of the vernacular *beste* is corroborated by its universal use in titles. Philippe de Thaun repeatedly refers to his model, the *Bestiaire*. Gervaise ends his book, "Ci fenist li livres des bestes." Guillaume le Clerc encapsulates the situation with a delightful unselfconsciousness: "Mult a a dire e a retraire / es essamples del bestiaire, / qui sont de bestes et d'oisels" (GC, 1167–9, "there is much to be said about the examples of the bestiary, which are about beasts and birds"). The compiler of LV begins by explaining that his text is called *Bestiaire* because "it tells about the natures of *bestes*." There may be no *animal* in the Middles Ages but, at least in French, all critters are gradually subsumed into *bestes*.

THE HUMAN BEAST

Given that, from the earliest bestiaries, human readers are the beneficiaries of the beasts' *senefiance*, the meaning of a beast is in a sense always already human. Variants of the formulation "this beast signifies every man" (e.g. of the antelope, G, 473–4) stretch to "man is this beast" (e.g. of the elephant, PT, 799–800). Whereas comparison with the elephant is positive, that with the antelope is not. A negative conception of the human *bestia* is also found in B-Is in Royal 2. C. XII,

26. See Reinsch, Introduction, 62–68, on the surprising range of species of fish named here.
27. In PT the partridge is placed last in the section on beasts and fire stones are placed last in that on birds. In G the crow is found with the beasts; the stag, swordfish, weasel, and aspic are surrounded by birds.

where the term *bestia*, defined in the chapter on the lion, returns only twice, both times deep in the chapter on the panther (B-Is, §24). "A beast with a spotted coat" ("bestia minutis orbiculis superpicta"), the panther allegedly evokes the beast-like sensuality of the Jews ("qui aliquando sensum bestiarum habebant"). Appeals to the bestial to denigrate but also particularize the human are an instance of what Derrida calls *bêtise*; similar strains recur in the pervasively anti-Semitic PT and GC.

But this hierarchy of reader (human) and read (beast) is increasingly leveled out as humans take their place among the critters. B-Is includes a chapter on a man—the prophet Amos —which Pierre de Beauvais is the only French author to retain; the LV *remanieur* not only keeps Pierre de Beauvais' chapter but repeatedly underlines Amos's presence by citing him in the glosses on other animals: the tiger (§7), aspic (§13), peacock (§19), monkey (§46), and partridge (§50). He thereby creates a kind of feedback loop whereby one critter, which happens to be a human being, appears as a guide to the meaning of others. Although Guillaume does not include Amos he also opens up the bestiary to the human by concluding with the parables of the talents and of the vineyard workers (GC, 3426–4100): by implication, these glossed tales of human behavior are analogous to those of other critters.

Immediately before his book on "animals" (Book XII), Isidore devotes a book of his *Etymologies* to "man and marvels" (Book XI, "De homine et portentis").[28] As part of their seismic restructuring of earlier bestiaries, SF texts integrate Isidore's accounts of the anatomy and ages of man as their penultimate chapters (§§121–22). An even more "zoological" reconceptualization of the human is found in §67 of LV ("De coi li home est fais et de sa nature"), a sustained exposition of man's relation to the four elements that has a parallel (and maybe source) in the *Bestiaire d'amours* (§15).[29] This chapter presents man as synthesizing all four elements, whereas some critters live by one alone: the mole on earth, a bird called the *garmalien* on air, the salamander on fire, and the herring on water. In the *Bestiaire d'amours* §15, the emphasis is rather on the generality of the senses in man as opposed to the exclusive dependence on one sense of certain animals.

---

28. In British Library Additional 28260, G is also copied immediately after a treatise on the ages of man.
29. Ed. Morini, *Bestiari medievali*, 365–424.

The treatment of the place of human beings in nature could be described as "scientific" in both these French texts.

At the same time as placing man among the beasts, the illustrators of SF bestiaries also regularly portray human beings alongside the other critters. A similar development can be charted in vernacular manuscripts from the very animal-centered images of PT and G to the later GC manuscripts. It is true, as Clark says, that the depiction of humans may have enhanced the attractiveness of SF bestiaries to laymen learning to master the written text;[30] it also reflects the bestiaries' increasingly inclusive attitude toward man. I disagree here with J. J. Cohen for whom there is a "classificatory 'order of things'" whereby "the symbolic function of the animal is primarily to reassure humans of their fundamental difference from other kinds of living things."[31] In the thirteenth-century bestiary, man is one of the beasts.

To say that "man is a rational animal" is to claim, of human creatures, that in addition to sentience and mobility they possess the faculty of speech. This claim operates according to the well-diagnosed procedure whereby what is claimed as proper to man is whatever is lacking to (other) animals: it assumes the *animal* and promotes the *animot*. But if the animal does not exist, or exists only sporadically, then neither does man as defined by Agamben's anthropological machine: the man who figures in a vernacular bestiary is not a speech-capable *animal* but a subcategory of beast. Before Derrida's *animot* comes not only a medieval focus on the *name* of individual species (the bestiary as wordbook), but also a peculiarly medieval form of *bêtise*. Like *bêtise* as Derrida defines it, the medieval version performs implausible inclusions and exclusions which result from the equivocation, in the word *beste*, between "all animals (including human ones)," "quadrupeds," "dangerous quadrupeds," and "animals inferior to human beings." These intellectual contortions are, however, very different from those critiqued by the French philosopher, which lump together all non-human animals as separate from human ones, and then re-ascribe their purportedly inferior nature to stigmatized humans ("qu'il est bête!" "how stupid he is!"). Whether as wordbooks or as essays in taxonomy, the bestiaries of the French and Latin Middle Ages do not operate an anthropological machine but a zoological one.

30. *Medieval Book of Beasts*, 62–64.
31. Quoted by Karl Steel, *How to Make a Human. Animals and Violence in the Middle Ages* (Columbus, OH: Ohio State University Press: 2011), 52.

MATTHEW SENIOR

"L'animal que donc je suis": Self-Humaning in Descartes and Derrida

> Everything that I am about to entrust to you no doubt
> comes back to asking you to *respond* to me, you, to me,
> reply to me concerning what it is to *respond*. If you can.[1]
>
> —Jacques Derrida

In *Renaissance Self-Fashioning: From More to Shakespeare*, Stephen Greenblatt examines a recurring social and psychological mechanism that he argues is central to Renaissance humanism. Following Jacob Burckhardt's famous dictum that in Renaissance Italy, "man became a spiritual *individual*, and recognized himself as such,"[2] Greenblatt adds an intersubjective dimension to this process: "Self-fashioning is achieved in relation to something perceived as alien, strange, or hostile. This threatening Other—heretic, savage, witch, adulteress, etc., must be discovered or invented in order to be attacked and destroyed."[3] Renaissance individualism is thus brought about by a turning inward, an isolation and intensification of the self, but also by a dialectical struggle against chosen Others.

The work of Charles Taylor, Giorgio Agamben, and Peter Sloterdijk also provides valuable historical analyses and philosophical models for the emergence of the individual in Western history. In *Sources of the Self*, Taylor cites the Platonic "Know thyself" as a foundational model of interiority in the West as well as the spiritual practices and writings of Augustine, whose pathway of intense self-scrutiny led to the discovery of God within his soul. *Noverim me, noverim Te* (May I know myself, may I know you), Augustine writes in the *Soliloquies*,

---

1. Jacques Derrida, *The Animal That Therefore I Am*, trans. David Wills (New York: Fordham University Press, 2008), 8.
2. Jacob Burckhardt, *The Civilization of the Renaissance in Italy*, trans. S. C. Middlemore (New York: Modern Library, 1954), 100.
3. Stephen Greenblatt, *Renaissance Self-Fashioning: From More to Shakespeare* (Chicago: University of Chicago Press, 1980), 9.

YFS 127, *"Animots": Postanimality in French Thought*, ed. Senior, Clark, and Freccero, © 2015 by Yale University.

founding in these sermons and in the *Confessions* a kind of auto-biographical writing that will give divine sanction to the exploration of the self.[4] For Taylor, Cartesian philosophy is linked to Augustinianism, but with an important secularizing turn. Descartes' form of meditation "is not carried out so as to make God appear at the very roots of the self, closer than my own eye [. . .] It is no longer a way to an experience of everything in God. Rather what I now meet is myself."[5] Descartes initiates a shift from an autobiographical subject dependant on God for the definition of its humanness to a *res cogitans* with a transparent, if fleeting, definition of itself and a distant, abstract relationship with God, as simply an idea of perfection found in the mind. It is this search for and creation of an illusive self – "What I now meet [and create] is myself," to amend Taylor's words slightly – that I wish to call *self-humaning*.

Agamben calls this process *anthropogenesis*, specifying that this event was not accomplished once and for all, at the beginning of history, but rather "is always under way, every time and in each individual who decides between the human and the animal, between nature and history, between life and death."[6] In *You Must Change Your Life: On Anthropotechnics*, Sloterdijk underscores the pervasive influence in Western culture of "man himself producing man," as Marx formulated this idea, and which echoes as a categorical imperative in the last line of Rilke's poem "Archaic Torso of Apollo," "You must change your life" (Du mußt dein Leben ändern). Sloterdijk finds this individual injunction to create the human in oneself in phenomena as diverse as Stoic philosophy, monasticism, the diaries of "cripples" during the nineteenth century, the rebirth of the Olympic Games in 1896, and L. Ron Hubbard's *Dianetics*.[7]

Although not discussed in depth by either Agamben or Sloterdijk, I will argue that Descartes, whose entire philosophy is technical and hyperbolically subjective, is a decisive figure in the history of anthropogenesis and anthropotechnics. With the *cogito* and the

4. Augustine of Hippo, *Soliloquies* I, 2, quoted in John Cottingham, "The Mind-Body Relation," in *The Blackwell Guide to Descartes' Meditations* (London: Blackwell, 2006), 179.

5. Charles Taylor, *Sources of the Self: The Making of the Modern Identity* (Cambridge: Harvard University Press, 1989), 157.

6. Giorgio Agamben, *The Open: Man and Animal*, trans. Kevin Attell (Stanford: Stanford University Press), 79.

7. Peter Sloterdijk, *You Must Change Your Life: On Anthropotechnics*, trans. Wieland Hoban (Malden, MA: Polity Press, 2013).

phenomenology of the human mind and body in the *Meditations*, Descartes rejects the prevailing biblical, Aristotelian, and Scholastic definitions of the human and replaces them with a subjective, existential enactment of humanness in which the only valid evidence for deciding what a human is must emerge from mental phenomena occurring within the philosopher-narrator's mind. Beginning with Descartes in modern philosophy, it will be an individual subject—no matter how fragile, fictive, or unreliable—who will be called upon to fashion his or her humanness and arbitrate what is or is not human in the external world.

I find confirmation of the persistence of this subjectivist, Cartesian strain in questions related to the human and the animal in the title of two of Derrida's late essays, "The Animal That Therefore I Am" and "But as for me, who am I (following)?"[8] Both titles are citations and puns of famous Cartesian doxologies. "The animal that therefore I am" instead of "I think therefore I am," from Part Four of the *Discourse on Method*, and the double meaning attached to "mais moi, qui suis-je," from the Second Meditation.[9] Having established, through the *cogito*, that he exists, Descartes asks himself several times who he is. The inversion and troping of the *cogito* and the *qui suis-je?* suggests that some aspects of the Cartesian revolution, the words themselves and the human identity they precipitate, are to be kept and reworked, responded to, "followed."

RENAISSANCE SELF-HUMANING

As Emmanuel Faye and others have argued recently, Descartes' secular humanism follows a tradition of reflection on the perfection and dignity of man reaching back to figures such as Siger de Brabant (c. 1240-c. 1284), Raymond Sebond (1385–1436), Charles de Bovelle (1479–1567), Giovanni Pico della Mirandola (1463–1494), and Michel de Montaigne (1533–1592).[10] For this line of thinkers, *perfectio ho-*

8. Both of these essays appear in *The Animal That Therefore I Am*, trans. David Wills (New York: Fordham University Press, 2008).

9. René Descartes, *Meditations on First Philosophy* in *The Philosophical Writings of Descartes*, trans. John Cottingham, Robert Stoothoff, and Dugald Murdoch (Cambridge: Cambridge University Press, 1984), AT VII:27. All subsequent citations of Descartes are taken from this edition, with volume and page numbers referencing the twelve volume Adam and Tannery edition (Paris: Vrin, 1964–76), abbreviated as AT.

10. Emmanuel Faye, *Philosophie et perfection de l'homme : De la Renaissance à Descartes* (Paris: Vrin, 1998); see also the volume edited by Faye: *Descartes et la*

minis meant the fullest realization of human nature in this life, on earth. In the writings of these philosophers, the earliest tradition in the medieval West of a secular ideal of human perfection emerges as the result of purely philosophical and scientific investigations into human nature. It is freed from the constraints of Christian theology, which views human nature as essentially flawed as a result of the Fall. Inspired by the example of Raymond Sebond, Montaigne declared his own work to be "purely human and philosophical, without mixture of theology."[11] Similarly, declaring his work *not* to be theology, Descartes announced the *Discourse on Method* as "a project for a universal science to raise our nature to its highest degree of perfection," turning his attention specifically to question of human perfection in the Fourth Meditation.[12]

In addition to the ideal of human perfection, the belief in an absolutely different and separate nature of man is another element of Renaissance humanism. This totally other nature of man is defined most memorably in Pico della Mirandola's *Oration on the Dignity of Man* (1487), in which man is called upon not only to reach perfection, but to fashion his own humanness. Borrowing a myth from Plato's *Protagoras*, Pico imagines that God gave Adam the freedom to fashion his own nature, as opposed to the animals, whose natures were fixed at the time of creation.

> We have given you, Oh Adam, no visage proper to yourself, nor any endowment properly your own, [. . . .] The nature of all other creatures is defined and restricted within laws which We have laid down: you, by contrast, impeded by no such restrictions, may, by your own free will, to whose custody We have assigned you, trace for yourself the lineaments of your own nature. [. . .] We have made you a creature neither of heaven nor of earth, neither mortal nor immortal, in order that you may, as the free and proud shaper of your own being, fashion yourself in the form you may prefer.[13]

In both the *Protagoras* and Pico's *Oration*, the first men composed themselves from animal body parts. We could call the self-creation in

---

Renaissance: Actes du colloque international de Tours, 22–24 mars (Paris: Champion, 1996).

11. Michel de Montaigne, from the essay "Prières," quoted in Faye, *Descartes et la Renaissance,*15.

12. Descartes, letter to Mersenne, AT 1:338.

13. Giovanni Pico della Mirandola, *Oration on the Dignity of Man*, trans. Robert Caponigri (Washington: Regnery, 1956), 7.

Plato and Pico auto-*bio*-graphy, in distinction to Descartes' anthropogenesis, which is, by contrast, auto-*psycho*-graphy since, as we will
see, animality and life—*bios*—is expelled from the core of human
identity and replaced with consciousness—*esprit, psuchē.*

At the basis of Pico's conception of man is the exercise of free will,
the choice of whatever animal parts one elects to compose one's identity. It is striking that in Pico's myth, Adam does not receive a face
from God. Man has no face common to his species; there is a radical distinction between the human and the animal face. Adam must
compose his own face, presumably from animal parts, as the first step
in the creation of his identity. The fashioning of a human face from
animal parts anticipates the revival of the physiognomic tradition
later during the Renaissance, in the engravings of Giambattista Della
Porta. The exclusivity of the human face in Pico, even though it is
fashioned of animal parts, seems to anticipate Levinas as well. Man
is neither an angel nor a land animal, although, as a consequence of
following either virtue or evil inclination, he can rise to the level of
the angels or fall to that of the beasts. Pico also still adheres to a cos-
mological definition of man, with the human as the privileged micro-
cosm of the cosmos. In the absolute freedom he bestows on humans
to rise or fall, Pico liberates human nature from the Aristotelian scale
of nature, anticipating Montaigne and Descartes. As will be the case
with Descartes, Pico's highest degree of self-humaning is reserved for
the "pure contemplator, unmindful of the body, wholly withdrawn
into the inner chambers of the mind."[14]

BUT WHAT IS A MAN?

The critique of the Aristotelian-Scholastic definition of man is one of
the important first steps in the Cartesian construction of the human
in the *Meditations.* It marks a decisive step in the radically subjective
anthropology of self-humaning. The critique of the definition of man
as a rational animal occurs early in the Second Meditation after hyperbolic doubt has swept away all belief in the existence of the material world. "I have convinced myself that there is absolutely nothing
in the world, no sky, no earth, no minds, no bodies."[15] A "deceiver
of supreme power and cunning" may even be deceiving the philosopher, who nonetheless is able to utter the single sentence that defies

14. Pico della Mirandolla, *Oration,* 11.
15. Descartes, AT 7:25.

all supernatural powers: "*I am, I exist.*" Immediately following this unshakable affirmation of being, the questioning of Aristotelian humanism begins. "What then did I formerly think I was? A man. But what is a man? Shall I say 'a rational animal'? No; for then I should have to inquire what an animal is, what rationality is, and in this way one question would lead me down the slope to other harder ones."[16]

Aristotle defined humans as "animals having logos" (*zoon logon echon*) in book 1.2 of the *Politics*; it is clear, however, that this definition does not separate humans from other animals as definitively as Descartes' radical dualism will. "Man is the only animal who has the gift of speech." "Man, when perfected, is the best of animals."[17] In both of these statements, speech or perfection are traits included within or added to an underlying animal nature. The human being, with all of its social trappings (most notably the family and the state), remains an animal. The state is a "creation of nature," as inherent to human nature as sexuality itself, which causes the first proto-state to be formed—the bond between man and woman, necessary for the propagation of the species. Although Descartes will privilege the same two Aristotelian criteria (reason and language) in separating humans from animals, he will do so in much more radical fashion. Descartes' essentially Lucretian view of nature, as a realm of inanimate atoms colliding and coalescing according to pure chance, devoid of any telos or preordained order, makes it impossible for him to accept Aristotle's view of a scale of nature, with a place reserved for man as the "best of animals."

To pick up again the thread of Descartes' search for a new definition of man, we recall that the narrator has reduced the phenomenality of his existence to that of a speaking subject. "I do not yet have a sufficient understanding of what I am, even as I am certain that I am."[18] The "I" cannot be affirmed as either a body or a subtle material soul. Regarding the body, the Meditator declares emphatically: "I am not that structure of limbs which is called a body."[19] Although Descartes showed great interest in anatomy throughout his work, he states here, categorically, that the "I" is *not* a human body. "I am not a body" is in some sense the motto of Cartesian anthropology and

16. Descartes, AT 7:26.
17. Aristotle, *Politics* in vol. 2 of *The Complete Works of Aristotle*, ed. Jonathan Barnes (Princeton: Princeton University Press, 1984), 1988.
18. Descartes, Ibid.
19. Descartes, AT 7:29.

all of the modern disembodiments that flow from it. At this point in the *Meditations*, and in some sense permanently, the essence of the human is not a body. Nor is the "I" a material soul. "I am not even some thin vapor which permeates the limbs—a wind, fire, air, breath, or whatever I depict in my imagination."[20]

The wind or pneumatic force alluded to here does describe very well the animal spirits that are concocted in the heart and move rapidly through the hollow tubes of the nervous system and the brain, as Descartes imagined them, but these winds, vapors, and particles are insensate and mechanical; they are not the "I," which remains resolutely immaterial and invisible. The sole function of the "I" is to think. "But what then am I?" – "A thing that thinks (*res cogitans*)."[21]

In this cutting off of the "I" from both the body and its vital principles, Derrida sees something profound and troubling about Cartesian philosophy, which substitutes the "I" in the place of the traditional conception of the human as a rational animal. In the second of three essays published together as *The Animal That Therefore I Am*, entitled "But as for me, who am I (following)?" Derrida observes about the disembodied Cartesian subject: "'I am,' in the purity of its intuition and thinking, excludes animality, even if it is rational. In the passage that follows this bracketing of the rational animal, Descartes proposes abstracting from his 'I am,' if I can put it this way, everything that recalls life."[22] Cartesian self-humaning is thus profoundly anti-natural and proceeds from an expulsion of animality from the core of the self. This trait will be found in the modern thinkers Derrida critiques: Heidegger, Levinas, and Lacan, all of whom, paradoxically, while deconstructing the Cartesian subject in different ways, retain and in varying degrees intensify Descartes' radical expulsion of animality from human nature. (As we will see, and as Florence Burgat points out in her essay in this volume, Sartre is an important Cartesian in this sense.)

As a final commentary on the rational animal, I would suggest that in a larger, symptomatic sense Descartes' questioning of "rational" as part of the definition of the human should be pondered as well. He refuses the word seemingly because its meaning is not transparent and leads down a "slope to harder questions." But I would argue that the

20. Ibid.
21. Descartes, AT 7:28.
22. Derrida, "But as for me," 71.

word is also expelled from the essence of the "I" because at this moment in the *Meditations* the narrator is not rational. The Meditator is not sure whether he has a body, whether the world exists, or whether his rational processes, such as mathematical calculations or logical deductions, are not the result of the deceptions of the Evil Genius. By doubting such certainties, Descartes asks if he is "like madmen, whose brains are so damaged by the vapors of melancholia that they firmly maintain that they are kings when they are paupers, [. . .] or say that their heads are made of earthenware or that they are pumpkins or made of glass."[23] The reply to this question is that in ordinary life the experiences of rational men and women in dreams are as extravagant as the illusions of the mad. By deliberately bracketing and relativizing all belief in the familiar material world, the self-made Cartesian "I" is beyond and contains both reason and madness. His mind is capable of embracing and staging all at once the perfect idea of God, the demonic deceptions of the Evil Genius, and all of the intermediary truths and half-truths that fill the human mind.

BARE WAX, BARE SPIRIT

Having rejected "rational animal" as his essence, and in effect substituted "thinking thing" as his definition, Descartes continues to tease out the hidden nature of the mind and make pronouncements about human and animal nature. One of the most decisive examples of this process occurs in the analysis of a piece of wax (*morceau de cire*) in the Second Meditation. In this passage we are asked to contemplate a piece of wax, at first solid, then melting, boiling, and finally burning up in smoke. In everyday language we say that we "see" the wax persist across these changes in state. But in order to "see" the wax persist, mental faculties must be engaged that go beyond vision and imagination. Only a human intelligence can strip away the changing outward appearances of the wax and grasp this substance in its intelligible dimension, as a collection of particles assuming various extensions in space. "When I distinguish the wax from its exterior forms, and, as though I had removed its clothes, I consider it totally naked, it is certain that, although there could still be errors in my judgment, I could nevertheless not conceive it as such without a human mind."[24] Mind, or to use Descartes' exact term, "spirit" (*esprit*), operates like

23. Descartes, AT 7:19.
24. Descartes, AT 7:32, translation modified.

a kind of vision, but an immaterial kind of vision capable of grasping objects beyond their vanishing mutable appearances.

As Descartes uncovers the characteristics of mind and the hidden nature of the self in the wax analysis, he observes that what emerges with the most distinctiveness of all is mind itself—even more clearly than the idea of the wax, which was seen "totally naked." "If the notion or the perception of the wax seemed more clear and distinct after not only the sight but also touch, and many other causes made it more manifest, how much more clearly and distinctly must I confess that I know myself now."[25] The "undressing" of the wax, and the simultaneous revelation of the immaterial mind are important anthropological moments in Descartes; they culminate in a clear and distinct emergence of the human—"I confess that I know myself now"—and an ensuing separation from animality. As Derrida comments, again from the "But as for me" essay, "In order, therefore, to gain access to the *je suis* as a human and not an animal mind, it is necessary to undress the wax."[26] And further, "The animal that I am not, the animal that in my very essence I am not, Descartes says, in short, presents itself as a human mind before naked wax."[27]

Paraphrasing Agamben and Heidegger, we could say that Descartes defines the human as *bare spirit*, a minimal, hidden, universal "common sense" existing outside of space, evincing itself in the leap beyond appearances in the undressing of the wax and a similar instantaneous and sovereign epiphany of itself in language, which, like the wax analysis, leads to a disqualification of the animal as a rational being.

OUTING THE ANIMAL

The sudden appearance of human rationality in language, and the capacity of language to instantly separate humans from animals is offered in the fifth part of the *Discourse on Method*. In this part of the *Discourse*, after presenting and defending his mechanist biology and arguing that animal and human bodies are very much like the automatons to be found in animated fountains in his day, Descartes asks how one could distinguish between an artificial animal and a real animal, and also how one could tell the difference between a real and

25. Descartes, AT 7:33.
26. Derrida, "But as for me," 73.
27. Ibid.

a mechanical human in such a scenario. For the mechanical animal, there is absolutely no difference, so it would be difficult. Between a mechanical and a real human however, *language* is the distinguishing factor. An automaton (and the distinction applies to all animals because they are indistinguishable from automatons) "could never use words, or put together other signs as we do in order to declare our thought to others." It could not "produce different arrangements of words so as to give an appropriate meaningful answer (*répondre au sens*) to what is said in its presence, as the dullest of men can do."[28] Animals do exhibit signs of their suffering and passions; they communicate their needs; both automatons and animals can be taught or programmed to mimic human language; but neither the machine nor the animal-machine can respond to "true questioning."[29] One can out a robot the same way one can out an animal—by simply asking them a question . . . to which neither can *respond*.

HEIDEGGER'S DESCARTES

Martin Heidegger has seen in Descartes' tendency to always prioritize the knowledge of his own mind over knowledge of the external world as the essence of the Cartesian revolution. In his 1949 lectures on Nietzsche, Heidegger affirms:

> At the beginning of modern philosophy stands Descartes' statement: *Ego cogito, ergo sum,* "I think therefore I am." All consciousness of things and of beings as a whole is referred back to the self-consciousness of the human subject as the unshakable ground of all certainty [. . . .] For representation as described, the *self* of man is essential as what lies at the very ground. The self is *sub-iectum*.[30]

Human exceptionalism, and man's unique rapport with Being, is taken even further by Heidegger in *Being and Time* and the *Letter on Humanism*. Like Descartes, Heidegger mentions the "Greek *zoon logon echon*" and criticizes the notion that man can be defined by setting him off, "as one living creature among others in contrast to plants, beasts, and God."[31] Even metaphysical projects such as

28. Descartes, AT 6:57.
29. Derrida, "But as for me," 82.
30. Martin Heidegger, *Nietzsche*, ed. David Farrell Krell, trans. Frank A. Capuzzi (San Francisco: Harper & Row, 1982) vol. IV, 86, 108.
31. Heidegger, "Letter on Humanism" in *Martin Heidegger: Basic Writings*, ed. David Farrell Krell (New York: Harper Collins, 1993), 227.

Descartes', in attributing to man an immortal soul, do not satisfy Heidegger's notion of ecstatic humanism. "Such standing in the clearing of Being I call the ek-sistence of man. This way of Being is proper only to man."[32] Animals, as is well known, are separated from human ek-sistent essence "by an abyss."[33]

SARTRE'S DESCARTES

In 1947, two years after his humanist manifesto "Existentialism is a Humanism," Jean-Paul Sartre penned "Cartesian Liberty," an introductory essay for an anthology of Descartes' major works. Declaring that for three centuries the French have "lived under Cartesian liberty," meaning the "independence of thought," Sartre recognizes in three moments of Cartesian philosophy (the *cogito*, the confrontation with the Evil Genius, and the idea of a God unfettered by natural laws) useful analogies and historical sources for his own philosophy of action. Certain declarations in Sartre's essay sound almost like Cornelian *stances*: "Every man is action" (Tout homme est action); "The man of action, contemplating his enterprise, can say: This is mine" (L'homme d'action, contemplant son entreprise, peut dire: ceci est à moi).[34] Sartre finds in Descartes several degrees of freedom, starting with the limited autonomy of assenting to mathematical proofs, passing next to the negative freedom of resisting and denying the falsehoods of the Evil Genius, and, finally, arriving at the model of absolute freedom represented by Descartes' God. At each of these stages there are ringing declarations of humanism and anthropocentrism. The understanding and affirmation of scientific truths gives existence to such truths in the world: "Man is the being by whom truth appears in the world."[35] The almost-nothingness of the *cogito* is an intimation of the nothingness of human nature. "I am in full exercise of my freedom when, empty and nothing myself, I *annihilate* everything that exists."[36] From the standpoint of Greenblatt's agonistic model of self-humaning, we could say that the

32. Heidegger, "Letter on Humanism," 228.
33. Ibid., 230.
34. Jean-Paul Sartre, "La liberté Cartésienne" in *Descartes: Introduction et choix par J.-P. Sartre* (Paris: Traits, 1946), 25.
35. Ibid., 16.
36. Ibid., 35.

Sartrean-Cartesian "I" overcomes the Evil Genius and appropriates his power to deceive. Hyperbolic doubt, according to Sartre, is related to absolute freedom. "It is in refusing until we can refuse no more that we are free. Thus methodological doubt becomes the prototype of the free act."[37]

Sartre interprets Descartes' conception of a God free to create any sort of laws of the universe, unrestrained by the laws of physics, as a sublimation and projection of Descartes' conception of a radically free human subject. It is telling that Sartre's hyperbolic humanism is an anti-naturalism. Through negativity, man can "withdraw from everything that in him is nature, his memory, his imagination, his body [. . . .] nothing shows better that man is not a being of nature."[38] A contemporary version of the human power to negate, which Sartre celebrates, might be the virtual and simulation. A powerful way to negate the real is to endlessly replicate it, to the point where it becomes impossible to distinguish the virtual from the real.

ANIMALSÉANCE

Derrida begins "The Animal That Therefore I Am" by recalling that his seminar at Cerisy-la-Salle is the third in what looks, retrospectively, like a progressive thematic itinerary, starting with the first seminar devoted to "The Ends of Man" (1980), then "The Crossing of Borders" (1992), and finally "The Autobiographical Animal" (1997), as if he were moving programmatically from the human toward "the animal in itself, the animal in me, and the animal at *unease* with itself" (my emphasis).[39] Derrida then opens his essay with a brief poetic exordium, a sweeping backward glance, as he becomes aware that an animal has been watching him for a long time.

> Since so long ago, can we say that the animal has been looking at us? What animal? The other.
>
> I often ask myself, just to see, *who I am*—and who I am (following) at the moment when, caught naked, in silence, by the gaze of an animal, for example, the eyes of a cat, I have trouble, yes, a bad time overcoming my embarrassment.

37. Ibid., 34.
38. Ibid., 36.
39. Derrida, "The Animal That Therefore I Am," 3.

Whence this malaise?
I have trouble repressing a reflex of shame. Trouble keeping silent
within me a protest against the indecency. Against the impropriety
[*malséance*] that can come of finding oneself naked, one's sex exposed, stark naked before a cat that looks at you without moving, just
to see.[40]

"What animal?" Derrida asks, and replies, "The other," meaning
that, from the outset, he considers himself to be a kind of animal and
the cat another—the other animal. The encounter produces an inexplicable malaise, a *malséance* specific to the exchange of gazes with
the cat, an "*animalséance*," the first of several animal neologisms or
puns (*animots*) that occur throughout this essay, hybrid words com-
bining human and animal emotions and ideas, forged in an attempt
to negotiate and "complicate" the borderland between human and
animal consciousness.

Naked and unknowing before his cat, the philosopher probes
and interrogates his *animalséance* in highly emotional and personal
terms, calling his feelings "*my* passion of *the* animal [. . .] an instant
of extreme passion."[41] This display and examination of an odd feeling,
establishing a mood in anticipation of an ontological breakthrough,
is in some ways comparable to the nausea that Sartre's hero Antoine
Roquentin feels in *La nausée* when he touches certain random objects or finds himself in familiar places.

Roquentin stoops down to pick up a piece of paper lying in the
street and suddenly has the bizarre sensation that the paper is touching him back: "objects should not *touch* because they are not alive."[42]
Entering a café, he has trouble recognizing the face of a familiar wait-
ress, Madeleine, and instead finds his attention wandering to strange
features on her face. "I did not recognize her. I looked at her large
cheeks which never stopped rushing towards the ears. In the hollow
of the cheeks, beneath the cheekbones, there were two pink stains
which seemed weary on this poor flesh." "What will you have, Mon-
sieur Antoine?" Madeleine asks. "Then the Nausea seized me, I
dropped to a seat, I no longer knew where I was, I saw the colors spin
slowly around me, I wanted to vomit."[43]

40. Ibid., 3–4.
41. Ibid., 11.
42. Sartre, *Nausea*, trans. Lloyd Alexander (New York: New Directions, 1964), 10.
43. Ibid.,18.

The familiar world of objects and categories such as inert matter, plant, animal, and human vacillate, providing glimpses into the true nature of things in their concreteness. The observing subject experiences anxiety as the web of familiar everyday objects, which he has fantasized and constructed as the Real, begins to crumble.

The notion that an unfamiliar emotion or sensation can herald an ontological shift or rupture can be compared, in both Sartre and Derrida, with Heidegger's strategic use of the word *Stimmung*, meaning "atmosphere," "tone," or "mood" in *Being and Time* (1927) and, more extensively, in his 1929–30 course, *The Fundamental Concepts of Metaphysics: World, Finitude, Solitude.*[44] In the latter work, Heidegger writes at length on the specific *Stimmung* of "profound boredom" (*tiefe Langeweile*) as a preparatory experience for the revelation of *Dasein.* In boredom, ordinary objects "have nothing to offer us" and yet we are still "riveted and delivered over to what bores us."[45] In a certain sense, objects of boredom, like Roquentin's objects of *nausée*, begin to strangely mistreat and abuse the subjects they hold captive. *Dasein* is an experience of being "thrown" and rejected by objects, and beginning to intimate, as a result of this disorienting experience, both the concealed being of objects, as such, as well as the separation and estrangement of the subject vis à vis these objects.

Along the lines of Roquentin, and in some sense similar to Descartes—traversing madness and hyperbolic doubt—Derrida gives free reign to and records the strange thoughts and fantasies that cross his mind as he is caught in the gaze of his cat; he experiences a kind of vertigo and loss of identity:

> In such moments, on the edge of the thing, in the imminence of the best or the worst, when anything can happen, where I can die of shame or pleasure, I no longer know in whose or in what direction to throw myself. Rather than chasing it away, chasing the cat away, I am in a hurry, yes, in a hurry to have it appear otherwise. I hasten to cover the obscenity of the event, in short, to cover myself. One thought alone keeps me spellbound: dress myself, even a little, or, which amounts to the same thing, run away—as if I were chasing myself out of the room—bite myself, therefore, bite my tongue, for example, at the very moment when I ask myself "Who?" But "Who therefore?" For I no

---

44. For discussions of *Stimmung* in Heidegger, see Agamben, *The Open*, 63–70; and Hans Ulrich Gumbrecht, *Atmosphere, Mood, Stimmung: On a Hidden Potential of Literature*, trans. Erik Butler (Stanford: Stanford University Press, 2012).

45. Quoted in Agamben, *The Open*, 64.

longer know who, therefore, I am (following) or who it is I am chas-
ing, who is following me or hunting me. Who comes before and who
is after whom?[46]

Like Roquentin, or like the Heideggerian subject thrown by *Dasein*,
Derrida feels, in the presence of his cat, "on the edge of the thing."
Anxiety and doubt lead to a revision of the Cartesian "Je suis," which
splits into two never fully reconcilable meanings: "I am" and "I am
following."

RESPONDING

Throughout this essay Derrida repeatedly poses the question of whether
animals can *respond* to human language, whether they can survive
the aggressive and dismissive linguistic "outing" Descartes inflicts
on them. "The said question of the said animal in its entirety comes
down to knowing not whether the animal speaks but whether one can
know what *respond* means. And how to distinguish a response from a
reaction."[47] On many levels, the answer to this question is affirmative:
the cat does respond to its name; it has its own language and its own
way of communicating its desires to be fed or let out of the apartment.

Alongside this examination of whether the "other animals" can
respond, I would argue that the outpouring of Derrida's *animalséance*
is an involuntary *response* to the animal. The cat triggers a series
of responses that are both human and animal, raising a number of
themes and questions (nakedness, shame, cruelty, the programmed
overproduction and slaughter of animals in industrial farming, etc.)
that will be pursued discursively and philosophically throughout the
entirety of *The Animal That Therefore I Am*.

The first of Derrida's unexamined, convulsive responses to the cat's
gaze is the impulse to cover himself; another response is the desire to
bite his tongue and refuse to talk. Inexplicably, or perhaps in profound
solidarity with the cat, Derrida becomes mute, entering into "the silence of the beasts" that Élisabeth de Fontenay describes so eloquently.

In the second paragraph, immediately following the description
of the encounter with the cat, Derrida explains in philosophical
terms what the charged exchange of glances with the animal revealed
to him.

---

46. Ibid., 9.
47. Derrida, "The Animal That Therefore I Am," 8.

Being *after*, being *alongside*, being *near* [*près*] would appear as different modes of being, indeed of *being-with*. With the animal. But, in spite of appearances, it isn't certain that these modes of being come to modify a preestablished being, even less a primitive "I am." In any case, they express a certain order of *being-huddled-together* [*être-serré*] . . .[48]

The specific terms that Derrida uses, being *"after," "alongside"* or *"near"* the animal are the very words that Heidegger uses in *The Fundamental Concepts of Metaphysics* to describe the limits of animal consciousness—the closeness yet inseparable distance between the animal and the open of *Dasein*, which prevents animals from grasping the Being of beings, "as such," and the concomitant grasping of themselves as conscious subjects.[49] Derrida draws near to but parts company with Heidegger: "it isn't certain that these modes of being [being after, alongside, or near] come to modify a preestablished being." What Derrida argues here is that there is no Being separable from or prior to "a certain order of *being-huddled-together* [*être-serré*]."

The inexplicable desire to flee the cat's presence, in the grips of a kind of claustrophobic panic, is the psychological response to the fear of being huddled together in an undifferentiated mass with the animal. Later in the essay Derrida will argue that the plurality of *"animot"* expresses, among other things, an "irreducible living multiplicity of mortals."[50] The preliminary affect of wanting to cover himself, flee, bite his tongue in silence; the strange reversal in which he feels simultaneously following and followed by the animal—in all of this, Derrida exhibits himself *responding* to the presence of an animal—staging, miming, creating, and testing, poetically, his humanness.

FOLLOWING, TRACKING, HUNTING

The same *nausée* that makes Roquentin feel like vomiting when entering a café is also capable of granting him "a small happiness of Nausea," when he listens to the ragtime classic "Some of these

---

48. Ibid., 10.
49. "We shall define the animal's specific being-alongside-itself—which has nothing to do with the selfhood of man comporting him- or herself as a person—this absorption in itself of the animal, in which behavior of any and every kind is possible as captivation." Heidegger, *The Fundamental Concepts of Metaphysics: World, Finitude, Solitude,* trans. William McNeill and Nicholas Walker (Bloomington: Indiana University Press, 1995), 238.
50. Derrida," The Animal That Therefore I Am," 41.

days." He hears the notes of the jazz music, the "dry little points. [. . .] They race, they press forward, they strike me a sharp blow in passing and are obliterated. I would like to hold them back, but I know if I succeeded in stopping one it would remain between my fingers only as a raffish languishing sound. I must accept their death; I must even will it. [. . .] I grow warm, I begin to feel happy."[51]

Similarly, Derrida's *animalséance* does have its ecstatic modulations—in the long temporal daydream he embarks on, leading from the lack of shame and nakedness on the part of his cat, all the way back to a fantasy of watching Adam name the animals, before the Fall, in Genesis. In this time before guilt and guilty confessions Adam is *free* to name the animals. God will not violate this essential human freedom; He abandons Himself to his "curiosity" in order to see (*pour voir*) how Adam will name the animals. There is thus a finitude to God in his waiting and derogation of the power of naming the animals to Adam. The immediacy and transparency of the Adamic names is lost in time. Denied the immediacy of this naming and response, Derrida is condemned to pursue an endless Cain- and Bellerophon-like tracking and hunting of the animal, which is a tracking and hunting of his own self and his humanity, in its obscure link to the animal. In the hunt and being hunted one never sees the wild and free animal clearly and distinctly (scientifically), but only momentarily and furtively. There is a relationship to the animal and to the self full of mystery and beauty. A beauty and a mystery that I have always found—to abandon myself, to respond, *à mon tour*, to the autobiographical pull of Derrida's text—in a few lines from Marie de France's lai *Guigemar*, at the moment when the Breton hero yields to his passion for hunting and enters the forest, beginning an adventure in self-discovery that starts with the pursuit of a deer.

> One day Guigemar felt the urge to hunt.
> He summoned his knights that very evening,
> His trackers and his *rabatteurs*.
> In the morning he rode into the forest,
> For Guigemar was a passionate hunter.[52]

---

51. Sartre, *Nausea*, 21.
52. Marie de France, *Les lais de Marie de France*, trans. Laurence Harf-Lancner (Paris: Le Livre de Poche, 1991), 31.

JEAN-LUC GUICHET

From the Animal of the Enlightenment to the Animal of Postmodernism

The aim of this article is to compare the relationship of man to animal (or to *animals*, if we heed Derrida's warning about the distressing but continual slighting of the necessary plural) in the eighteenth century on the one hand, and in these early years of the twenty-first century on the other. My ultimate purpose is to get some sense of the present state of this relationship and its underlying dynamics in our so-called postmodern world. Earlier centuries had gradually created a deep rift between man and animal, a rift generally unknown—or at least never so deep—in the ancient world. In the eighteenth century, to the contrary, just as in our own day, the man-animal relationship tended to close up to the point of more or less reconstructing —at least theoretically—that lost continuity. This means that we may legitimately ask whether today's view of animals is simply a legacy of the Enlightenment. The answer is that understanding the structure of the prevailing man-animal relationship ultimately means seeing it as the completion of the eighteenth-century view, at least as represented by some of that period's most outstanding thinkers; this rounding-out process, however, was in retreat or stagnant during the nineteenth and twentieth centuries (up until the 1970s, roughly speaking). To assess such developments over the centuries, it behooves us—aside from the necessity, here as elsewhere, of eschewing the myth of a progress supposedly reaching perfect fulfillment in our era—to articulate the more or less implicit criteria generally deployed, namely continuity, community, and communication.

To take Diderot, Condillac, and Rousseau as the chief thinkers on this issue in eighteenth-century France, it does seem that the Enlightenment in its critical campaign against the Christian religion and the earlier metaphysical—especially Cartesian—tradition, was

YFS 127, *"Animots": Postanimality in French Thought*, ed. Senior, Clark, and Freccero, © 2015 by Yale University.

striving to reconstruct the continuity between man and animal that these movements had denied or at least vigorously downplayed. This critical enterprise was radical inasmuch as it undermined the very foundations of these tendencies: the notion of the soul—a divisive or hierachizing barrier—was demolished by Diderot; the idealist or intellectualist theory of knowledge, which restricted true knowledge to the human mind alone, was refuted by Condillac, who went further in this direction than Locke before him; lastly, the two assumptions hitherto grounding ethical theory, first original sin and secondly the pre-eminence of reason, both of which precepts allowed man alone to participate in the world of what is right and of values in general while deeming his animal dimension to be the source of his fall, were challenged by Rousseau when he made sensibility the ethical and anthropological foundation-stone. Today, in view of the broad decline of the Christian religion's domination of society and of people's minds—along with, in the scientific realm, the impact of Darwinism, genetics, the neurological sciences, ethology, and especially primatology—it would seem that a decisive rapprochement of man and animal has once again been achieved, providing the trends set in motion by the Enlightenment with their final concluding point, on this as on other issues. Ethics in our present-day societies, moreover, is based more and more upon naturalistic and compassionate considerations, and no longer in any way upon religious or metaphysical ones: ours is by no means an intransigent morality of duty and austerity, of transcendence and detachment, but on the contrary a less rational, more emotional morality of closeness and attachment to oneself and others which thus tends to rejoin the Rousseauist approach. At the same time, the removal of guilt from sexuality has dissolved the theme, so long dominant, of an original sin that corrupts the purity of the divine in man and in creation; the connotation of bestiality ascribed to animals since the Middle Ages has thus been likewise removed. Lastly, the gradual extension of equal rights to slaves, to women, to racial minorities, to children and adolescents, and eventually to the handicapped, is now tending, by a sort of contagion, to be applied to nonhuman living beings.

Let us now take a closer look at our three leading Enlightenment thinkers. Rousseau's main concern, in my view, seems to be the creation of a new picture of man. According to him, man cannot be defined simply in terms of man himself, as a separate entity. Far from it, for man can be understood solely on the basis of a primary animality that makes him first and foremost a being of nature—the being, precisely, portrayed in the first part of Rousseau's *Discourse on the Origin and Basis of Inequality among Men* (also known as the *Second Discourse*). That said, humanity is truly constituted only by the achievement of that perfectibility which is unique to man, or in other words by the historical process that mars his initial naturalness. Thus, apparently for the first time, humanity is apprehended as a degradation of animality—not with a pejorative intent, however, or out of skepticism or some religious purpose, but rather to present a positive account of the social and historical figure of man and of the capacities developed in conjunction with this figure. True, "the man who meditates is a depraved animal,"[1] yet that man is, irreducibly, the one that we are, fated to reflect because he can no longer slough off the self-consciousness that he has acquired, and that is now consubstantial with him, so as to avoid the problems that this raises, with all their ethical and sociopolitical corollaries. This radical shift from one kind of self-understanding in man to another corresponds to the switch from an anthropology of difference to an anthropology of differentiation. The original animal dimension of our being emerges thereby as essential: the animal becomes a counterpart for the human in a relationship that is not only one of difference but also one of composition. Despite the alterations in the human component, its primary animality survives as a point of reference, a form of completeness, equilibrium, and autonomy that is irremediably lost but for which a replacement must now be found within the eminently relative existence that has become ours. Fundamental tendencies that reside within us and endure despite all the layers superimposed by centuries of socialization continue to express that primary animal nature, self-love and pity being the main instances. Far, then, from being identical to original sin, animality in man—the core of sensibility—becomes, in Rousseau's view, a force for authenticity and regulation that serves, if one can maintain its integrity and vitality, as a guarantor of the relationship to oneself and to others.

Condillac, for his part, restricts the scope of the question of knowledge from the outset. He is not concerned primarily with animals, for the simple reason that he is not concerned with man either—unlike Rousseau, who focused his thinking on the nexus of issues

1. *Discours sur l'origine et les fondements de l'inégalité parmi les hommes* (1755). In *Œuvres complètes* 3 (Paris: Gallimard, Collection La Pléiade, 1964), 138.

uniting the two kinds of beings. All the same, inasmuch as he started out from and kept coming back to Locke's problem of the origin of knowledge, Condillac ended up by reconstructing the path of the development of experience, which is also that of the development of the mind, a shared path nothing about which to begin with distinguishes man logically from animals. Theirs are two minds thrust into the empirical venture of the construction of the self by the self—a procedure devoid of constraints or programming of any kind, whether in the form of innate ideas or of some sort of instinct—and gradually mustering all the intellectual, communicational, and social tools needed to deal with the problems thrown up in the course of experience. The important point is that Condillac, with a commitment to a radical and consistent approach that distinguished him from his master Locke, did not separate sensation and reflection but coupled them together from the start—an approach echoed by the Rousseau of the *Second Discourse*: "Every animal has ideas because it has senses."[2] Thus, even if the animal's development comes to a stop, the route is one and the same for animal and man, and the two are kept apart initially by no compartmentalization. The channel for all beings is unique and diversifies only *a posteriori*, as a function, precisely, of the circumstances and bifurcations presented by experience, by different needs, and lastly by the specifics of each's sensory apparatus. With respect to these last, it is touch that turns out to be decisive, for it permits the vital activation of the immanent reflexivity of the tangible, this by virtue of man's particular aptitude—given his hands with their mobile fingers, relatively independent of each other, and his bare skin—for touching and sensing touch. Since perfectibility in Condillac's view also characterizes the animal, the difference between animal and man is thus a matter of mere circumstance and thus in effect contingent.

Diderot, who aspires to a thoroughgoing materialism, sees animality as the universal form of a being that is conceived as entirely corporeal in nature. In his view, every individual is an organized entity and varies solely as a function of that organization. The greater the organic complexity, the more complex a being becomes in terms of desires, needs, faculties, and relationships with others and with the world, and as things stand at the moment the human individual represents the most highly realized exemplar of that complexity. But no

2. Ibid., 141.

call from off the shared path makes itself heard, no solicitation that could prevail upon the human subject to head in a different direction than that taken by other living beings. Adopting a completely Lucretian position, Diderot portrays the human animal as the happy outcome of chance combinations of matter, thus making the notion of a soul, hitherto the metaphysical basis of the difference between humans and animals, quite redundant.

Some qualifications are nevertheless in order. In the first place, collective attitudes in the eighteenth century were only partly affected here (as in many other spheres) by the kind of critical thinking engaged in by our three thinkers. Moreover, as potent as it might have been, the new conjoining of man and animal was very far from being complete. On the contrary, Enlightenment man may be said to have always so arranged things as to remain in top position and preserve a measure of dignity that animals could never claim. Buffon is a prime example here: his *Natural History* presents one monograph after another pointing up the thoroughly anthropomorphic qualities and shortcomings of one animal species or another, whereas his *Discourses* stress that man differs from animals in an irreducible, indeed metaphysical way. The fact is that during the Enlightenment the postulation of continuity between the two kinds of beings had in essence two foundations only: a physiological one owing to the progress of anatomy and a philosophical one associated with the spread of the empiricist theory of knowledge and the speculations of materialism; still lacking were the scientific advances mentioned earlier that came in the wake of Darwinism. It is hardly surprising, therefore, that man, no matter how strong the tendency of critical thought to conjugate him with animals, should eventually retain a separate status. We have already seen how Rousseau never truly contested this privileged position of the human being: even if man viewed as thoroughly immersed in the pure state of nature—and let us not forget that for Rousseau that state was purely hypothetical—is apparently indistinct from other animals, he still, thanks to his metaphysical freedom and perfectibility, possesses a behavioral polyvalence unknown elsewhere in the world of living things. Furthermore, that perfectibility, once stirred by circumstances, will elevate the human subject by endowing him—despite all the deviations and corruption of social arrangements—with the possibility of exercising moral autonomy. Even on the plane of the commonality of man and animal, Rousseau finds a way to preserve their distinctiveness: in his eyes they share the capacity for compassion, but only so long as it is understood that compassion takes two forms, the first being an immediate, particular, and strictly negative form, the exclusively animal form of the repulsion felt by man-in-the-pure-state-of-nature in face of the injury or distress of another sentient living being, and the second being the truly human form, far more sophisticated and authentically moral, the compassion that Émile first experiences only at sixteen years of age—which confirms that it is far from being animal.

As for Condillac, at the very moment when he finds himself most deeply committed to this continuity between man and animal, he feels the need to distance himself from it by reaffirming the distinctiveness of the two kinds of beings in a rush of spirituality apropos of which it is hard to say to what degree it is attributable to a simple concern to conform to prevailing opinion and to what degree it reflects a heartfelt conviction.[3] In any event, the philosopher's reassertion of this distinction effectively smuggles back in the difference between man and animal which—while the two pursue the same course, that of experience—causes the animal to halt very soon and man to continue indefinitely. Condillac certainly holds—unlike Rousseau, and before Rousseau, Descartes and Buffon—that perfectibility is common to animal and man, but only in man is it indefinite, so that the portion of infinity to be found here below belongs exclusively to human beings.

Diderot is certainly much bolder, for he carries the commonality of the two kinds of beings onto the metaphysical plane and, following La Mettrie, asserts their complete material—and hence ontological—unity. Here too, however, man—though reduced to a combination of animal elements—is described not just as different but also as unique. Man alone, in fact, thanks to the size of his brain and his exceptional sensory equilibrium, achieves a rational power and an autonomy of judgment that distances him decisively from animal impulsiveness. Thus, however strong his links to the world of the senses may be, no matter how analogous his reason may be to animal instinct (for hu-

3. "We may conclude that, although the soul of the beast is as simple as that of man, and that in this respect there is no difference between the one and the other, the faculties that are our portion and the purpose to which God appoints us demonstrate that, were we able to penetrate the nature of these two substances, then we should see that they are infinitely different. Our soul is therefore not of the same nature as that of beasts." Étienne Bonnot de Condillac, *Traité des animaux*, ed. M. Malherbe (Paris: Vrin, 2004), 182.

man reason is merely a more perfected version of that instinct[4]), man is distinguished by a higher rationality whereby, thanks to his understanding, he is able to assume the mantle of a supreme judge.[5] Here we catch Diderot returning, albeit on a materialist basis, to what is in the end a rather idealist or spiritualist vision of the human mind, which he deems alone capable of jurisdiction and government, especially in view of the fact that man has the exclusive possession of genuine language—merely embryonic in animals—a fact that qualifies him definitively as a being who determines rights, a being apt for deliberation and assembly. This is the thesis of Diderot's *Encyclopedia* article on "Natural Right": "If animals were on an approximate level with us, [. . .] if they were able to convey clearly their feelings and thoughts and know ours with the same clarity: in a word, if they were able to vote in a general assembly, it would be necessary to summon them there, and the cause of natural rights would no longer be pleaded before *humanity* but before *animality*."[6]

The limits Enlightenment thinkers placed on the conjoining of man and animal might nevertheless be interpreted as even further confirmation of the continuity between their century and ours. On this reading we, for our part, have simply gone further—but thanks to them—than our eighteenth-century predecessors. Perched as it were on their shoulders, we would have dared to proceed farther down the path they opened up, being at once more liberated with respect to traditional anthropocentric moral and metaphysical norms and better informed by virtue of decisive scientific advances in the interim.

Nonetheless, this notion of a postmodern culmination of the Enlightenment approach to animals can be contested by a set of counter-

4. "Man is also an animal species; his reason is nothing but a perfectible and perfected instinct." Denis Diderot, *Réfutation d'Helvétius* (1773), in *Œuvres 1 (Philosophie)*, ed. L. Versini (Paris: Robert Laffont, 1994), 829.

5. "But it is not thus with man. There is such a harmony between his senses that none predominates sufficiently over the others to lay down the law to his understanding; on the contrary, it is that understanding, or the organ of man's reason, that is the strongest. It is a judge who is neither corrupted by nor subjugated to any of the witnesses. It preserves its entire authority, and uses it to perfect itself. It combines all manner of ideas and sensations, because it feels nothing strongly." Ibid., 815.

6. *Encyclopédie 1*, ed. A. Pons (Paris: Flammarion, 1986), s.v. "Droit naturel." English translation: Stephen J. Gendzier, ed. and trans., *Denis Diderot's The Encyclopedia: Selections* (New York: Harper & Row, [1967]), s.v. "Natural Right."

arguments in the light of which our century may seem on the contrary to have slid back relative to this putative progress.

First of all, even if one assumes that the theory of evolution was the chief lever of the reversal that began at the end of the nineteenth century, it would be utterly naïve to maintain that it quite simply eliminated mankind's distinctiveness. The fact is that, while in phylogenetic terms this theory unquestionably brought animal species and the human species closer together, it did so only at the cost of an extreme temporal distancing that tended to neutralize this effect and buffer it no less considerably by surreptitiously introducing hierarchy. In the eighteenth century, by contrast, the time interval, far from countering man-animal continuity, was either absent (as in the creationist conception) or so short that it allowed animal features to emerge on the surface of the human countenance through an interplay of anamorphosis and analogy, which may be found in Diderot,[7] among others, and that inspired physiognomy, fast developing at that time. During the Enlightenment animality thus actually spurred humanity forward (which also explains the violence of the defensive reactions in a still potent theological context).

Secondly, even as the theoretical continuity between man and animal has unquestionably been reinforced in our time, actual proximity has declined and the density and variety of animal presence in the immediate space of our surroundings has evaporated (household pets being an exception that does not invalidate this general trend). A reversal within the man-animal relationship is thus apparent as between the pre- and post-Enlightenment periods: during the Cartesian seventeenth century proximity predominated without continuity, whereas in our own neo-Darwinian times continuity prevails without proximity.

As for the practical treatment of animals, it has never been more "dehumanized" and ethically indefensible than it is today, because man has replaced cruelty with a ghostly form of existence—especially under industrial farming conditions—that is so impoverished and paradoxically "de-animalized" as to be historically unprecedented.

---

7. Consider for example the famous reciprocal transformation of the dog and the Sorbonne professor (see *Réfutation d'Helvétius*, 823). In Darwin this immediate proximity between man and animal is discussed far more in his work on the expression of emotions than in that on the evolution of species (even though the two areas are obviously related).

Furthermore, the differentiation between man and animal that once prevailed—even into the eighteenth century, as we have seen—did not stand in the way of a very strong investment of animals with meaning. Just the opposite, in fact, for animals in various avatars reflected human beings, their diversity, their obsessions, and their conflicts. Paradoxically, humans contrasted themselves to animals while at the same continually projecting themselves onto them, and deemed man and animal fundamentally distinct yet incessantly drew upon the inspirational force of the animal world. By contrast, today's embrace of inter-species continuity is accompanied by man's withdrawal of investment from animals inasmuch as, being merely a positive reflection of him, they no longer offer anything more than a redundant portrait. The animal mirror of man, far from displaying the traits of human personality in outline, as it once did, has now become completely smooth and self-satisfied, devoid of any real personality, as part of the same tendency which has rendered animals "nice" and stripped them of any true consistency and depth, making even wild animals less and less wild. This infantilizing, even de-animalizing sugar-coating of beasts leads eventually to a watered-down and uni-lateral vision of them while by extension doing much the same to images of the human downgraded into an anthropomorphically satu-rated world where the wild in the sense of the savage has been oddly expunged from nature.

What seems to be disappearing as a result of these historical vi-cissitudes of the man-animal relationship is the animal's otherness; as though the most interesting aspect of animals were the degree to which they resemble us, whereas in the end the very opposite may well be the truth of the matter. Perhaps this explains the develop-ment, as a repercussion, of the vogue for exotic pets, for animals markedly different from us such as iguanas, chameleons, various snakes, or spiders, all clearly far harder to anthropomorphize. But even if these animals restore some measure of otherness to the rela-tionship, they remain strictly marginal and no doubt reflect a mere reaction within the overall human-animal landscape. So imperative, indeed, is our desire to have resemblance trump difference that our underestimation of the animal's otherness leads to the repression of our own human specificity, which we come to look upon as a shame-ful pretension. Here it is worth noting the moral implications of the constraint and even the contradiction embodied in an excessive iden-tification of man and animal, which may quite simply serve to stymie any prospect of humans adopting an ethical attitude of respect and responsibility toward animals, this on the spurious grounds of the unlikelihood of an animal conceiving of, much less assuming such a biologically useless if not harmful attitude toward another animal, particularly one of a different species.

Thus the claim of a continuity between man and animal has now been strengthened more than ever before while at the same time being broadly deprived of its substance and benefits. To be more precise, the fact of the phylogenetic continuity, because it is henceforward fully established, has after a fashion anesthetized the issue of the difference and polarized efforts to identify resemblances or common features systematically on other levels. What is at stake here for mankind has been pushed aside and all the emphasis placed on the cognitive faculties of animals and on the ethical corollaries of the re-valuing of their capacities. Reflection on the animal question might seem to have been waylaid, even alienated, by the question of animal cognition, triggering, curiously, a return to the perspective of late Antiquity, preoccupied above all by the matter of animal intelligence and the ethical implications thereof (though the theological debates on metempsychosis should not be overlooked).

And yet, and this is the point, it appears impossible to maintain that all discontinuity between man and animal has been eradicated, leaving a completely unbroken continuum. Far from it, in fact, for discontinuity has re-emerged, and this in a version so radical that it seems to invalidate the very possibility of any real continuity. The version of things to which I refer was first proposed by Heidegger. In light of it, we may proceed once more today to evoke change in our conception of the man-animal relationship and even to envisage the rupture of that relationship.

The relevance of Heidegger's thinking on this subject resides in fact in the way he radicalizes the question by showing that it cannot be broken down by positing an animal dimension along with a specifically human dimension in man, as was done traditionally, or at least in the Aristotelian tradition. Even in their most glaring animality, human beings always appear completely human,[8] for man differs from

---

8. This is not to say that the human being can never in any way be described as inhuman: for one thing, the term "inhuman" denotes the opposite of the human not in a general sense but rather qua moral value; and for another, by extension, only humanity is capable of inhumanity, since all negation implies the pre-existence of the positive that it negates.

animals not partially but coextensively: there can be no question here
of components or levels that can be apprehended and isolated within
the body of man's being and then compared with animal reality, because the basis of the difference is an attitude toward the world and
that attitude is a metaphysical one. To be exact, this human attitude or relationship—which defines the *Dasein* as such—consists in
an openness to other beings and to the world as given in their own
independent existence, and this distinguishes man from the animal,
which is not open but trapped according to Heidegger within an environment. Everything depends, therefore, on the way the question
of this difference is envisaged, and approaching it in the right way—
namely as a *whole*, without any break-down into elements (which
would mean accepting different levels of identity and, step by step,
anthropologizing the animal and animalizing man)—reveals the radical nature of the distinction. The fact is that, even when we proceed
in this way, whatever we recognize as animality in man remains irreducibly a *human* animality, which changes everything. What is so
often referred to—questionably—as the animal side of man is thus
never accessible as such to man himself but instead proves, invari-
ably (as Condillac and Rousseau clearly understood with respect to
the question of origins), to be always already understood and con-
verted into man's humanity. Inversely, to be sure, one could take this
to mean that humanity is never pure, nor purely separate, for it is always more or less a conversion of animality—an idea, of course, that
Heidegger would never have countenanced.

It seems to me, therefore, that Heidegger reached a threshold on
the animal question that made it impossible thereafter to frame the
question in the terms previously used. It is in the wake of this step
that Derrida's thoughts on animality were developed. His thinking
is especially interesting in that it clearly embraces the human discontinuity of the human postulated by Heidegger without, however,
echoing Heidegger's underestimation of the animal's being. Derrida
even calls the ignoring of this difference of man the second biggest
"stupid mistake" relative to the animal question[9] —a second error
often overlooked but just as massive as the first that Derrida evokes

---

9. "I have thus never believed in some homogenous continuity between what
calls *itself* man and what *he* calls the animal [. . . .] That would be worse than sleep-
walking, it would be simply too asinine (*bête*)." Jacques Derrida, *L'animal que donc je
suis* (Paris: Galilée, 2006 [1997]), 52. English translation by David Wills: "The Animal
that therefore I am (More to Follow)," *Critical Enquiry* 28/2 (Winter 2002): 398.

elsewhere, and that consists, as already noted, in the homogenization of animality through the use of the singular "animal."

In a way, then, Derrida goes at once further and not as far as Heidegger. On the one hand, unlike Heidegger who does not quit a meditative position, he commits his thinking to a quite experimental process, as he recounts in *The Animal That Therefore I Am*. Furthermore, this experimentation, which is also a mise-en-scène, initiates a quite unprecedented way of envisaging the man-animal relationship neither as an opposition nor as a conjunction, but instead as a kind of exposure: naked in face of the frank gaze of a cat, stripped of all outward signs of the human, the subject is revealed in his own animality, thus reversing the traditional relationship of human dominance of the other (animal) by means of look, speech, and disposition/requisition/manipulation. Submitting in a sense to this mute summons, the subject or "I" puts himself in question without any prior assumptions and, letting himself be carried along by the motor force of the situation itself, experiences a veritable inverse *cogito*, one articulated by heteronomy and no longer reflected back to the self according to an unimpeachable formula of autonomy and sovereignty.[10] The position of judge that Diderot, as we noted earlier, reserved for man as the subject of reason and jurisdiction is thus usurped by the animal, whose silence no longer stands for a lack or a weakness but rather for a strength, that of a hieratic attitude of oversight and mystery reminiscent of the cats captured in the statuary of ancient Egypt. At this point it is in his entirety that the human subject, transfixed in his very being as it were by the gaze of the animal, henceforward unsure of that being and of the nature of the humanity of the human, is summoned to explain himself.

On the other hand, Derrida seems elsewhere to lag behind Heidegger with respect not to the attitude and involvement of the subject but with respect to the determinants of animality itself. Contrary to the German philosopher, who describes animals as "world-poor," Derrida declines to characterize the actual being of the animal while treating its inner reality as a sort of undecidable vanishing point, certainly a determining factor but quite indeterminate in itself. This en-

10. See Jean-Luc Guichet, "Ruses et distorsions animales du cogito: *L'animal que donc je suis* de Jacques Derrida," in *L'animalité —six interprétations humaines*, ed. Jan-Ivar Linden (Paris: L'Harmattan, 2011), 47–59.

sures the distinctiveness of the human being while endowing man with no sort of superiority over animals, which remain indefinable in the metaphysical sense.

It is important to note that this metaphysical differentiation in no way justifies making the difference in question into a basic attribute of man. What is in play here, as we have seen, is a particular attitude and by no means a property of nature, human or otherwise. It so happens that this attitude, or relationship, is manifested at present by human beings, but we are entitled to assume—although Derrida does not himself clarify this—that it is an essentially accidental phenomenon and in no way entails a priori that no other imaginable being could ever embrace it. On the contrary, since this specific attitude is an alteration of an earlier manner of being in the world which may be roughly described as animal, it is arguable that in any case it presupposes animality as its starting-point and may therefore—being by definition a corollary of a process of de-animalization—affect any animal, provided certain conditions are met (mastery of a symbolic language definitely being one of them).

At the same time it seems to me that this exposure of the subject has a compensatory function, that it expresses a kind of remorse, and that in any case it is a secondary phenomenon with regard to the condition imposed overall on animals in the world of today, a condition more like incarceration than any kind of opening, more like a compartmentalization than an intensification of the relationship.[11] So has discontinuity won out after all?

Throughout his account of this situation, which is at once compelled and exploratory, Derrida continually stresses the impossibility of communication with the animal whose gaze nevertheless penetrates to the human's very depths. But of course the power of that gaze resides precisely in its unreadability: does its determinative force derive from the animal itself, as source, or is the animal simply the catalyst of the human's own relationship of estrangement from himself, perhaps even of his own *animal* relationship to himself? The gaze that opens me up to this animal otherness sends me back mercilessly at the same time to myself in terms of a solitude that is irreducible because it is unreadable. The experience that Derrida presents to

11. Moreover, in his book Derrida clearly denounces today's industrialized treatment of animals.

us here would seem to expose the present-day relationship of man to animals as one of non-communication, with the narcissistic relationship to oneself as its sole horizon.[12]

This metaphysical condition of solitude is thus also a historical condition. At least since the domestication of the dog in Paleolithic times, community between animal and man had never been broken. Even if, beginning with the Christian Middle Ages and up until the seventeenth century, the distinctiveness of man seems to have become more and more marked, this difference was always embedded in a human world populated—not to say overpopulated—by animals. Today, whereas the continuity between the two kinds of beings has, since the Enlightenment, been ever more firmly established or reinstated, the ancestral form of man-animal community has simultaneously, and paradoxically, been eroded. In the first place, we are experiencing a crisis in our relationship to a nature from which we are gradually being excluded by the combined effects of our exponential urbanization and our reduction of the overall animal population along with that of the diversity of species. Furthermore, in addition to the gradual decline of wild animals we must also consider the withdrawal of stock animals confined to spaces set apart in accordance with an overarching industrial logic. The old farm animals, which occupied a transitional place between wild animals and household pets—for while they were domestic in one sense they also kept a measure of independence, while epitomizing the complete life cycle of animals until their eventual slaughter—have indeed vanished from the human landscape. The disappearance of animals splits the man-animal relationship in an almost schizophrenic way between, on the one hand, a superficially anthropomorphic vision exemplified by pets (as also by the media's idealized wild animals), and on the other, the objective but masked reality of the alienated animal of industrialized food production and science. And so, paradoxically, while the continuity between man and animal has never be so widely recognized in theory, it is countered by a de facto separation that condemns present-day mankind to a wilderness devoid of animal life (the growing importance of household pets seeming to me, as already noted, to be a phenomenon that is more of a reaction to, than a negation

12. I do not have the space here to consider Deleuze's thinking on animals, and the same goes for many other present-day authors, but it seems to me that the thesis of becoming animal—in the sense of a change with no set goal or category, not even animality—does not imply any actual communication in the man-animal relationship.

of this broad tendency). Now, it is arguable that animal company is the guarantor of an essential aspect of man's humanity. The result, once again paradoxical, is that de-animalization is correlated with a de-humanization of the world entailing a human solitude which may be described as animal in that it strips man of the open character that Giorgio Agamben, following Heidegger, considered a defining quality of the human.

The confinement of animals and their disappearance from the space reserved to human beings compromises man's aspiration to open being by depriving him of contact with a true otherness that has the capacity—as a radically distinct external point of view that cannot be assumed by him—to serve as mediation in his relationship with the pure objective otherness of things and of nature. Whether animality is reduced to a reflection of humanity or to the role of a replaceable cog in an industrial process, the animal is at once de-animalized and de-subjectivized. In consequence, too, human life—henceforward a closed circuit—can no longer be constructed in its humanity on the basis of an animality that is a given and comprehensible as such; and this is even more true if, as it seems to me, that humanity consists in fact not in a set of personal and positive characteristics but essentially in a de-animalization, so that it is fundamentally the fruit of a negative process. To this extent, by losing animals—and their diversity— man loses himself too, thus demonstrating the profound truth that identity consists primarily in being different from others, which also means being the same as them in some sense. These questions must by no means await our own times to be answered at last, for the eighteenth century—which could never have even imagined separating man and animal within the world they shared—furnishes the tools needed to investigate the lot of modern man, who is doomed to mull narcissistically over identity issues, unable to find the wherewithal in animality to nourish his humanity, as always in the past, in terms of imagination, of meaning, of thought, and, in short, of difference.

—Translated by Donald Nicholson-Smith

JEAN-CHRISTOPHE BAILLY

Animals Are Masters of Silence

This talk has been planned for many months but as usual I got to it only belatedly.[1] This was not just because as a rule the feeling of a degree of urgency, even of lateness, helps me settle on the opening, the outline, and the form of what I propose to say, but also, this time, because the subject, the question of animals, so vast per se, is now so frequently raised—so frequented, so to speak—that, just like those it concerns or is supposed to concern, namely animals themselves, one sometimes conceives a desire to flee and find oneself a good hiding-place and never emerge from it. To which, of course, is added the fear of finding oneself too tightly constrained by the necessity to say once more what one has already sought to say, especially considering that one can hardly count more here than anywhere else on a boundless field of expression: just because a problem comes at us from every side—or perhaps indeed precisely for that reason—our angle of attack or approach is not infinitely variable.

As I thought to dispel such doubts, or to proceed despite them, and to arrive at my subject, the first question that arose, of course, was what might have precipitated this flood, this mass of concern with beasts and our relationships with them.

(In the context of our discussion of *animals*, assuming always—and and it is not certain—that the word "beast" is somewhat less generic, a little more precise, more suggestive of cries, smells, and fear, then it is worth reviving the term from time to time.)

The issue of the frequency with which this anxiety about beasts arises today (and the trend is recent, no more than a few years old),

---

1. Editor's note: This is a translation of the text of a talk delivered in Poitiers on February 4, 2010, for a conference titled "Le sens de l'animal / Pourquoi l'animal?" hosted by La maison des sciences de l'homme of the University of Poitiers.

YFS 127, *"Animots": Postanimality in French Thought*, ed. Senior, Clark, and Freccero, © 2015 by Yale University.

specifically anxiety about our past, present, and future relationships with animals, is a question that to my mind can have no other causes than a certain hesitancy and a certain suspicion: hesitancy with respect to human certitudes and the suspicion that a wrong path has been taken, both of them internal responses to what is experienced as a foreshadowing or annunciation of the pure and simple disappearance of animals from the face of the earth. A catastrophic hypothesis, undoubtedly, but sadly a working one, so to speak, a hypothesis that comes to mind as soon as the slightest serious thought is given to the threats hanging today over environments and over most biotopes. It is beneath the shadow cast by this hypothesis (which ranges from negative reverie to the coldest calculation) that the question of animals flourishes, directing its widest possible focus upon the animal world in its entirety and viewing wild animals (and, after all, they were all wild once) not only as survivors but also as witnesses, as demonstrations to humanity, infinitely necessary to man's equilibrium and intelligence, of an effective otherness that is lived day to day.

(Let me recall *en passant* that it is no coincidence that the most ancient traces that humans have left us—whatever their motivations may have been—are pure recordings of that otherness, for the animal pictures of prehistory testify to a primal act of recognition fundamental to the emergence of mankind. The very first people, the furthest from us in time, that we can identify as modern humans, which is to say those from the Aurignacian period, from the era of the Chauvet Cave, are the ones who painted animals almost exclusively, despite all the other things they *could* have painted.)

I tried to evoke the disappearance of animals to which our times expose us—hypothetical of course, but already initiated for several species—in a show entitled *Sur le vif, fable mélancolique sur le déclin des espèces sauvages* ("From Life: A Melancholy Fable on the Decline of Species"). Written and produced with Gilberte Tsaï, and put on in 2003, this show, to our great sadness, did not enjoy the success that we had hoped for. I say "sadness" advisedly, fully aware that one should never take success or anything of the sort for granted, that such an attitude is a bad one and almost inevitably leads to disappointment. But in this case our sadness was more than disappointment, for it embodied something more, namely a feeling of injustice: the fact was that with this show, which pleaded the animals' cause, and thus assumed a specific posture, that of being and conceiving of itself as a defense and an illustration, we had the feeling we were preaching in the wilderness or missing the target completely, and I am well aware that we could easily blame ourselves for that and transform our sadness into self-criticism, but what I am trying to convey by recalling this is something of a different order, namely that animals were in a sense implicated in our sadness, which ultimately resembled, at least as I remember it, the inexpressible aspect of the kind of pain we feel upon the loss of a domestic animal—a sort of enormous woe, specific, distinct, and oppressive, but a woe that is greeted, more than other woes, by incomprehension, and that retreats more than others into itself, so great is its exposure to the prejudice, after all massively shared, according to which a loss of this kind is not too serious and indeed in reality, by the yardstick of human suffering in general, amounts to nothing at all.

The thesis of our show, in fact rather clearly anti-humanist in nature, was precisely that all death is serious, that any erasure of existence confronts us with the gravity of death just as any emergence of existence confronts us with the gravity (or the mystery) of life. This was the conclusion, I believe, to which the show led, and all the more so inasmuch as the whole animal issue was on display in the finale in the shape of a mourning, an adieu. We contrived this by means of masks: on stage for the closing scene were a bear, an ass, a fox, an eagle owl, and a Barbary macaque—members of a kind of committee, come, like delegates on a mission, to bid us farewell, to acknowledge us for the last time, having resolved to leave for elsewhere. Of course this was merely a fable, and within it a reversal, because the animals were granted the ability to choose, and they chose to abandon humans to their own devices, whereas in reality they have barely any other choice vis-à-vis humans than to take flight. Be that as it may, they leave in the fable, and that is the point of the fable, and that is what I want to get to here, for of course they were never really there, all our efforts notwithstanding: behind the masks and the imagery, and first and foremost because they could talk, these were not animals. The aporia of the show is also that of these remarks today, and ultimately of every discussion of beasts, especially where the aim is to evoke and magnify their silence, their detachment with respect to language. Animals do not talk, and it is against this backdrop of silence, from within this silence, punctuated perhaps (not to say certainly) by cries, but fundamentally silent in terms of what we understand as meaning, that they scrutinize us.

The conceit of the fable is to have animals talk, to bestow the gift of the *logos* upon them, not in order to get them into line, but rather to get us out of it, or out, as Francis Ponge used to say, of our groove—but ready to get back into it very quickly, as soon as it becomes apparent that the animals are stand-ins or effectively allegorical representations of the human comedy or *fabula*, albeit characterized by a certain alienation effect: there are certainly moments in La Fontaine when the fox is just a fox, the wolf a wolf, the rat a rat. But this weak if essential breath of animality is as nothing, naturally, alongside what was attempted, much later and at a far remove from any allegorizing instrumentalization, by Kafka, in whose work (I am thinking above all, but not exclusively, of "The Burrow") the animal habitus seems poured into the mold of human speech in an amazingly discreet and convincing way. Yet there is nothing for it: beyond the fable, beyond its almost *sotto voce* conjoining of what it says and whatever it might embody of non-human feelings, there lies a great gulf, a gulf that language indicates but can never bridge, because in point of fact language itself exemplifies it. My intent in this paper is to inflect things towards a modesty born of astonishment, to help detach what is "properly human" from its canker of pride while at the same time, conversely, declining to correlate the lack of articulated language, as is so often done in an automatic and unthinking manner, with imbecility, or at least with a necessarily subordinate standing. True, it would not get us very far were I to do no more than state and repeat that animals cannot speak, even when we assign speech to them, but we may manage a step forward by asking ourselves, by contrast, in what a world of nameless things might consist, and how in such a world, to which we have had but a furtive access in a distant and unremembered childhood, something resembling meaning—though not our kind of meaning—might emerge and, in some way, inasmuch as we are open to perceiving it, reach us.

What is at stake here is the immediacy of living things to themselves—to the mass of entangled, diverse, and extraordinary actions that constitutes them. Indeed, like a breaking wave, a world without names is a world of actions, actions whereby animals, according to their abilities as species and as individuals, seem to wrap themselves in the world and create it before our eyes, certainly just as we ourselves do, but also in another way, with quite different styles and, it must be said, a gift for envelopment that surpasses ours. What is thus displayed—and it is directly linked to their silence, in direct harmony with the fact that they do not speak (to us)—are *modi operandi*, practices, avoidances, gratifications, in short everything we are accustomed to place under the heading of behavior, which, as we know, as readily includes the motions of a squid and the bounding of a wild animal as the giraffe's gentle gait or the flapping of a duck's wings as it rises from a pond. All and everything in the animal world—or, in other words, everything that beasts can do, and everything they do.

Of these habitual or experimental courses of action and of the interruptions that punctuate them, of what really happens to animals, we know precious little, and even if we are able to form a vague picture of them, it is only via the filter of our own impressions. So what we need to have at our disposition is a translation of the impression itself, an access route to the modes of existence and duration of animals' impressions and sensations, or otherwise stated the means to picture as though from within the quality and form of the percepts and emotions thanks to which life unfolds for animals. Curiously, verbs, in the infinitive form, would seem to offer something of a doorway to this universe closed to us and without names: being generic, it is as though they dwell in a realm where meaning is fully present, a realm preceding denomination proper; whereas nouns or adjectives stand out as points, infinitives manifest themselves rather as lines, or cause lines to emerge, and we may say of such lines not only that animals draw them but also that we can follow them, and thus read or decipher them. Think of the words *fly, swim, breathe, sleep, keep watch, flee, leap, hide*, and so on, ending with *die*. It is clear that thanks to this verbal form something of the life and vivacity of animals is nevertheless captured: very little, no doubt, but just enough so that by virtue of this connection the verb itself is recharged and opened up. Take *fly*, for example; or *sleep*, for another. To fly—something we cannot do and of which at bottom we know practically nothing. To sleep—something , by contrast, of which we have practical experience, but about which we do not know everything.

So let us follow these two lines, these two silent lines stretching before us just as they do before animals. First, flight—truly a line in the strictest sense, a rapid and ephemeral line that is erased no sooner than it appears, erased indeed in its appearing, making the being that draws it, so very light, perhaps no heavier than a few grams, into a projectile launching itself into space: *envoyé en l'air*, or sent up into the air, to use a familiar French vulgarism that has the trivial meaning of "getting off," but which, taken literally, describes birds, or bats, who are indeed sent up into the air, send themselves and see themselves up in the air, and are perhaps also driven there, but in any case have a kind of knowledge at their disposal that one can of course file away as a mere *savoir-faire* or acquired technique but which seems however to be something quite else, something that can embody, as Rilke suggested, an entrance into the Open, and let me make it clear, for it must be clear, that the open—which I feel should have no initial capital letter so that it too may remain infinitive, and infinite—is by no means a simple metaphor or abstraction, or at least if so, then it is one established in the most concrete manner as a withdrawal or absence of matter, which is to say that to fly is to experience distancing and actually inhabit the in-between, the empty fullness of the interval, and that this experience entails a joy that is visible (and audible), as manifested in the wildest way in the circlings of starling flocks or in streaks of swallows at dusk, or again, and surely no less intensely, in the night-gliding of various owls, barn owls or eagle owls, barely brushing the darkness and leaving traces if anything even slightly more deeply plunged in silence. And should the word "joy" shock, so be it, for here too the issue is the need for a translation capable of bringing the meaning of what we as humans know of joy into conjunction with the miracle of that escape from gravity that birds epitomize in their upward soaring; capable too, perhaps, of precipitating a retroactive effect, with the meaning and sensation of flying, thrust very deep into the imaginary realm, opening space up, as though from within, so that our contemplation is impregnated by it and our thinking flooded by the radiant and dilated sense of what opens up and is nothing but opening up.

Just how far removed we are from all acquaintanceship with flying (it hardly seems necessary to point out that being ensconced in a fuselage has nothing to do with flying) was brought home to me one evening, in tragic fashion, when I saw a man land a few steps away from me and my partner after throwing himself out of a hotel window on Rue de l'Odéon in Paris. The result of this act, the fall, followed by the collision with the ground, was not the worst of it, or at any rate not the most terrifying thing. The man's body, as disjointed as a rag doll, was in one sense neither more nor less than a body damaged by an accident with respect to which a series of actions needed to be undertaken, but what I really remember is the terrible image of that man, that rag doll, still in the air, arms more or less crossed,

that scarecrow so horribly weighted down by his despair, so powerfully attracted by the ground, and so indisputably incapable of flying
(and indeed it was into this indisputability that he had fallen) that it
was not only his person but the whole of humanity that seemed fated
to crash into the ground with him. This memory, and the use I am
making of it here, are certainly not trivial matters, but at least it is
possible, by confining them to the objective dimension of the purely
negative, to picture, by contrast, the consistency of a world of taking
wing, of paths curved or straight, diving, climbing again, voluntary,
free, traversing space in every direction while leaving no trace. In
other words: the open—but the open as dictated by the birds, sung by
the birds, and continually refined by them.

Let me turn now to sleep, where we are on familiar, everyday
ground, confronting something whose contours are well known to us
and whose depth we intuit, something that is inscribed within us as
a long discontinuous line drawn taut every night and loosened every
morning. A line that we do not think of most of the time, wanting
simply to follow it and plunge into the strange realm of forgetful-
ness to which it leads, but that brings itself back to mind as soon as
we lose track of it, which shows how much our equilibrium depends
on the rhythmic recurrence of its return. Rest thus gives us access
to the most secret part of ourselves, not only the portion, often so
spectacular, that appears with dreams, but also the more distant and
almost unknown one that emerges and gains in strength when the
agitation caused by dreams has subsided and when, deeply asleep, we
find ourselves in a sense curled up, and this less in ourselves than in a
space that welcomes us but which is bound to retreat from us eventually; here, and here only, we perhaps reach a zone or an indistinct yet
fundamental frontier where a hermetic connection is restored, in all
its original violence, to a world of which the only outward sign is our
breathing and which constitutes a kind of threshold to which we are
delivered as we sleep.

My feeling is that this threshold, at once intimate and far away,
to which the night delivers us and where each of us descends alone,
is accessible to all sleeping creatures: to observe an animal sleeping
and see its body gently or at times feverishly rise and fall is in a way
to confirm that it too has been brought to this threshold, this frontier where being seems to retreat into itself and accept itself utterly
in its existence, and this in a manner highly generic yet at the same

time distinct, extending to all living beings (humans, animals, and very likely plants) but at the same time actualized in the particularity or singularity of each individual being, in which therefore, to an observer, all of life seems to gather. The reverie that unfolds for sleeping animals is at once ample and melancholy: ample because it has the characteristics, naturally, of a broadening of the consciousness of our existence, and melancholy because this very broadening is based on a shared transience, as decreed for all mortal beings. Postulating a kinship or generalized connectedness of this kind is certainly not meant to revive some notion or other of paradise. Rather, the purpose is merely to admit the existence in its own right of a common foundation, allowing this to come into view and expose in the simplest possible manner the corollary existence (I make no bones about the terms) of a stock of experience common to man and beast, a stock from whence we draw the greater part of our energy but that our activity, as developed over the centuries, has gradually obliterated, so that the signs of it have become almost indecipherable for us.

These are the signs that, when they do reach us, we place in the sole (and, in my view, inappropriate) category of "animality." The fact is that it makes no more sense to go looking for "animal" aspects of humans than to attribute, as we so often do in a sentimental way, something "human" to animals. The common foundation of experience that I am referring to has nothing about it of a vague communality with ill-defined borders; on the contrary, it is the precise space where each species (and each representative of each species), by nourishing itself there in its own way and at its own specific rate, is able to actualize its form and achieve individuation. Individuation is extreme in every being, as witnessed in each of us, and biodiversity here is a term with only the faintest resonance as a designation for the extraordinary propensity of the multiple to extend and ricochet in a space wide open and hospitable to every kind of finitude. Nothing here, in the context of what is in effect the precondition of existence, is more eloquent than the situation that arises when two individuated forms face each other, and, rather than avoid each other by fleeing, grant themselves a moment of suspense during which to look at each other. What I am referring to, of course, is the always unique experience of eye-to-eye contact. An experience that I have often spoken of, because it is, I believe, the source of my feelings and my distress concerning animals, its first effect being to place before our eyes, in the shape of a look that is not like ours, that is not "human," nor ever can be, the existence of another gaze, and hence the existence of otherness as such.

Such a shared moment, so long as we take the time to let it operate, the possibility of which certain painters have demonstrated for us—and here what I have in mind is the insistence, so exactly portrayed, in the eye of the ass that looks at us from behind, at the level of the white satin trousers in Watteau's "Gilles" (or "Pierrot")—such a moment, then, whereby we try to grasp what the eyes of the animal looking at us, and at which we are looking , tell us about what in the animal resembles what we for our part call thought, always concerns otherness as such, always implies a "two-sided" relationship which, precisely because it has no resolution, opens the door not to the other or to the secret of the other but rather to the full recognition of that other. Even domestic animals, the house cat, or a puppy, occasionally reveal themselves to us in their otherness by detaching themselves from the husk of protective sentiments in which they are imprisoned. But no matter the animal, the important thing, so impressive and in some cases so unforgettable, is the completeness with which, in the absence of any constraint, existence condenses into the singularity of the being that embodies it and bends it to its own ends; the common foundation is also what creates in us—and in animals—the experience of these extraordinarily diverse ways of embodying and holding fast to existence.

Over and above the exchange itself and its most characteristic property, namely the simultaneous presence of two visions, two gazes, two ways of being, what one is led to conclude is that the world exists and can be looked at in different ways, that the very moment that links us unfolds in a plurality of worlds; for along the line denoted by the verb "to look for," it is not the same world that appears when the line passes through the eyes of a lynx, a sparrowhawk, a steer, a bat, an antelope, a snake, or a human being—just as things are not quite the same from one human being to the next. It goes without saying that within each species there comes into play (indeed as the rule of the game) a community or a certain consistency of behavior and points of reference upon which each member may more or less count, though obviously with great variation from one species to another and depending on the specific forms assumed by individuation and by social life. But it is also a given that, without our being in any sense able to partake of whatever representations animals create of their world, we can nevertheless attempt to follow their lead and in that way broaden our own apprehension and our own angles of approach, striving to let ourselves be penetrated by a little of what animals are in the world and by what is at their disposal as a world, even if this were to be no more than that poverty which Heidegger disparagingly clad them in and that is at once their destitution or distress and the state whose sway over them they contest as best they can, and this by means of a wealth of skills that it would not be useless, I believe, to enumerate.

I suddenly realize that by proposing that we allow ourselves to be penetrated by animals' worlds and ways of being in the world, I am merely reiterating what has long been expressed, through myths and even more through rites and customs, by populations of hunters, by peoples who may be described, to use the words of Georges Bataille, as peoples of a "lost intimacy," or, to continue with the terms that I have been using here, those who, among humans, have never ceased to rely on a common existential and experiential foundation. How to reconnect here—for the intimacy has indeed been lost—is the real question. This is also the standpoint from which we may surmise that animals are for us silent masters. The truest, the most authentic approach would unquestionably be to go over to the other side and, since it is impossible to endow animals with a faculty of speech that they can never have, introduce them into the open and shadowy space of our thoughts through one of their number, one moreover which has, according to various traditions, been taken as the very incarnation of perspicacity and discernment. I am referring to the lynx.

The fact is that from the moment I began thinking about this paper, the lynx came into my mind. I thought that in one way or another the lynx would, and must be, present, or at the very least pass through, and that it should thus be the lynx, there before us, that would represent the figure of the silent master. But it would be a miracle if a lynx could immediately appear among us, and not only do I lack miracle-making powers but also, among wild animals, and especially among felids, the lynx is one of the hardest even to spot. It was not, however, as a symbol, even as a symbol of inconspicuousness, that I would have wished a lynx with us, among us, beyond my words or prior to them, but rather as an instance, an *exemplum* of an animal, so that through it something of the animal's worlds might be vouchsafed us, not excluding its brutality. Out of disappointment and curiosity, therefore, I set out to inform myself as best I might, learning along the way that the lynx also bears the name *loup-cervier* [literally: deer-hunting wolf], which makes one wonder whether it is not a lynx that Alfred de Vigny evokes in his poem "La mort du loup"; and that the expression "lynx-eyed" is derived not from the keen sight of the lynx, whose vision is not particularly sharp, but from a deformation of the name of the Argonaut Lynceus, who was, by contrast, according to myth, a kind of seer. But what caught my attention most forcefully, apart from the lynx's head and silhouette, both truly of a flawless beauty, was the very highly developed character of the animal's sensory apparatus, except, apparently, for the sense of smell: its vision, despite my remarks above; its hearing also, thanks notably to the fine tufts of hair on the tips of its ears, which give the lynx an owl-like look among felines and probably serve to capture sounds; and its sense of touch, enhanced not only by the very large cushions under its wide and powerful paws that ensure an extremely silent step, but also by the vibrissae of its whiskers and other appendages that support a sort of hypersensitivity, a feeling of electric, patient, and smooth contact with the universe.

Sadly, as may be very quickly ascertained, nothing in these words of mine or in the information they convey has the concrete value of a single dab or a single scoop of snow from a lynx's paw, so perhaps, after all, we must resort entirely to fables and give substance in this way, a very different and probably very remote way, to our idea of the lynx, just as the Northwestern Indians described by Claude Lévi-Strauss do with theirs, in their imaginary and familiar fashion, through their stories in which animals are endowed with strange powers that intervene in an accidental manner and underpin lineages and kinships for human beings. The idea of the lynx to which I allude, however, is one that arises quite apart from the familiarity upon which myths repose; it reposes, in fact, on nothing, and is indeed perhaps without repose—nothing but a shadow in motion whose passage among us I would truly have loved to see in the shape given to it by the animal: pure intimacy with itself and, for us, an almost pure "extimacy," a passage, in exchange for our silence, of a silent form; a master, a phantom, even a god if you wish—or a beast.

—Translated by Donald Nicholson-Smith

BÉNÉDICTE BOISSERON

After Jacques Derrida (More to Follow): From A-cat-emic to Caliban

> I often ask myself, just to see, who I am—and who I am (following) at the moment when, caught naked, in silence, by the gaze of an animal, for example, the eyes of a cat, I have trouble, yes, a bad time overcoming my embarrassment.
>
> —Jacques Derrida, *The Animal That Therefore I Am*

Can the animal respond? asks Jacques Derrida. Can the subaltern speak? asks Gayatri Chakravorty Spivak. Together, the two questions draw an analogy between Animal Studies and Postcolonial Studies, fields that came to life when the silent one started to talk, or rather, when the invisible one was finally seen seeing. As Derrida says in *The Animal That Therefore I Am*: "*to see and to be seen* through the eyes of the other,"[1] the "other" being the cat staring at his naked body in the bathroom. Postcolonial Studies, starting with the Negritude of Aimé Césaire, Léon-Gontran Damas, and Léopold Sédar Senghor, introduced western consciousness to the experience of being seen by the other. "Here are black men standing, looking at us, and I hope that you—like me—will feel the shock of being seen,"[2] Jean-Paul Sartre writes in his introduction to the *nègre* (as in Negritude) voice. But more than merely *being seen*, it would be more accurate to say that Animal and (Post)-Colonial Studies are located in the fragile instance right before self-consciousness, in the fraction of a moment when the naked one is about to realize that he or she is being looked at by the silent one. "I am seen and seen naked, before even seeing myself seen by a cat."[3] This article will focus on the prescience of the gaze forcing one to look up in order to respond to the silent stare.

1. Jacques Derrida, *The Animal That Therefore I Am*, trans. David Wills (New York: Fordham University Press, 2008), 12.
2. Jean-Paul Sartre, "Black Orpheus," trans. John MacCombie, in *The Massachusetts* 6/1 (Autumn, 1964-Winter, 1965): 13.
3. Derrida, *The Animal That Therefore I Am*, 11.

YFS 127, *"Animots": Postanimality in French Thought*, ed. Senior, Clark, and Freccero, © 2015 by Yale University.

This focus has a dual function. On the one hand, the article will address the question at the heart of Colonial and Postcolonial Studies, namely how to name the one that we do not know. This question runs, in Animal Studies, from J.M. Coetzee to Derrida (*animot*); and in Postcolonial Studies, from the *nègre* to Christopher Columbus's cannibal. On the other, this article will focus on the very nature of the academic lecture. It will argue that, when Derrida delivers a lecture about the anguish of seeing his cat seeing him naked, the guest speaker is indirectly addressing, incidentally, his own nakedness in front of the staring audience. Therefore, this article will also be, and first of all, about the prescience of the audience's stare on the speaker who has to talk about the animal, a living entity that he does not really know. In sum, it is about the predicament of having to talk about what one does not know.

When J. M. Coetzee was invited to deliver a series of lectures on ethics for the Princeton's Tanner Lectures in 1997, the South African writer chose to give a fictional presentation on animal rights, a short story entitled *The Lives of Animals*. Rather than following the conventional format of the academic lecture, Coetzee ventured into the hybrid world of scholarly fiction writing. In a *mise en abyme* technique, Coetzee's lecture told of the protagonist Elizabeth Costello delivering a lecture on animal rights to an audience of college professors. Adding to the embedded pattern, Costello addressed in her lecture a short story by Franz Kafka, "A Report to an Academy," about a human-like ape (Red Peter) presenting to the Academy of Science the story of his anthropomorphic transformation. Coetzee, like Costello and Kafka, is a writer, not a scholar or specialist of Animal Studies, which makes it challenging for all three to talk about animal philosophy. As it were, Coetzee was able simultaneously to establish and disclaim his author-ity by repeating seemingly ad infinitum the theme of the non-scholar addressing an audience of scholars on the question of animals, "I am not a Kafka scholar,' Costello says, 'In fact I am not a scholar at all,'"[4]—just like Coetzee who, despite his lack of—so to speak—credentials, delivered an academic lecture on animal ethics.

First comes the lecture, then the audience's response and along with it, the anguish of having to respond to the response. Coetzee presumably sought to circumvent the usual protocol by hiding his voice,

4. J.M. Coetzee, *The Lives of Animals* (Princeton: Princeton University Press, 1999), 27.

and hence his author-ity, behind heteroglossic chatters. Because Costello is not perceived—to quote Mikhail Bakhtin—as "an object of authorial discourse, but rather a fully valid, autonomous carrier of [her] own individual world,"[5] Coetzee's protagonist can make claims of her own, independently from the author. But the problem is how to respond to a character's claims that are precisely unclaimed by the author. This question sums up the situation of the philosopher Peter Singer, as he tries to respond to Coetzee's lecture. As Singer admits in his response to Coetzee's lecture, "I don't know how to go about responding to his so-called lecture."[6] Singer chooses to speak through the voice of a fictional alter ego, which is his own way of circumventing the challenge of responding to Coetzee's lecture.[7]

Singer's response to Coetzee invites us to ponder the role of the response in an academic lecture. Coetzee uses a smoke and mirrors strategy in order to avoid answering for—as in *répondre de* (being accountable for)—his claims. In a further attempt to highjack the second step of the lecture (the response), Coetzee includes, in his own lecture, the reactions of Costello's audience as well as her Q & A session. In so doing, Coetzee instigates in his audience a vicarious impression of having already responded to his lecture, thus preventing the real audience from having to respond. Yet, the response is always infallible, as Singer's response shows. No matter how inhospitable the lecture may be, the response never fails; it *always already* follows the lecture. The book *The Lives of Animals* is a collection of essays from the Tanner Lectures that includes not only Coetzee's lecture, but also the responses to his lecture by four scholars (Marjorie Garber, Peter Singer, Wendy Doniger, and Barbara Smuts). The structure of the book attests to the impendingness of the response since after the lecture inevitably come the responses. *The Lives of Animals* (first the lecture, then the responses) serves as a reminder that, in spite of all, Coetzee must own up to his words; meaning, he must—as the French puts it—*répondre de ses actions*. Coetzee is compelled to respond

5. Mikhail Bakhtin, *Problems of Dostoevsky's Poetics* (Minneapolis: University of Minnesota Press, 1984), 5.

6. Coetzee, *The Lives of Animals*, 91.

7. Singer chooses to follow Coetzee's postmodern technique through a fictional dialogue between his daughter and himself discussing how to respond to Coetzee's lecture. The daughter has been invited to offer a response to Coetzee's lecture in Princeton. Singer suggests she respond with a fictional piece, which he is himself precisely writing.

to (*répondre de*/own up to) his words, even if it means *répondre de* the impossibility of responding to his lecture. In this regard, Coetzee's lecture is not only an exercise in showing the infallibleness of *répondre de* academically, but also of the intrinsic act of *répondre à*, in the sense of *following after* and mostly *abiding by*. Costello follows after, takes after, Kafka's "Report to an Academy." The embedded pattern in Coetzee's lecture, however, exceeds what meets the eye. Presenting itself as an always already *response to* a previous lecture, Coetzee invites his followers to follow the trace of his itinerary, which leads us inevitably to Jacques Derrida.

There are only a few months separating Derrida's July 1997 lecture in Cerisy (France) from Coetzee's October 1997 lecture at Princeton University, yet Coetzee's *The Lives of Animals* comes across as a cross-Atlantic follow-up to Derrida's *The Animal That Therefore I Am*. Probably unbeknownst to him, Coetzee is made to take after Derrida, in the literal sense of following right after Derrida. At the château of Cerisy-la-Salle, Derrida presented a ten-hour lecture, the theme of which was "The Autobiographical Animal." The introduction to the lecture, which would be the only piece included in the conference proceedings, was later published under the title "The Animal That Therefore I Am (More to Follow)." "More to Follow [*à suivre*]" indicated Derrida's intention to publish other parts of his lecture at a later date. In 2003, he fulfilled his promise by publishing another piece from his lecture, "And Say the Animal Responded?" But " More to Follow" does not only offer a promise to publish more pieces from the lecture, it also invites a follow-up. Coetzee soon enough heard the invitation and followed after him. But in addition, "More to Follow [*à suivre*]" is meant to engage the audience to follow Derrida, "to follow' in the sense of understanding and following his train of thought, his lecture being a *suite* requiring some following:

> If I am following this suite [*si je suis cette suite*], and everything in what I am about to say will lead to the question of what "to follow" or "to pursue" means, as well as "to be after," back to the question of what I do when "I am" or "I follow," when I say "*Je suis*," if I am (following) this suite then, I move from "the ends of man," that is the confines of man, to "the crossing of borders" between man and animal.[8]

8. Derrida, *The Animal That Therefore I Am*, 3.

The English translation of *L'animal que donc je suis* by David Wills contributes to Derrida's text an even more ventriloquistic complexity. Given Derrida's ample use of homonyms, Derrida's language can only be partially translated; as such it always retains a polyglossic nature populated with markers of *restance*:

> *Qui suis-je?* Or *Que suis-je?* Who or what am I (following)? Henceforth it is disturbed by an ambiguity that remains, within it, untranslatable, in what remains small, the small, the small word falling in the middle of this three-word interrogative proposition, namely, the little homonym *suis* [. . . .].[9]

Lawrence Venuti, in *The Translator's Invisibility*, indicates that non-transparent translations are based on a so-called "foreignizing method." Translators who observe this method "register the linguistic and cultural difference of the foreign text, sending the reader abroad."[10] Following Venuti's logic, we can say that, for the sake of accuracy, in his English translation, Wills is compelled to keep Derrida's French text "foreign." Derrida's text is like an animal that leaves a track for the others to follow. Like a pack animal or a horde, Derrida's writing is inherently multiple. His voice is, to paraphrase Gilles Deleuze and Félix Guattari (*A Thousand Plateaus*), "molecular" because diffractive, polysemic, and polyglottic.

But what about the animals? "The animal, what a word!"[11] Derrida says. And indeed, it is all about the word, *animot*, the *mot animé* that the followers animate, bring back to life as they follow the suite and repeat it in their own variation. Derrida's lecture presents itself as a dare to whoever follow his animal scent. Derrida carried the habit of writing down his lectures verbatim before delivering them. The transcription of what he is about to say pinpoints again, in a sort of inverted sequence of events, the iterable nature of Derrida's lectures. First comes the written word that will be then delivered orally, which can be seen as an expression of self-reflexive ventriloquizing. Once the words reach us, in their published version of "L'animal que donc je suis (à suivre)" and even more so in their English translation "The Animal That Therefore I Am (More to Follow)," Derrida's lecture has

9. Ibid., 64.
10. Lawrence Venuti, *The Translator's Invisibility: A History of Translation* (London and New York: Routledge, 1995), 20.
11. Derrida, *The Animal That Therefore I Am*, 23.

acquired such iterability that it has already fulfilled its promise of having had more to follow, the theme of the scholar presenting on animals having been repeated many times, in different versions, within the same lecture.[12] The emphasis put on iterability and following (taking after) communicates a fear of finitude, what Derrida calls in his lecture "the reckoning [échéance]."[13] Derrida quotes Plato on the silence of writing: "No matter what question one asks them, writings remain silent, keeping a most majestic silence or else always replying in the same terms, which means not replying."[14] Derrida's written lecture is a double silence: there is not only the silence of the written word as mentioned by Plato, but there is also the silence of the audience staring and waiting for the end (*échéance*) of the delivered lecture before responding. Here is the true anguish: the fear of silence or of the reckoning, the moment when one will have to respond after everything has been said.

As previously mentioned, Derrida presented his lecture "The Animal That Therefore I Am" (which includes the introduction "The Animal That Therefore I Am (More to Follow)") at a Cerisy conference in July 1997. Coetzee *follows closely* Derrida, but not only chronologically. Beyond the obvious question of animals and the common year in which the two lectures were delivered, what essentially brings Coetzee and Derrida's lectures together is the fear of the response. This fear is the *punctum*, as Roland Barthes names it in *Camera Lucida*, the thing that speaks to you, the relatable experience that is so familiar and yet never explicitly voiced. "Everything that I am about to entrust to you no doubt comes back to asking you to *respond* to me,"[15] Derrida tells his audience at Cerisy. It is a plea for a response that also translates the anguish of *répondre de*, to be accountable for the words delivered in his lecture. "I no longer know how to respond, or even to respond to the question that compels me or asks me who I am (following) or after whom I am (following) [. . .]."[16] In the preface to *The Animal That Therefore I Am*, the editor Marie-Louise Mal-

---

12. As Matthew Calarco indicates, in "Tracking the Animal in Derrida," his book review of *The Animal That Therefore I Am*, Derrida wanted to, and started to, alter his text before considering it for publication. He only published two parts of his lecture, "The Animal That Therefore I Am (More to Follow)" and "Say the Animal Responded." The remaining chapters were published posthumously.

13. Derrida, *The Animal That Therefore I Am*, 22.

14. Ibid., 52.

15. Ibid., 10.

16. Ibid.

let addresses Derrida's profound anguish, which she sees as an anxiety caused by time elapsing, again the idea of reckoning [*échéance*]. Mallet notices a leitmotif around time, or the lack thereof, in the transcription of Derrida's lecture, leading her to conclude that Derrida was extremely concerned about what she calls "the tolling of a bell."[17] Given Derrida's motifs in his entire body of work based on the question of delaying (*différance, iterability, restance,* to name a few), Derrida's fear of reckoning (*échéance*) comes as no surprise. Derrida's lecture itself, as an initially written text, is a plea for a *suite* against a finitude, a plea for something that will carry on his words in spite of their oral evanescence. In *Limited Inc.,* Derrida writes:

> A written sign, in the current meaning of this word, is a mark that subsists, one which does not exhaust itself in the moment of its inscription and which can give rise to an iteration in the absence and beyond the presence of the empirically determined subject who, in a given context, has emitted or produced it. This is what has enabled us, at least traditionally, to distinguish a "written" from an "oral" communication.[18]

Derrida's written lecture as something that "subsists" and "does not exhaust itself" helps understand the anguish mentioned by Mallet. As the editor explains, the anxiety that she detects in Derrida's lecture about the time elapsing includes the obvious, namely "the end of a colloquium, the little time remaining in fact, the fear, also, of taking up too much time and attention on the part of an audience that, nevertheless, was asking for nothing else."[19] But there is something more in Derrida's anguish. "Jacques Derrida's readers and friends will recognize there an anxiety, an anguish, a 'trembling' of the voice that they have often heard [. . .]" Mallet says, "his thinking always forged ahead toward an uncertain future to come, in the first instance through this concern for 'doing justice' to the text."[20] In other words, Mallet convincingly argues that Derrida's anguish comes from the fear of not owning up to his words, of the inability to *répondre de ses mots.*

But what if the "trembling of the voice" did not only reflect a concern for doing "justice to the text" but also for the simple and

17. Ibid., xii.
18. Derrida, *Limited Inc.* (Evanston: Northwestern University Press, 1988), 9.
19. Derrida, *The Animal That Therefore I Am,* xii.
20. Ibid.

commonly shared anguish of standing alone, naked, with a text in one's hands? What if in Derrida's *The Animal That Therefore I Am*, the silent cat looking at Derrida's naked body were a modest detour, on Derrida's part, to address the real anguish: the silent audience facing him in his "haunted castle"?[21] Even more to the point, what if *The Animal That Therefore I Am* were, in truth, about a naked Derrida standing in front of a silent audience not responding since, in a lecture, the response always follows (*"suivre"*) and never is (*"être"*)? As Mallet says in her preface, "the conference continued with the other programmed lectures, but participants were expecting more: the question of the animal in Heidegger, which had been pointed to many times during the lecture, remained in abeyance. On the last day, therefore, July 20, at the end of the proceedings, Derrida agreed to improvise a response to that expectation."[22] The last day, at the last moment, Derrida had to *répondre de ses mots*, and follow up on his Heidegger promise. In spite of his insistence on not being the last to speak—"don't think for a moment that I am insisting on having the last word [. . .] be really the last to speak"[23]—Derrida has to keep speaking, forever catching up on a failed promise.

As we tease out the polysemy in his neologism *animalséance*,[24] referring to the discomfort of a naked Derrida in the presence of his staring cat, we see that the animal is not the cat but Derrida, the only one truly *à poil* (meaning in French both "furry" and "naked"). "Nudity gets stripped to bare necessity only in that frontal exhibition, in that face-to-face,"[25] Derrida argues, the frontal exhibition being also the nature of the academic lecture. The guest speaker is in *malséance*, he is the only one *animé* (animated) in a room filled with static listeners. Derrida is, most of all, the animal *traqué*, tracked down like a deer caught in the headlights of the audience's silent stare. "An animal looks at me,"[26] the speaker says, as he looks at himself being looked at by the silent audience. Derrida presents a new genre of academics, the a-cat-emic, the academic animal feeling the anguish of the reckoning, the moment when the lecture comes to a close and it is time to *répondre de* (be accountable for his words)

21. Ibid., 23.
22. Ibid., xi.
23. Ibid., 141.
24. Ibid., 4.
25. Ibid., 11.
26. Ibid., 6.

and *répondre à* (answering to) the audience. The a-cat-emic reminds us of Rodney Wainwright, David Lodge's character in *Small World*, an Australian academic who, having only written the introductory pages of his paper, dreads the moment when he will reach the end of his unfinished paper, when he will have to face the failed expectations of the audience.

"Animals are my concern,"[27] Derrida asserts. Indeed, the real question raised in *The Animal that Therefore I Am* is: *est-ce que l'animal le regarde*? (is the animal looking at him)—in the polysemic sense of looking at him and concerning him. But equally, the underlying question is: *est-ce que le public le regarde*? (is the audience looking at him) —in the dual sense of looking at him, and should this gaze concern him. This brings us back to Coetzee's embedded theme of the non-scholar addressing an audience of scholars on the question of animals. Kafka, Costello, Coetzee, and Derrida, none of them are scholars of animal ethics; they all are in the situation of asking themselves if the animal *les regarde*—concerns them. Does the animal question fit their competence since they have never before presented anything, explicitly, on the animal question? Coetzee tries to avoid answering the question by, again, having the fictional audience answer it for him. After her philosophical lecture, 'The Philosophers and the Animals," Costello is scheduled to conduct a creative writing seminar entitled "The Poets and the Animals." When Norma, Costello's daughter-in-law, hears that Costello's seminar will address animals in the field of creative writing, she says: "I'm glad it's on something she knows about. I find her philosophizing rather difficult."[28] Once again, Coetzee hides behind the veil of vicariousness to avoid having to face the audience's dissatisfaction about his unaccredited philosophizing. Derrida, on the other hand, is relentless in proving that animals *le regardent*, concern him, hence the leitmotif in his work about his long-term interest in animals. "[. . .] for a very long time, since I began writing, in fact, I believe I have been dedicated to the question of the living and of the living animal. For me that will always have been the most important and decisive question;"[29] "They [animals] are the critters [*bêtes*] that I have been (following) from the start, for decades and from one ten-day confer-

27. Ibid., 35.
28. Ibid., 47.
29. Ibid., 34.

ence to the next;"[30] "they multiply, lunging more and more wildly in my face in proportion as my texts seem to become autobiographical, or so one would have me believe;"[31] "I therefore admit to my old obsession with a personal and somewhat paradisiacal bestiary."[32] A few years after the *Animal autobiographique* series at Cerisy, in a lecture from December 12, 2001, Derrida reiterates his long-time concern for the animal question, what he calls then *carnophallogocentrism*:

> [. . .] which has interested me for a long time and touches on what so many philosophers and anthropologists hold to be proper to man and human law [. . .] I have been emphasizing wherever (i.e. just about everywhere) I have been interested in the great question of the animal and what is proper to man, as everything I nicknamed *carnophallogocentrism* [. . .].[33]

The animal in Derrida essentially revolves around a question of "since when." Since when have animals concerned him? As he says above, "for a long time." And here, "since so long ago" [*depuis le temps*]: "Since so long ago, can we say that the animal has been looking at us?"[34]

In his anguish to do justice to the animal question, Derrida invites his audience to track the *restance* of the animal presence in his body of work, as a way to prove that "for a long time," animals have been his concern. As he says, "Still, short of outlining a philosophical autobiography, short of retracing my steps along the paths of philosophy, I could have, or perhaps should have undertaken an anamnesic interpretation of all *my* animals." Adding promptly, "I won't do that,"[35] Derrida indirectly invites his followers to follow up on his aborted intention of tracking the animal traces, *dépister la piste* (14).[36] In *Zoographies*, Matthew Calarco expresses his surprise at hearing Derrida's claim that animals have been his concern for a long time. The author writes:

30. Ibid., 35.
31. Ibid.
32. Ibid., 37.
33. Derrida, *The Beast and the Sovereign Vol. I*, trans. Geoffrey Bennington (Chicago: The University of Chicago Press, 2008), 36.
34. Derrida, *The Animal That Therefore I Am*, 3.
35. Ibid., 35.
36. Derrida follows here the psychology of *the pretense of a pretense*, a technique described by Lacan and quoted by Derrida in *The Animal That Therefore I Am*: "Why tell me that you are going to do X in order to have me believe you are going to do Y, whereas you are indeed going to do X" (128). Derrida says he could retrace his animal presence yet he will not, while indirectly doing it anyway.

This statement will likely appear odd both to longtime readers of
Derrida and to those readers who are familiar with debates in animal philosophy. While Derrida's name and work have, in recent years,
been generally aligned with progressive political discourses and movements, only rarely has the importance of his thought been recognized
for issues concerning animals.[37]

The double-entendre in *regarder, looking/concerning*, epitomizes
the a-cat-emic anguish of doing justice to the text. Coetzee, Costello,
and Derrida are committed to doing justice to the animal question,
in spite of their incapacity or their unwillingness to trace back their
credentials on the subject.

That being said, Derrida is knowingly and purposely a marginal in
the field of Animal Studies, his voice being at the limit of this field.
As he says, "limitrophy is therefore my subject. Not just because it
will concern what sprouts or grows at the limit, around the limit,
by maintaining the limit, but also what *feeds the limit*."[38] Derrida's
concept of *animot* is in fact antonymous with the "animal question."
In fact, *animot* is— from Descartes on—what *questions* the animal
question, as it challenges human entitlement to authoritatively name
the animal as a non-responsive being. For Derrida, the people who
studied and named the animals never thought that those animals
could address them. "They have taken no account of the fact that
what they call 'animal' could *look at* them, and *address* them from
down there, from a wholly other origin."[39] Derrida's use of the word
animot, in that respect, underlines the awareness of the animals' capacity to respond by looking back, by addressing the presumptuous
people who have named them. *Animot* allows Derrida to show that
he is on the defensive when it comes to subjectifying the other in the
act of naming (*animot* as a word [*mot*]). *Animot*, as in the phonetic
plural of animals (*animaux*), also permits Derrida to insist on the in-
commensurability of the animal, animals being a "multiplicity" that
cannot be "homogenized"[40] into a generic living species. Derrida's cat
is the real cat staring at him, not the cat as an empty signifier symbol
of the animal species. *Animot* deals with all those who have studied,

37. Matthew Calarco, "Tracking the Animal in Derrida," *Humanimalia* 1/1 (September 2009): 103.
38. Derrida, *The Animal That Therefore I Am*, 29.
39. Ibid., 13.
40. Ibid., 43.

looked at the animal, without seeing that the animal was looking back at them. In that, Derrida *follows* Sartre.

Sartre writes: "For three thousand years, the white man has enjoyed the privilege of seeing without being seen [. . .]. Today, these black men are looking at us, and our gaze comes back to our own eyes."[41] What Sartre describes in his 1948 preface to the Negritude anthology[42] is comparable to what Derrida will address, close to sixty years later, in his lecture "The Animal That Therefore I Am." In both cases, the philosophers focus on the discomfiture of specularity, the beholder of the initial gaze losing his composure as s/he feels the "shock"[43] of being seen, or as Derrida puts it, "a reflex of shame."[44] In both cases, the element of unexpectedness is what creates the unease, *malséance /animalséance*.[45] The impertinence of the eyes unexpectedly meeting is crucial in both Sartre and Derrida. But what makes it even more impertinent is the untimeliness of the experience, given that Derrida and Sartre belatedly become aware of the cat's and the *nègre*'s already existing stare. They have been caught, initially unbeknownst to them, in their nakedness, literally *à poil* for Derrida and nakedly white for Sartre—"our white heads are no more than Chinese lanterns swinging in the wind." To add insult to the injury, Sartre says that the *nègre* shows no interest for the object of his gaze. "A black poet—unconcerned with us—."[46] *Le noir ne nous regarde pas*, we are not his concern, after all. "*Maman, regarde le nègre, j'ai peur!*"[47] "Mummy, look at the Negro, I'm afraid!," this is how Frantz Fanon in *Peau noire, masques blancs*, addresses the question of Black interpellation (Althusser). As Fanon explains, the Black man is negatively defined through the White gaze, the White gaze being the sovereign authority, the one that names and defines the other. But here comes the *noirséance*, which is as alienating as the *animalséance*: the White man looks at himself being looked at and sees that his existence is not the Black man's concern, *ne le regarde pas*, it is an empty stare.

41. Sartre, "Black Orpheus," *The Massachusetts Review* 6/1 (Autumn, 1964-Winter, 1965): 13
42. Léopold Sédar Senghor, *Anthologie de la nouvelle poésie nègre et malgache de langue française* (Paris: Presses Universitaires de France, 1948).
43. Sartre, "Black Orpheus," 13.
44. Ibid., 4.
45. Derrida, *The Animal That Therefore I Am*, 4.
46. Sartre, "Black Orpheus," 13.
47. Frantz Fanon, *Peau noire, masques blancs* (Paris: Seuil, 1965), 90.

Some may argue that comparing the animal with the colonized is problematic, just as, in *The Lives of Animals*, fictional characters took offense at Costello comparing the holocaust genocide with the slaughter of animals in abattoirs. But given that Derrida addressed the animal question at the level of words (*mots*), as he showed concerns for those who name the silent others, the comparison is not only appropriate but also pressing. Hélène Cixous once said, "whoever cannot hear the cat's speech is just one step from not hearing a woman's speech or a Jew's or an Arab's or that of the subject of one of those species that bear the destiny of banishment."[48] What brings Animal and Postcolonial Studies together is not so much the "destiny of banishment" as that of being named as an unresponsive entity. The "shock of being seen" described by Sartre is due to the long-lasting expectation that the named one does not talk back, does not respond.

"And Say the Animal Responded?" is chapter three of *The Animal That Therefore I Am*. We find its postcolonial counterpart in *The Empire Writes Back* by Bill Ashcroft, Gareth Griffiths, and Helen Tiffin. *The Empire Writes Back*, published in 1989, borrowed its title from a 1982 piece by Salman Rushdie from *The Times* entitled "The Empire Writes Back with a Vengeance." In it, Rushdie posits that the English language needs to be decentered, as "the Empire is striking back."[49] Ashcroft's *The Empire Writes Back* looks at the revisional methods used by authors from the Commonwealth who aimed at decolonizing the English language. "They [colonized peoples] need [. . .] to escape from the implicit body of assumptions to which English was attached [. . .]."[50] Ashcroft and his co-authors pinpoint the moment when the silent one was finally ready to return the stare, to talk back, and in so doing to strip English of its Western clothes.

The word *Caliban*, almost an anagram of "cannibal," may be the best illustration of what postcolonial revision means in terms of staring/striking back. Caliban originally refers to a character, half-human and half-animal,[51] in Shakespeare's *The Tempest*. Prospero occupies

48. Hélène Cixous, "The Keys To: Jacques Derrida as a Proteus Unbound," *Discourse* 30/1–2 (Winter/Spring, 2008): 93.
49. Bill Ashcroft, Gareth Griffiths, and Helen Tiffin, *The Empire Writes Back: Theory and Practice in Post-Colonial Literatures* (London: Routledge, 2002), 7.
50. Ibid., 10.
51. For a detailed study of the transformation of Shakespeare's Caliban over the centuries, see Virginia Mason Vaughan, "'Something Rich and Strange': Caliban's Theatrical Metamorphoses," *Shakespeare Quarterly* 36/4 (Winter, 1985): 390–405; and

Caliban's island and forces the native into servitude. This character has been subject to a series of postcolonial revisions in which Caliban has turned into a rebel and defiant colonized. In Aimé Césaire's *A Tempest*, one of the most celebrated works of black revision, Caliban asks the colonizer Prospero to call him "X," as not only a reference to Malcolm X, but also to naming as a means of colonial subjection. Caliban, as an anagrammatical subversion of cannibal, precisely refers to the colonial institution of naming as empowerment. Both words hark back to Christopher Columbus's 1492 encounter with the Caribbean natives, when Columbus was told that a neighbor tribe was named *Caribs*. The communication was in translation from the Taino Indian language to Spanish and Columbus misheard the name, thinking the tribe's name was "cannibal." Columbus went back to Europe with the false assumption that the Caribs were named cannibals, and who could have corrected him since, as we know, Columbus was the one responsible in the Americas for naming what the westerner saw as the other? What matters is not what the tribe's name was in reality, but what the colonial decided it was. As George Lamming observes:

> Columbus's journal speaks about meeting a Caribbean aboriginal on arrival and conversing with him. Yet, as far as I know, Columbus spoke not a word of any aboriginal Caribbean language, and the aboriginal spoke neither Italian nor Spanish; it is peculiar that they could understand each other; what Columbus really did was to create what he ordered, because he represented power."[52]

Much of the colonial history of the Caribbean can be read through the question of naming as an institution of power. But also, as Celia Britton argues in *Edouard Glissant and Postcolonial Theory*, the subaltern sometimes purposely embraces the imposed name and flaunts it back in the Western face as ironical empowerment. This is what, Britton adds, Mireille Rosello calls "mimetic opposition," when for example the Caribbean people take over "the enemy's prejudices and us[e] them for their own ends."[53] All this to say that Caliban, half animal and half human, is a postcolonial follow-up (though preceding

---

Shakespeare's Caliban: A Cultural History, in collaboration with Alden T. Vaughan (Cambridge: Cambridge University Press, 1993).

52. George Lamming, *Frontiers of Caribbean Literature in English* in *Warwick University Caribbean Studies* (London: Macmillan Caribbean, 1996), 2.

53. Celia Britton, *Edouard Glissant and Postcolonial Theory: Strategies of Language and Resistance* (Charlottesville and London: University Press of Virginia, 1999), 28.

Derrida) to *animot,* and it is something reminding us that the word it-self, the naming is what carries the danger of striking back when least expected. Ironically enough, in contrast to what Derrida has claimed, it is not the real cat, the real *nègre* or the cannibal looking back at us but the name itself with its empty stare no longer concerned by us.

CARLA FRECCERO

"A Race of Wolves"

Marie de France, La Fontaine, Hobbes, Derrida, and other figurations;
werewolf trials, fairy tales, Angela Carter and postmodern wolf-
human mergers such as those in the Stephenie Meyers "Twilight"
series—"wolf" is everywhere in the Western imagination, from moral
fables to political allegories to juridical encounters and the queerness
of transpecies becomings.

My interest in wolves, and wolves and humans, emerges from
my work on the genealogy of the cynanthrope, the merger of dog
and man. Cynanthropes were thought to live on the edge of civilization and to be intelligent and rational like humans but also ferocious and hostile toward strangers, devouring their enemies. They
are examples of what I call "carnivorous virility," a cultural fantasy
that the merger between dog and human restores to human men a
measure of primitive strength, virility, and savagery.[1] The figure of
the cynanthrope is a "material-semiotic" figure: material because it
was thought to exist as an entity—there are depictions of it—and it
persists in fantastic forms of masculine-canine becoming; and "semi-
otic," that is, meaningful (it persists because meaningful). The story
of the cynanthrope is also queer insofar as the merger in question—a
transpecies coupling—may also be said to be between men. But animal theory (and I include humans here) is also queer because it opens
up questions of non-normative subjectivities, sexualities, and desire.
It de-normativizes or de-centers the human by showing how the human is one subject-position among others. I call what I do figural historiography, using feminism, queer theory, critical race theory, and

1. See Carla Freccero, "Carnivorous Virility, or Becoming-Dog," in *Interspecies*,
ed. Julie Livingston and Jasbir Puar, special issue, *Social Text* 29/1 (2011): 177–95.

YFS 127, *"Animots": Postanimality in French Thought*, ed. Senior, Clark, and Freccero,
© 2015 by Yale University.

animal studies to discern the material semiotics in figures of wolf-human interactions. Such theory (and, I hope, my story) aims to tease apart the long and tangled inter-implications of sex, species, and race.

There's an intimate historical connection between species and race. That period in the eighteenth and nineteenth centuries in Europe that saw an intensification of taxonomizing and typologizing of the human "races" and that gave rise to eugenics, also saw the burgeoning of the study of biological classification culminating in evolutionary theory. Likewise, the period of European abolitionist activism corresponded to animal welfare movements, especially in Britain, and some of the great humanitarian denunciators of slavery also denounced cruelty to animals, if not their "slavery" as well.

And yet, the intimacy of species and race as conceptual categories has engendered, if anything, an aversion to their co-articulation in current critical cultural discourses purporting to understand both racialization and speciation. This has occurred, I think, for a number of reasons: on the one hand, scholars of racialization are all too aware of the history of ideological analogism. Racists and civilizationists have long compared groups of humans they regarded as inferior to themselves with non-humans and have thereby justified all manner of abuse. Likewise the "less-than-human" status afforded some humans has led to a rigidification of species hierarchy, tantamount to reinstating the great chain of being, whereby the human occupies an exceptional status in the order of the living, with no comparison allowed. The counter-discourse that would distance the non-human animal from the human—as in the expression "human life," so nicely questioned by Judith Butler in *Undoing Gender*—like the counter-discourse that distances some humans from other humans and hier-archizes them, unwittingly reinstates modalities of exclusion by relegating some of the living to non-viability, to unlivable lives.[2] Finally, there is also the fear that, by privileging the living-in-general over the specificity of the human, there will be a turn away from human injustice toward other humans, which is the problem that progressive liberalism always seems to grapple with when adjudicating bids for greater enfranchisement or liberation: first us then them.[3] This

2. Judith Butler, *Undoing Gender* (NY and Oxford: Routledge, 2004), 12–13.

3. For a brief survey of some of the difficulties of reading species and race together, see Claire Jean Kim and Carla Freccero, "Introduction: A Dialogue," in *Species/Race/Sex*, ed. Claire Jean Kim and Carla Freccero, special issue, *American Quarterly* 65/3 (2013): 461–79.

prioritization or progressivism has, however, reached its limits in the current era of planetary life dubbed "The Anthropocene," where the material foundations of all biological life are put into question by human agency in the environment that makes all "life" possible. It is thus no longer an option to think progressive enfranchisements of orders of the living, for the very reason that the interconnectedness of the living in the present—and the interdependence of life—will in fact determine the contours of the future—its length and duration, its quality, its very possibility.

How, where, and why do wolves signify, and what are the material histories, cultures, and encounters that make lupine figures ubiquitous in human oral and scriptural cultures? This figural historiography follows twisted paths and sometimes denatures temporal chronologies and ideologies of reproductive futurism: it is a queer transspecies racial/civilizational narrative, a story about indigeneity and autochthony. The contradictory figuration of wolves throughout Western history and literature offers insight into the complexities and contradictions at work in cultural productions of species, sex, gender, and race, for each of these are bound up with animality. But it's not enough to address the non-human animal merely for his or her representational value; I am thus also trying to find a way to think about and with wolf and wolf figures for (that is, in the interest of) wolves as living beings in themselves.

However fictionally and allegorically ubiquitous, material wolves —(I originally wrote "in their integrity," but what could I have meant? Am I in search of the authentic wolf, the never-before-eradicated and re-seeded wolf, am I looking for "wild" wolves? Indeed, wolves are also asked to stand in for a nostalgia for the wholeness of the human and the natural, a nostalgia that is both spatial and temporal)— are largely absent from most peoples' lives (not all, but most), except where they are protected or where, as in parts of Eastern Europe and Asia, there hasn't been as much systematic eradication. There is thus a work of transspecies mourning to be done here that also seeks to come to terms with the spectral returns of lupine being within the cultures that have expelled and eradicated it. It is what Jacques Derrida calls a "hauntology,"—a way of thinking and responding ethically within history.[4] For Derrida, spectrality describes a mode

4. See Jacques Derrida, *Specters of Marx: The State of the Debt, The Work of Mourning, and The New International,* trans. Peggy Kamuf (New York: Routledge,

of historical attentiveness that the living might have to what is not present but somehow appears as a figure, a "non-living present in the living present" that is no longer or not yet with the living, and hauntology is the practice of attending to the spectral.[5] There is both a powerful analogy and a relation here—the indigeneity of the wolf and perceptions of the wolf's competition for resources with humans (settler colonialists?) suggests, first, that—as Brian K. Hudson has argued—there are threads to be woven between first beings and first peoples;[6] and second, that wolves may he privileged among first beings for understanding spectrality's force, its ethical insistence, in the present.

I begin with a proverbial wolf; I am looking for the *lupus in fabula* (the wolf in the story), which is a way of saying "speaking of the devil" . . .

In the 1963 Warner Brothers' cartoon featuring Ralph E. Wolf and Sam Sheepdog, a wolf and a sheepdog share a companionable dailiness and friendship involving coffee together in the morning and a return home arm in arm at the end of the day.[7] In between they assume their role as enemies: the sheepdog guards the flock, while the wolf devises numerous stratagems to steal the sheep, foiled at every turn by a seemingly dopey yet powerful and alert guard dog. The cartoon, with its reference to the workaday world, cleverly points to the human cultural roles within which dog and wolf are forced to play out their opposed roles, and marks as capital the framework for their opposition: there is an invisible boss and a system within which they must perform: someone—presumably human—owns the flock, and both are employed in its maintenance and devastation. The cartoon is knowing and innovative in that it remarks on the "insiderness" to human culture of the wolf—he is *supposed* to try to steal the sheep,

1994). Originally published as *Spectres de Marx* (Paris: Galilée, 1993). For a beautiful application of hauntology that compellingly charts the subjective and collective effects of traumatic historical events, see Avery Gordon's analysis of Toni Morrison's *Beloved* in *Ghostly Matters: Haunting and the Sociological Imagination* (Minneapolis: University of Minnesota Press, 2008), 137–92. See also Freccero, *Queer/Early/Modern* (Durham, NC: Duke University Press, 2005), 69–104.

   5. *Specters of Marx*, 254.

   6. Brian K. Hudson, "First Beings in American Indian Literatures," in *Animal Studies*, ed. Brian K. Hudson and Dustin Gray, special issue, *Studies in American Indian Literatures* 25/4 (2013): 3–10.

   7. "Woolen Under Where," *Merrie Melodies*, dir. Phil Monroe and Richard Thompson (May 11, 1963; Burbank, CA: Warner Brothers Pictures), television.

although, in a fort-da of mastery and triumph over trauma, he will never succeed. Instead, his actions confirm and reconfirm the superior agency of the human creation: the sheepdog. No matter how much the thief tries to bring down the empire he is foiled.[8] In its material realization—its production—one discerns the racial valences implicitly at work, from the whiteness of Sam Sheepdog to the brownness of Ralph E. Wolf, who is modeled on the cartoon image of Wiley Coyote and thus also carries with him the degraded and degrading spectral image of the Native American as companion/twin and competitor for resources of the land.

The cartoon suggests that the economic system of private property (and primitive accumulation) require an enemy. And "enemy" is most often what wolf is, especially in the economic arena. The archive of wolves and humans in intimate naturecultures is a record of economic competition, top-of-the-food-chain predators finding themselves side by side, the one in the *polis* (the city), the other on its borders (wolves in literary records are always in the forest, a wild space, the space of romance; wolves thus occupy the genre of romance, or they are *unheimlich*, uncanny, "home-like" yet not, and thus also occupy the genre of horror). Both parties—human and wolf—are interested in the flesh of ungulates, whether they be the domesticated sheep and cattle whose accumulation furnished primitive wealth, or the "wild" deer whose abundance furnished royalty with hunting grounds.[9] And they do, or did, populate the world—of wolves, Garry Marvin says that they're "the most widely distributed of all land mammals, apart from humans," and Aleksander Pluskowski notes that they have adaptive success "in being able to survive in virtually any environment."[10] They were both (humans and wolves) found in

8. Given the historical moment of the cartoon, one can speculate about its allegory: does it reference the red evil at the heart of nineteen-fifties' America? Is it a domestic racial threat? Or is it invoking the failure of World War II's axis of evil (one of Mussolini's fascist youth organizations was called the *figli della lupa*, children of the she-wolf)?

9. For an interesting discussion of aristocratic enclosure of forest land and the privatization of hunting rights, see Matt Cartmill, *A View to a Death in the Morning: Hunting and Nature Through History* (Cambridge, MA: Harvard University Press, repr. 1996).

10. See Garry Marvin, "Wolves in Sheep's (and Others') Clothing," in *Beastly Natures: Animals, Humans, and the Study of History*, ed. Dorothee Brantz (Charlottesville and London: University of Virginia Press, 2010), 66; and Aleksander Pluskowski, *Wolves and the Wilderness in the Middle Ages* (Woodbridge: The Boydell Press, 2006), 25.

almost every corner of the earth—and the fact that, now, the one is far more widespread than the other is related to their having shared so much territory. And if *homo homini lupus*—a man is a wolf to/ for other men—a phrase whose originating context is economic, then wolves too are often wolves for other wolves, since in reserves and parks it would seem that half if not more of their fatalities are due to predation by other wolves . . . in territorial disputes.[11] Their sociality—both human and wolf—is the nuclear family, sometimes extended—clans, packs—and when rival children are born, it has been a customary strategy to kill them, wolves killing wolves, and humans humans. As Ferdinand, in a brilliant economy of phrasing, declares to the Duchess of Malfi concerning his murder of her children, "The death of young wolves is never to be pitied."[12] Both humans and wolves also practice cross-species infanticide: one systematic practice for eradicating wolves in pre-modernity was to find the den and kill all the cubs in spring or summer, while wolf attacks on humans primarily target children.[13] In "Little Red Riding Hood" there's a specificity to the gender of the child—she's female—which adds a dimension of genetic and reproductive competition to the fantasy of wolf/human competition—the transpecies miscegenation so sought after in other contexts (male human hybridized with male wolf), when posited as between male wolf and female human, is a threat.

Do wolves (and wolves and humans) have a history? And what have they learned? Like humans, wolves excel in visual observational learning. They have learned to fear firepower and know the distances they need to keep from guns.[14] It also seems to be the case, from documenting human-wolf encounters, that there are "no examples of humans being incorporated into long-term predation strategies" on the part of wolves.[15] The obverse is certainly not true, as the example of the *Luparii* attests. *Luparii* were designated wolf-hunting

---

11. "Gray Wolf," *Wikipedia.org*, last modified June 2, 2014, http://en.wikipedia.org/wiki/Gray_wolf.

12. John Webster, *The Duchess of Malfi*, ed. Leah S. Marcus (London: Methuen Drama, 2009).

13. Pluskowski, *Wolves and the Wilderness in the Middle Ages*.

14. Pluskowski makes the fascinating point that "modern wolves have had many generations of experience with firearms and their general timidity may be related to this. But this shyness is conditional and wolves have been known to overcome their fear of people in a number of situations . . . it is likely that wolves in medieval northern Europe were even more fearless," *Wolves and the Wilderness in the Middle Ages*, 108.

15. Ibid., 108.

royal officials receiving bounties for killed wolves, from the ninth century on in Europe. Wolves prefer wild ungulates to tame ones, given the choice, and they only kill tame ones in surplus (which has led, among humans, to their reputation as greedy, vindictive, and wantonly destructive). A longer cultural history would explore the many micro-decisions, genetically selective and conscious (as well as unconscious) that led eventually to dog for, as Donna Haraway and others have argued, dog is a naturecultural history of mutual domestication, wolf-for-human, human-for-wolf, the results being (for the wolf-become-dog) smaller brains, smaller teeth, neoteny, and an ability to read humans visually and vocally—a kind of language acquisition.[16] Wolves, for the most part, recognize dogs and their human and wolf allegiances. There seems to be no wholesale strategy to become-dog on the part of wolves, while it is unclear, at least for most of this history, whether humans have practiced a systematic strategy of the becoming-dog of wolf. For a long time humans have intended genocide for wolves. Where wolves have survived, it is mostly because they found places to live that were inaccessible to human hunters.

The phrase *homo homini lupus*, man is a wolf to other men, is from Plautus's *Asinaria*, and it is the phrase the merchant in the text utters: "One man to another is a wolf, not a man, when he doesn't know what sort he is."[17] But this phrase's more famous future is a political, not an economic one, and it takes out the qualifying phrase: Thomas Hobbes's *homo homini lupus* is the evil twin of the other Latin adage, commented on by Erasmus and Hobbes, *homo homini deus*. Man is wolf and god, god and wolf are man's possibilities, man is somewhere between wolf and god, if he is man. This is the subject of Jacques Derrida's 2001–2002 seminar, *The Beast and the Sovereign, La* (feminine*) bête et le* (masculine*) souverain*, which is also *The Beast is the Sovereign*.[18] Derrida addresses both the feminiza-

16. Donna Haraway, *When Species Meet* (Minneapolis: University of Minnesota Press, 2008). See also *The Companion Species Manifesto: Dogs, People, and Significant Otherness* (Chicago: Prickly Paradigm Press, 2003).

17. Titus Maccius Plautus, *Asinaria*, act 2, scene 4 in *The Comedies of Plautus*, trans. Henry Thomas Riley (London: George Bell and Sons, 1912), http://data.perseus.org/catalog/urn:cts:latinLit:phi0119.phi002.opp-eng1.

18. Jacques Derrida, *The Beast and the Sovereign*, Vol. I, ed. Michel Lisse, Marie-Louise Mallet, and Ginette Michaud, trans. Geoffrey Bennington (Chicago and London: University of Chicago Press, 2011). Originally published as *Séminaire, La bête et le souverain, Volume I: 2001–2002* (Paris: Galilée, 2008).

tion of the non-human animal in human schemes of representation and points out the identity/twinning between one kind of sovereign and another, both exceptions to the law of the *polis*. He performs a *genelycology* of sovereignty, noting the ways wolf and sovereign mirror each other, become each other, and raise questions of reason and force in government. In the long and ancient *genelycology* of political animals, and in the naturecultural formations that give rise to wolf-with/against/for-human and human-with/against/for-wolf, he finds many places where humans, most often male humans, derive their heroic, exceptional, savage, strong, noble, ferocious, status from the wolf beside them: 1) as their twin brother—Derrida cites an Ojibwe hero legend of fraternal rivalry between brothers, one human, one wolf; 2) as their wolf mother (the one who suckles Romulus and Remus), also invoked in the context of fraternal rivalry in the founding of the nation-state; 3) as their wolf father and brothers (Rudyard Kipling's Akela, the adoptive father of Mowgli the man-cub and Mowgli's brothers, the wolf pack); 4) as the wolf who is preserved in their names, nicknames, and totems.[19]

Derrida wants us to consider "this becoming-beast, this becoming-animal of a sovereign who is above all a war chief, and is determined as sovereign or as animal faced with the enemy. He is instituted as sovereign by the possibility of the enemy, by that hostility in which Schmitt claimed to recognize, along with the possibility of the political, the very possibility of the sovereign, of sovereign decision and exception."[20] He invokes Carl Schmitt's concept of the political, which bases the conceptual realm of state sovereignty and autonomy upon the distinction between friend and enemy.[21] For Schmitt, an enemy establishes the very notion of the political. The enemy is a hostile equal, another like the self. As Derrida writes, of the interspecies twin hero legends:

> His brother is the wolf, his next of kin is the wolf. For this man, the twin brother is a wolf: a friendly wolf, a friendly brother whose death leaves him inconsolable, beyond all possible work of mourning; or else an enemy wolf, an enemy brother, a twin brother he will have

19. Derrida, *The Beast and the Sovereign*, Vol. I, 9–11.
20. Ibid., 10.
21. Carl Schmitt, *The Concept of the Political*, trans. George Schwab (Chicago: University of Chicago Press, 1996).

killed, and whom he will not have mourned here either. Those close
to me, brothers, friendly or enemy brothers are wolves who are my
kind and my brothers.[22]

In his study of Albanian shepherds, Marvin observes that the wolf is
accorded the subjectivity of enemy in Schmittian terms, as a brother/
other with agency and intention: "The wolf is a stranger, an Other,
the wild outsider who continues to be wild and does not succumb
to domestication and incorporation," he writes, and although apparently in Norway shepherds are economically compensated for wolf
depredations, farmers, he argues, nevertheless want revenge, as from
an enemy with purpose and intent.[23]

This sovereign/tyrant who is a wolf lives in the literature of fables
and popular stories as well, and he (for he is often if not always a
male wolf) is also a noble animal, unlike the degraded servant, the
dog, whose collar of servitude, famously in Aesop, Marie de France,
and Jean La Fontaine, among others, will not be adopted by the wolf
for an easier life. There is thus a contradiction in representations of
the wolf's relationship to human social orders that also informs his
racialized human counterpart: the wolf is wild, noble, possessing a
primitive strength and natural dignity, and yet he is capable of an
inhuman savagery that the human (sovereign) must suppress in himself. In the medieval *lai* "Bisclavret," Marie de France's knight-wolf
demonstrates his civilized (and thus, ironically, his dog-like) nature
through his recognition of and submission to the king.[24] For Marie,
there must be two wolves, a bad one and a good one, in order to reha-
bilitate wolfish-ness: Bisclavret (Breton) is not a *loup garou/garwaf*,
the Norman terms for werewolf, because "A werewolf is a savage
beast;/ while his fury is on him/ he eats men, does much harm."[25]
The difference in the two contradictory valences of the wolf-man hybrid is marked by a linguistic, which is also a racial/national, difference (England and France): "In Breton, the *lai's* name is *Bisclavret*—
the Normans call it *Garwaf*."[26] The medieval (were)wolf thus already
exhibits the conflicting values of the nation-racial difference that this

22. Derrida, *The Beast and the Sovereign*, Vol. I, 10–11.
23. Marvin, "Wolves in Sheep's (and Others') Clothing," 70, 72.
24. Marie de France, *Lais de Marie de France*, trans. Alexandre Micha (Paris: Garnier Flammarion, 1994), 126–43.
25. *The Lais of Marie de France*, trans. Robert Hanning and Joan Ferrante (New
York: E.P. Dutton, 1978), 92, ll. 9–11.
26. *The Lais of Marie de France*, 92, ll. 3–4.

species merger is thought to embody. And yet, in the story, the wolf is asked to stand in for something particularly "savage" about sovereign power—for Bisclavret uses his savagery righteously to punish his adulterous wife and her usurping husband (he attacks them both and tears off his former wife's nose). The King, in turn, tortures the wife to elicit a confession. Peggy McCracken, analyzing this tale from the point of view of translation, notes that for Marie, translation frequently occurs at the site of an animal's name, as here, thus signaling "a translatability between human and animal forms," insofar as translation is a figure for the transformation that also occurs thematically between humans and animals in the *Lais*.[27] As the tale bears out, and the twinning of beast and sovereign suggest, the difference asserted between *Bisclavret* and *Garwaf* may be "merely" skin deep. The wolf is the sovereign turned tyrant or he is the tyrant in the sovereign. The beast is the sovereign, the sovereign is the beast.

Jean La Fontaine nicely encapsulates this "fabular" or "fabulous" dimension of the political when he comments on problems of power and subordination in the fable of the wolf and the lamb, whose first line serves as a refrain for Derrida's seminar: "La raison du plus fort est toujours la meilleure" (the reason of the strongest is always the best, or "might makes right").[28] The wolf, in an extravagant performance of ressentiment, feels wronged from the outset and seeks to blame the lamb, who very reasonably—that is, using rational faculties (La Fontaine knew—and disagreed with—Descartes' theory of the animal machine)—explains that he could not possibly be the culprit (first, because he drinks downstream from the wolf, second, because he was not born when the wolf was insulted/slandered the year before). The lamb addresses him as "Your Majesty": "'Sire,' répond l'Agneau, 'que votre Majesté/Ne se mette pas en colère'" ("'Let not, Sire,/Your Majesty feel so much ire',", ll. 10–11), and it is clear that he is dealing with a powerful and arbitrary ruler. That ruler—both plaintiff and judge, as the explicitly juridical language suggests—feels wronged in advance and seeks vengeance. The story ends as one might expect, the wolf carrying off and eating the lamb, "sans autre forme de procès," (l.29), which, in a literal translation, means without any (other) form of

27. Peggy McCracken, "Translation and Animals in Marie de France's *Lais*," *Australian Journal of French Studies* 46/3 (2009): 206–218.

28. "Le loup et l'agneau," fable X in Jean de La Fontaine, *Fables*, ed. Antoine Adam (Paris: Garnier Flammarion, 1966), 59–60. See also *Selected Fables*, ed. Maya Slater, trans. Christopher Wood (Oxford and New York: Oxford University Press, 1995), 18–20.

trial. It also points to the juridical context of sovereignty enshrined in the seventeenth-century writ of *habeas corpus* that sets the terms of both sovereignty and subjection in Giorgio Agamben's discussion of sovereignty.[29] Ultimately, this framing of wolf-lamb relations that pits an arbitrary, ruthless, and unjust power against innocence and reason will binaristically inform all future representations of savage and civilized in Western narratives of humans and of wolves and humans.

In Marie's *lais* the bisclavret (the name is both generic and proper), though a "bête" or beast and thus feminine when referred to in the third person, is nevertheless most often subjectively described through masculine pronouns (the name permitting this transition between feminine beast and masculine werewolf); in La Fontaine's tale, "majesté" and "bête" both feminize the wolf, while "loup" masculinizes him. Derrida's beast and sovereign thus also flicker between genders, the feminine beast and the masculine sovereign alternating sexual ontologies. The racialized/savage man, the beast in the man, and "woman" are, in the carnophallogocentric poetics of the West, conjoined by their proximity to the wolf. Anne Carson writes:

> The wolf is a conventional symbol of marginality in Greek poetry. The wolf is an outlaw. He lives beyond the boundary of usefully cultivated and inhabited space marked off as the polis, in that blank no man's land called to apeiron ("the unbounded"). Women, in the ancient view, share this territory spiritually and metaphorically in virtue of a "natural" female affinity for all that is lawless, formless and in need of the civilizing hand of man.[30]

This also proleptically informs Freud's argument that women incompletely sublimate and are thus more tied to the instinctual drives of animality than men; women are connected, like wolves, to the wild and to earth, and they are amoral. This is perhaps what motivates some of the postmodern twists in tales of Red Riding Hood, such as the television series' *Once Upon a Time*'s "Red Handed," where there's a mere red cloak between Little Red Riding Hood and the

---

29. Giorgio Agamben, *Homo Sacer: Sovereign Power and Bare Life*, trans. Daniel Heller-Roazen (Stanford, CA: Stanford University Press, repr. 1998). Agamben also discusses "wolf" and Marie de France; for him, the metamorphosis of the knight into wolf signals the "state of exception," 104–111.

30. Anne Carson, "The Gender of Sound," in *Glass, Irony and God* (New York: New Directions Publishing Corporation, 1992), 119–42.

wolf.[31] When wolves are gendered, maternal wolves confer salutary savagery.[32] They figure importantly in fantasies of nation-building, for the heroes in the archives of *genelycology* will need the ferocity of a wolf for the future founding and ruling of their nations; like Marie's king, they will need wolf-ness at their side or within them to mete out punishment without weakness. True to the feminist observation that masculinist cultural fantasies consign women to the roles of mother and whore (the virgin occupies a special status in this wolf tale, as Angela Carter's reworkings of wolf stories suggest), the other female wolf, the "she-wolf," is rapacious, a sexual and economic predator. The medieval and early modern nickname for prostitutes was *"lupae,"* (she-wolves), because they aggressively stripped their clients of wealth.[33]

Do modern versions of the conjoining of human and wolf and the figuration of the human in wolfly terms forge alternatives to the traditional narratives that link wolves to primitive masculinity and tyrannical savagery? Can refigurations of the relationship between wolves and humans have an effect on—transform and refigure—the species, race, and sex nexus in which this relationship is knotted up? And what might this have to do with wolves?

Consider Stephenie Myers's *Twilight* series, where the werewolf is a Native American man. The wolf, like the racialized other of a white European cultural imagination, connotes sexual potency, vigor, a carnality that supplements—with sexualized embodiedness—civilization. But here, those values are positive (even if they can't compete with the effete sophistication and capitalist wealth of the extremely

31. "Red-Handed," *Once Upon a Time*, dir. Ron Underwood (March 11, 2012; Burbank, CA: ABC Studios), television.

32. I understand this fantasy as consonant with early modern (Italian) practices of sending children of the nobility to be wet-nursed by rural peasant women, in spite of the high rates of mortality thereby entailed. The wet-nurse was thought to confer the sturdiness and vigor of peasant rurality through her breast milk.

33. For Angela Carter's re-workings of Red Riding Hood, see *The Bloody Chamber and Other Stories* (New York: Harper & Row, 1979); see Kimberly Lau, "Erotic Infidelities: Angela Carter's Wolf Trilogy," *Marvels & Tales* 22/1 (2008): 77–94. "Shakira's song, "She-Wolf," builds on this conceit of the lustful she-wolf and at the same time disavows it. A sexually rapacious and predatory savagery is conferred on the woman and experienced by her as a form of liberation from the excessive docility required of her by her workaday life and boyfriend. See Shakira, "She-Wolf," *She-Wolf* (2009, Epic, CD). For "lupae" and "lupanar" (the ancient Roman term for a brothel, from wolf-den), see "Lupanar (Pompeii)," *Wikipedia.org*, last modified May 10, 2014, http://en.wikipedia.org/wiki/Lupanar_%28Pompeii%29.

pale and sparkling vampire-husband).[34] It remains to be seen whether the refashioning of feminine agency and sexualized transpecies proximity to wolves—wolves of color, it seems, specifically—has any kind of subversive role to play in reworking cultural fantasies about the wolf in the man. Modern revisionist (and sometimes feminist) narratives of this species merger (popular film and TV adaptations, especially of Red Riding Hood) seem usually to reinscribe racialism by linking werewolfism to genetics.

Karen Russell's "St. Lucy's Home for Girls Raised by Wolves" presents a feminist way of valorizing the connection between women and race, gender and species that critiques masculinist racialized fantasies of culture and articulates wolf-women in their own terms.[35] Too often, even in their feminist incarnations, women and wolves co-exist in mutual relation to a now-positively valorized wildness and nature. Russell's story nevertheless offers a way to think about wolfliness that queers the stories of lone heroic or rapacious individualists. She describes a devastating rite of passage whereby young girls raised by wolves are taken from their packs to convent schools to learn to become human, an allegory for the boarding schools to which Native American children were forcibly taken to "educate and civilize" them into Western Christian North American values (thus troping, again, the connection between wolves and indigenous Americans). The process involves unlearning collectivity and solidarity, unlearning the Deleuzian pack or swarm in favor of the oedipalized individual.[36] Indeed, so many of the Western cultural fantasies of being-wolf exaggerate what is, in wolf land, an extreme exception: the lone wolf. Wolves live in packs, in collectivities, and a feminist Deleuzian becoming-wolf that refuses masculinist heroic or demonic individualism might offer a line of flight for both women and wolves.

This essay began by addressing wolves and humans, their similarities, their proximities within the naturecultures where they co-exist, their mutual relations, their difficult entanglements, and their cultural histories. But there is no means to address wolves "as such," just

34. Stephenie Meyer, *Twilight* (New York: Little, Brown and Company, 2005–2008).

35. Karen Russell, "St. Lucy's Home for Girls Raised by Wolves," in *St. Lucy's Home for Girls Raised by Wolves* (New York: Random House, Inc., 2006), 225–46.

36. Gilles Deleuze and Félix Guattari, "1730: Becoming-Intense, Becoming-Animal, Becoming Imperceptible . . . ," in *A Thousand Plateaus: Capitalism and Schizophrenia*, trans. Brian Massumi (Minneapolis, London: University of Minnesota Press, 1987), 232–309.

as there is also no way to address "the human" as such. What such cultural analyses can do is to think through the material-semiotic—the meaningful enfleshment—of bodies, histories, and meanings called human and non-human animal. To forego any "representation" at all (in both the sense of figuration and the sense of political representation) is to risk relinquishing all responsibility (in the sense of responding and responding to) for the co-articulations of lives, histories, and cultures called human and animal. Wolves, even, perhaps especially the ones with which humans now choose to repopulate the wilderness, are, for human culture, spectral. The spectral wolf, which includes a long line, a *genelycology*, a multiplicity of wolves brutally and deliberately exterminated over centuries and centuries of human culture, haunts human myths, human stories, human psyches, and continues to haunt the figure of the human-as-animal in literature, political theory, and popular culture. This haunting also shows us the degree to which human and animal share not only a history of comparison and analogy—some humans are like animals, some humans have been animalized—but also a history of traumatic expulsion from the land in the name of certain "human" rights and property claims. It is for those who recognize the connection—not the analogy—of this relationship to forge alternatives to the story of competing rights and hierarchically differential valuations of "life."

VINCIANE DESPRET

Do Animals Work? Creating Pragmatic Narratives

Here we ascend from earth to heaven.[1]

They [humans] begin to distinguish themselves from animals as soon as they begin to produce their means of subsistence, a step which is conditioned by their physical organization. By producing their means of subsistence, men are indirectly producing their actual material life.[2]

Of all philosophers, Marx understood relational sensuousness, and he thought deeply about the metabolism between human beings and the rest of the world enacted in living labor. As I read him, however, he was finally unable to escape from the humanist teleology of that labor—the making of man himself. In the end, no companion species, reciprocal inductions, or multispecies epigenetics are in his story.[3]

One of the most advantageous paths, but the least attended to as such, in an effort to get beyond the division between "sciences of nature" and "human sciences" is the consideration of work. For thousands of years, domestic animals have worked beside human beings.[4]

DO ANIMALS WORK?

Certainly some animals deserve to be called "workers." We readily admit this in the case of service dogs, and in the cases of horses or oxen who pull heavy loads; it also appears to be true of certain animals who are used by professionals, such as police dogs, rescue dogs, rats who locate buried land mines so that they can be safely neutralized, and messenger pigeons, among others. Donna Haraway, in

1. Karl Marx, "The German Ideology" in *Literary Theory: An Anthology*, ed. Julie Rivkin and Michael Ryan (London: Blackwell, 1998), 656.
2. Marx, *The German Ideology*, 653.
3. Donna Haraway, *When Species Meet* (Minneapolis: University of Minnesota Press, 2008), 46.
4. Jocelyne Porcher and Elisabeth Lécrivain, "Bergers, chiens, brebis, un collectif de travail naturel?" *Études rurales* 189 (2012): 121.

YFS 127, *"Animots": Postanimality in French Thought*, ed. Senior, Clark, and Freccero, © 2015 by Yale University.

When Species Meet, has proposed looking at the "collaboration" of laboratory animals in this light, a suggestion that unequivocally reflects the attitude of animal-handling technicians toward the animals they use in their experiments.[5]

The area of public performances and show business can offer an introduction to this way of looking at things. In an essay about what he calls the anomalies of the theater, the "alien bodies" of the stage: stage fright, embarrassment, laughter, and . . . animals on stage, theater historian Nicolas Ridout remarks that the presence of animals in the operation of traditional theater is always problematic, and it is rare that real animals are used (of course, in this instance, the theater is to be distinguished from the circus). According to Ridout, when animals have parts in a stage production, they create a certain tension or uneasiness, and he attempts to analyze this. In his view, the presence of animals explicitly cast in roles on stage makes visible things that are supposed to be invisible: on the one hand, the work actors are doing (everything in the theater has to do with a kind of register of action that imitates spontaneity); on the other, an unpleasant feeling connected to the light the animal seems to cast on the human actors. "The strangeness of the animal on stage comes not from the fact that it ought not to be there, has no business being there, but rather in the fact that there is suddenly nothing strange about it being there, being exploited there, as any human performer."[6]

Certainly the presence of animals on stage—to the extent that they are not just there "to be there," that is, they are often there (paradoxically) as a sign of something else (they may be representing something, acting as a symbol for something else)—does not in itself have the power to create this uneasiness. This feeling emerges when animals really act on stage—when they are claimed as "real actors." Some theatrical companies, such as the Societas Raffaello Sanzio, have experimented with this, particularly in a performance of the *Oresteia* in 1996, which was staged from a deliberately polemical point of view.

Here Ridout elaborates on Romeo Castellucci's analysis. Castellucci wonders about a time when animals will disappear from the

---

5. Haraway, *When Species Meet*; Vinciane Despret, *Penser comme un rat* (Paris: Quae, 2009); Robert Kirk, "Between the Clinic and the Laboratory: Ethology and Pharmacology in the Work of Michael Robin Alexander Chance, 1946–1964, *Medical History* 53/4 (2009): 513–36.

6. Nicolas Ridout, *Stage Fright, Animals, and Other Theatrical Problems* (Cambridge : Cambridge University Press, 2006), 127.

stage, and speculates about the moment when the gods were removed from it. The polemical gesture of reintroducing animals on stage, he argues, is equivalent to returning to the theological and critical roots of the theater, that is, to the theater before tragedy, in its infancy—in the etymological sense of "infancy" (*infans*: the condition of those who are without language). Ridout quotes Castellucci: "If there is a polemic regarding tragedy it is without doubt related to the role of the author, to the movement of writing and therefore to that incredible pretension of verticality that is differentiated in terms of gender."[7] For Castellucci, this "incredible pretension to verticality," which differentiates a non-human from a human animal, is echoed in the allusion to infancy and is carried forward in the difference between genders. It is linked to the mythical reconstruction of an origin and to the appearance of the authorial function. The function of the author in the theater, in this reconstruction, is thought to be co-emergent with the separation from the animal, the assumption of power by men (over women) and the division of labor between humans and animals, men and women, manual laborers (rendered proximate to infancy and animality) and intellectuals. In other words, and still according to this constructed mythical origin, "the division of labor, the death of God, the establishment of human dominion over the animals and the birth of tragedy may all be seen as simultaneous (. . .); Western theater has kept the animal offstage in order to hide its origins in these moments of inaugural violence and the institution of division of labor."[8]

It does not matter whether this mythical reconstruction is plausible, and Ridout states this clearly: "What was the animal doing on stage before the birth of tragedy, what was the pre-tragic theater? We do not know."[9] What matters is what we are sensitized to by the mythical and fabulous origin, what the origin makes visible that was not previously visible, and the new questions we are thereby authorized to ask, but which we had not thought to formulate. Thus, the mythical origin indeed creates stories (fabulous, "fabulating"); it seeks some means of making a vanished experience available again in the contemporary world. It can move us to story making, to the

7. Ridout, *Stage Fright*, 111.
8. Ibid., 114.
9. Ibid., *Stage Fright*, 111.

creation of memories, the construction of a history that renders the present and the future richer in possibilities.[10] Ridout adds:

> In the shudder, the unease, the disquiet and the caution with which we greet the appearance of the animal on the stage, we are responding to this looking back, and in that looking back the recognition of some kind of complicity in domination and submission. What we experience is a form of shame, I think, at being discovered in our own acts of domination, over animals and over ourselves. The truth of the division of labor makes itself felt, and what we are ashamed of is that we never saw it before, not until the animal returned to the stage and made us stare it in the face, smell it, sense it in our shuddering.[11]

What the reconstruction makes visible, what I would like to cite as evidence, is a little different from the usual historical reconstruction. Primary violence is not located in the fact that animals have been transformed into "potential instrument(s) of satisfaction," but in the carrying out of a division of labor in such a way as to exclude them. Animals do not appear to work; in the referential framework that emerges from this division of labor/exclusion from labor, it is held that what animals do, they do "naturally," as if answering *our* needs is the same thing as acting according to nature. Thus, in its initial movement, the division of labor is a matter of dividing those who explicitly, really, work, from those who are only following a bent in their nature, a necessity of a biological rather than a historical sort.

RECREATING HISTORY WITH ANIMALS

When the French historian Eric Baratay began looking at the possibility of writing a history from the animal's point of view, the methodological and epistemological difficulties of the project led him to adopt a number of strategies. In order to write a history from the point of view of an animal, such that it should not simply be a human story in which animals play symbolic roles or function as

10. On the concept of that which is "fabulatoire," see Donna Haraway, "Sowing Worlds: A Seed Bag for Terraforming with Earth Others," in *Beyond the Cyborg: Adventures with Haraway*, ed. Margaret Grebowicz and Helen Merrick (Columbia University Press, forthcoming) and Isabelle Stengers and Vinciane Despret, *Women Who Make a Fuss: The Unfaithful Daughters of Virginia Woolf*, trans. April Knutson (Minneapolis: Univocal Publishing, 2013).

11. Ridout, *Stage Fright*, 137.

mere instruments, one must, he says, look for places and moments in various stories "when the animals start paying attention to what humans are offering or demanding, and then either accept, play for time, resist, refuse . . . stories in which they exhibit unusual skills or behaviors (. . .) We could describe [this process] as one of acculturation, that is, not just humans imposing their will but also acceptance from the animal, dialogue between the two, influence of the animal upon the human."[12] This strategy leads him to write a chapter about the work of horses in certain mines. The active participation of the horses is corroborated by examples, testimonials, and archives that preserve stories told by mine managers, who were able to depend on their horses for many different skills, including the remarkable one of finding their own way in and out of the mine. These men tell stories about horses doing things without being told,

> going forward on their own, to the place where wagons were loaded, as soon as the gong had been struck the usual number of times, which were nonetheless different depending on which gallery the wagon was close to; they slowed down the wagon convoy by pushing against it with their chests if anything untoward happened in the front (. . .); they pushed open swinging doors with their heads, undoubtedly in order not to [have to] start going again [once they had come to a halt]. They refused to work after the quitting time, appearing to know the time by themselves; when they were untied, they returned to the barn immediately, finding their way in the dark through winding passages.[13]

He remarks that the most frequently recounted episode involved horses refusing to pull extra wagons hitched onto the usual load. Some horses just stopped pulling if the number of wagons went beyond the norm (it was imagined that they might be able to estimate the number based on the difference in noises produced by the wheels when there were more of them rolling). Some horses would respond to repeated urging in this situation by kicking off the chain that hooked them to the lead wagon. "In this case there was evident resistance, though from good co-workers."[14] Some horses distinguished between drivers, as miners observed, refusing to work for one and then consenting to work for another, whom they knew would drive them gently and pay attention to their comfort.

12. Eric Baratay, *Le point de vue animal* (Paris : Seuil, 2012), 67.
13. Ibid., 121.
14. Ibid., 122.

Despite epistemic, conceptual, and ideological obstacles, some authors interested in the animal's point of view still manage to unearth convincing testimonials; they succeed in asking this question seriously and in searching for serious answers (not just thinking about "good intentions") regarding certain animals who work and work together with humans. It is, however, an altogether different situation when we consider how we think about animals that we raise in order to kill and eat them.

Jocelyne Porcher, a sociologist who studies breeding practices, places this question at the center of her research. She began her study by asking breeders: could one in any way say that their animals collaborate with them and work with them? Would that make any sense?[15] This is not something easy to think about—not for us, and not for the breeders, for the most part. The general response is that humans work, animals don't. Yet Porcher heard many stories about animals who did in fact participate in the work of those who were raising them, and animals who acted in deliberate ways of their own volition. This leads Porcher to suggest that work may not be visible, and also that what work is may be difficult to conceive. It is said without saying; it is seen without being seen.

When a proposition is difficult to respond to—do animals work ?—it often indicates that the answer to the question will change something. And that is the thing that guides Porcher as a sociologist: if the proposition is accepted as true, that will change something. Because such a question is never asked "just to see" in her sociology; rather, it means taking a pragmatic position, involving a question whose answer turns out to have consequences.

Porcher notes that few sociologists or anthropologists have tried to imagine that animals work. Richard Tapper is one of the few. Taking a perspective that is very close to that assumed by Marx in *The German Ideology*, but this time including animals, which Marx would not have permitted, he examines the development of the relationships between humans and non-human animals, judging that this relationship must have followed a historical progression similar to that undergone by the relations of production between different groups of men. In hunting societies the relationship between humans and non-human animals is communitarian, because animals are part of the same world as humans. The first examples of domestication appear

15. Vinciane Despret and Jocelyne Porcher, *Etre bête* (Arles: Actes Sud, 2007).

to be similar to types of slavery. Pastoralism is similar to contractual forms of the feudal type. In industrial systems, the relationship is based on means of production and capitalist relationships.[16]

But Porcher discards this otherwise attractive hypothesis. And this is no doubt the way she would treat Castellucci's analysis: for if Castelluci's or Tapper's reconstructions are valid because they raise the possibility that animals may indeed work, they also close these relationships up in a single schema, that of ownership and exploitation. From this vantage point, Porcher writes, "a different ending is impossible to imagine." What these reconstructions (by Tapper and as recounted by Ridout) put in play has to do with what we inherit. The verb "to inherit" is not merely receptive; it implies a task, a pragmatic act (appropriation). One's heritage is something constructed, and it is constantly transforming itself retroactively. It makes us capable of something other than simply carrying on a tradition; it demands that we be capable of responding and that we in fact respond to our heritage. Things are inherited, but we become ourselves in carrying out the gesture of inheriting. "Re-member," as Haraway would say; enact the past, and collect and compose. To inherit includes giving oneself an account of a certain task, which is more than just remembering. To make a story is to reconstruct, to fabulate, and to offer other presents and futures to the past. "Good stories reach into rich pasts to sustain thick presents to keep the story going for those who come after."[17]

What sort of history would allow us to suppose that the relations that have linked stock raisers or breeders to their animals might change? To ask the question of work properly, Porcher says, "One must consider animals as other than victims, natural and cultural idiots that need to be liberated despite themselves." The allusion is to liberationists who would like to "liberate the world of animals," that also implies freeing the (human) world of (the presence of) animals. And this critique is part of Porcher's basic stance; for Porcher, humans and animals must always be imagined together.

Ceasing to consider animals as victims means considering a relationship that is other than one of exploitation, in which (since they are not natural and cultural idiots) animals involve themselves, giv-

16. Porcher, *Vivre avec les animaux, une utopie pour le 21ème siècle* (Paris: La Découverte, 2011).
17. Haraway, "Sowing Worlds."

ing, receiving, exchanging, just as breeders are not "exploiting," but are giving, receiving, exchanging, raising, and growing with, their animals.

This is why the questions, "Do animals work? Do they collaborate with their owners actively?" are important in pragmatic terms. Without a history to learn and a story to tell, we must address this question to the present. Putting this question to breeders is not a means of knowing through information – "what do breeders think of x?" – but a real experiment. If they are asked to think, and actively, it is not to gather data or opinions but to explore these propositions with the breeders, to make them hesitate, to try an "experiential" experiment: What does it mean to speculate in such a way? And if we try to think that animals work, what would "work" mean then? How can we make visible and expressible that which is invisible and hard to think about? I will come back to this point.

THOSE WHO WORK ARE NOT THE ONES WE EXPECT

I said that the question of considering whether animals do work is not an easy one. It is still more difficult if we consider that the only place it can be brought forward is the place where only the meaning associated with exploitation can matter. In other words, animals' work is invisible except in places where both humans and animals are greatly mistreated.

In fact the places where the question of animal work manages to be formulated, the places where the evidence of such work is found, are the places where animals are industrially "produced." Porcher explains this apparent paradox: in industrial animal raising and feeding, animals are sequestered and removed from their own world, then placed in a world so completely human that "their behaviors appear very definitely as belonging to a work relationship." Men and animals are involved in a competitive production system that seems to favor considering an animal as a worker who also has his or her job to do. The animal may be punished if someone thinks he or she botched a job (for example when a sow eats her farrow). Workers in these systems, says Porcher, especially in relation to intensive hog feeding, end up thinking of their jobs as a kind of personnel management. The expression is not used, but its content is constantly invoked. Productive sows must be distinguished from unproductive ones, and the capacity of the animals to reach expected production levels must be monitored. "Representing oneself as a sort of 'Director of animal resources' is something that attests the wide diffusion of thinking like a manager, and the place this thinking has assumed in animal production operations."[18] The animal in such a frame seems to occupy the place of an obscure underclass, malleable, serviceable, and disposable in the end. The typical tendency of industrialization not to use human workers unless it is absolutely necessary, since they are costly and error-prone, appears here: machines replace humans for cleaning tasks, and there are even mechanical boars that can detect when sows are in heat. On the other hand, the possibility that animals work, in modern feeder operations, appears harder to render perceptible.

I said above that when we put the question to stock raisers, most often we got a subdued response: no, humans work, not animals. But when Porcher conducted the interviews for her thesis on the relationship between breeders and their animals, she ended up hearing many anecdotes that made her think that, in fact, the animals did collaborate, that they were involved, that they sometimes wanted to help, and that they did some things on their own initiative.[19]

Porcher and I decided that, since we had worked cooperatively on this inquiry in order to try to resolve the difficulty, we would share with the breeders the manner in which we had formulated the question.[20] In fact, we adopted a pragmatic approach, pragmatic not in the sense of revealing a reality, but in order to make a reality perceptible, to actively make it exist. Then we wagered, as it were, that we could reach this goal through a simple methodological postulate: the problem needed to be part of the solution. So we decided to ask the breeders to help us. We introduced ourselves to them, explaining exactly what our problem was, and asked them to work with us on that basis. We said to them: "During the preceding inquiries, Jocelyne heard many anecdotes from stock raisers that tended to indicate that animals collaborated actively in working. But when we asked them the question, the breeders we had been talking to said no, animals do not work. And yet there were these stories. So, in your opinion, *as a*

18. Porcher and Schmitt Tiphaine, "Les vaches collaborent-elles au travail? Une question de sociologie," *MAUSS* 35 (2010); Porcher and Schmitt, "Dairy Cows: Workers in the Shadows?," *Society &Animals* 20/1 (2012).

19. Porcher, *Éleveurs et animaux, Réinventer le lien* (Paris: PUF, 2002).

20. Despret and Porcher, *Être bête.*

breeder, could you help us learn how to ask our question so that it has a chance of making sense to other people?"[21]

When we asked the question that way, it started the breeders thinking. It was interesting, however, that some of the breeders chided us gently, saying, "Isn't your job to ask questions? And aren't you trying to get us to do your job?"

WHAT YOU NEED IS TRUST

But we had an answer for those remarks. Very simply: "We are not doing anything other than what you have described to us, what you do with your animals: we are letting you do something." The majority of breeders, once they also had explored the manner in which we were obliged to formulate our question, answered, saying things like: ". . . in fact, our system of stock raising is based on letting the animals do as much for themselves as possible." I can cite an excerpt from Eric Simon, who articulated this with particular clarity—and his response exhibited a characteristic that we have often observed: the stock raisers indicated to us that we should not put this question to industrial animal feeder operations and to small traditional or organic operations in the same way. "Let's say, "he explained,

> that a system with buildings and cages is set up to put the animal in a place where the breeder can do things that may be required more easily. So we would say that the contribution of the animal is reduced, but the breeder tries to be able to do as many things as possible. We others are out here in the open air, and the object is to put the animal in a situation where it can do as much for itself as possible. For example when hogs are farrowing, the problem is how to set things up so that the sow is calm enough, that she can feel herself in a universe that is sufficiently reassuring so she can farrow correctly in a short enough time, and roll over on a minimum of piglets. So from our side, we try to work on this problem using equipment and also our relationship with the animal, when is the right moment to go into the farrowing shed, things of that nature, whether to put in more or less straw. But we say to ourselves: OK, it's the sow's job to farrow. That is, personally, I don't try to speed up the farrowing. I hardly ever give oxytocin injections. (. . .) I make sure to move my sheds around

21. For a further analysis of the methodological and epistemological consequences of this inquiry, see Despret, "The Becomings of Subjectivity in Animal Worlds," *Subjectivity* 23 (2008).

so that the ground underneath is dry enough, because if the ground is wet, she doesn't like it, she moves too much. We want to put straw out, but not too much because if there's too much straw, it doesn't work. At some point I ask Gibelin how much straw to put in. So I'm saying to him, where should I put the straw? How much should I put in? And he starts talking to me, and he says, whatever you do, it's not going to change things, because the straw is her little nest, and she's the one who arranges it. It's like your wife; if you started cleaning the house she will never be happy with it, because it will never be done like she does it. He says to me: the sow is the same way. She's going to come after you whatever you do and put things the way she wants them. (. . .) The word, it's the technological mastery over everything. There, we accept that there are some things that we don't master, and we say, I have confidence. I trust. (. . .) There is a delicate balance to find, between doing enough so that everything works, and then at some point saying, OK, I've done what I had to do; now it's her turn.

References to confidence and trust occurred often in the interviews we conducted, and also references to responsibility. What we have discovered links up with what Haraway says with regard to animals in laboratories: "animals as workers in labs, animals in all their worlds, are response-able in the same sense people are; that is, responsibility is a relationship crafted into intra-action through which entities, subjects and objects, come into being."[22] And in fact, the breeders did not hesitate to speak of the responsibility of which their animals are capable: "There is a hierarchy of value," said André Louvigny, "and of responsibility within the herd, certainly, the fact of coming in to eat, and of having the same place to lie down every night. (. . .) And then," he continued, "there are those who show the way sometimes, the ones who work most closely with humans." And at that point one of us spoke up and said, "So in the end they do work with you." And he answered, "Yes, they work with us, it's the older ones who teach the young how to act around the breeder, that's certain. That's why we like to keep the oldest cattle sometimes, it's good to have them around because they have the right habits, and they trust us. They help the others stay calm. They calm things down, if other cattle are nervous about something, they help quiet that down." Louvigny was talking about a cow they call a lead cow. A lead cow is not a dominant

---

22. Haraway, *When Species Meet*, 71.

animal, but one who trusts the breeder, and one the herd itself trusts, an animal the breeder can count on to help move the herd around. In the words of Paul Marty: "the lead cow is always the same one, she's not the dominant of the herd but she is in front" (it was frequently explained to us that the most dominant animal in the hierarchy of the herd would be found in the middle of the herd). Marty continued:

> That is a good cow, because thanks to her I can go all over the place. Often I am alone, I walk in front and they follow me. Other times, it's surprising, afterwards I want to round them up, and they won't cooperate. But if I want to put them in another field, I could lead them to the end of the world because of that lead cow. (. . .) That cow, I walk in front of her, she will follow me anywhere. That's it. And I can certainly say that that cow, yes, she really does participate because she saves me time. (. . .) Sometimes I trick her, and she knows it, when I call the cattle, for example, in the spring to weigh the calves, in the beginning they follow me, but when they figure out what's happening at that season they don't help me anymore.

That last sentence is important. What it implied allowed Porcher to go further with her inquiry. Marty's last observation shows that the work animals do appears more clearly in those moments when animals refuse to cooperate. This is apparent when breeders, many of whom talk about this theme, spontaneously bring up the subject of limits. I ran across this theme very often myself in interviewing animal technicians working in laboratories, doing experiments: what they call paying attention to the animals refers to more than questions of well-being, and implies that we are able to feel the limits that animals ask us to take into account. With regard to cows, we have often heard breeders say: "They show us that there are limits, beyond which we must not go." The question of limits is at the center of the relationship between breeders and their animals. And this is what guided the following part of Porcher's inquiry.

For if, in the framework of our research together, when we insisted, some breeders ended up saying "perhaps they do," and "if you look at it like that we may believe that animals work," it took time and patience and required that we acknowledge the anecdotes we were told as having more than one meaning; it was an experiment.

Because work often leaves no evidence behind, Porcher decided to modify her research tools. She addressed her questions to the cows.

ASKING THE ANIMALS

Ethology has taught us that certain questions cannot be answered unless one constructs concrete conditions beforehand, not only those that allow the questions to be asked, but also those that render those who ask capable of discerning the answer, capable of grasping it when it emerges.[23] With one of her students, Tiphaine Schmitt, Porcher spent a long time observing and filming the cows in one particular herd kept in a barn. She noted all the occasions when the cows had to act on their own initiative, follow rules, and work cooperatively with the breeder, anticipating his actions so that he could finish his work. She also paid attention to the strategies the cows created to maintain a peaceful environment, to the polite maneuvers, the social grooming, and the peace-maintaining gestures of the cows, such as giving way to a congener, letting an other supplant oneself, etc.

What she observed is precisely the reason why the work was invisible: work only becomes perceptible when the cows resist, refuse to cooperate, and place limits on what can happen, because this resistance shows that when everything goes correctly, it is because of an active investment on the part of the cows. When everything happens as it should, we don't see the work. If we now reread Baratay's testimony, we see clearly that the conditions under which the animals' work can appear are the conditions in which the animals show that they can resist, that they can throw their heads in refusal, and even sabotage the work and its possibilities. We find again, implicitly, this very condition in the testimony of animal technicians working on scientific experiments : if the animals will not cooperate, there can't be an experiment. Thus when the cows go peacefully to be attached to the milking machine, when they do not kick up a fuss, when they go in order, when they move away from the machine after the milker has finished, when they move here and there to allow the breeder to clean their stalls, when they do what has to be done in response to an order, and when they do what they must so that everything happens as it is supposed to, we do not see this as their willingness to do what is expected of them. Everything begins to look like a machine that is functioning, and their obedience looks "mechanical," a word that conveys its meaning very well. Only when there are conflicts that disturb this order of things, for example when it is time for

23. Despret, *Quand le loup habitera avec l'agneau* (Paris: Seuil, coll. Les empêcheurs de penser en rond, 2002).

one cow to be attached to the milking machine, or when the cows do not move around to allow cleaning, or when they go somewhere other than where they are being driven, when they balk, or when they are simply slow to move, in short, when they resist, then we begin to see, or rather to interpret in other terms the situations in which everything goes as planned. Everything goes as planned because the cows have done their part. Thus the moments without conflict no longer appear as something merely natural, self-evident, or mechanical. They require from the cows the activity of pacification, in which the cows make compromises, groom each other, and exchange gestures of politeness.

A similar observation, though there are important differences, emerges from the research conducted by the sociologist Jérôme Michalon with animals such as dogs and horses who are asked to serve as therapeutic assistants for humans with various kinds of problems.[24] These animals often have a passive air and seem to simply be letting things happen, but when things become difficult for them, when they "react," one can tell that their cooperation is based on a remarkable ability to hold themselves back, an active restraint, and even a determination to contain themselves. But none of this is perceived, since it seems to be something that goes without saying.[25]

In the observations made by Porcher and her student, many things that seemed to go without saying suddenly attest to a whole range of kinds of work that amounts to cooperation with the breeder, invisible work. Only by observing the many ways that cows can resist the breeder, bending or breaking the rules, hanging back or otherwise doing something other than what is expected of them, were the researchers able to see clearly that the cows understand what they are supposed to do and that they are actively invested in the work. In other words, when the cows show that they are unwilling to do what

24. Jérôme Michalon, *Panser avec les animaux, Sociologie du soin par le contact animalier* (Paris: Presses de l'Ecole des Mines, 2014).

25. As psychoanalyst Christophe Dejours writes about human work: "Being intelligent in work always means standing back from procedures and instructions. Working well implies violating recommendations, regulations, procedures, codes, specifications and normative organization. In many work situations, however, the monitoring and surveillance of gestures, movements, operating methods, and procedures are rigorous if not severe, with the result that intelligence in work is often condemned to remaining unobtrusive, or even hidden." See Christophe Dejours, "Subjectivity, Work and Action" in *Recognition, Work, Politics: New Directions in French Critical Theory*, ed. J. P. Deranty et al (Leiden, the Netherlands: Brill, 2007), 78.

is wanted, the effect of their willingness, their "good will" appears. Cooperation becomes perceptible when compared to recalcitrance.[26] Practical or collective intelligence appears when intentional mistakes are made, or when feigned misunderstanding leads to active disobedience. Work is rendered invisible when everything is going correctly, or to put it another way, when everything goes as it's supposed to, which is the conclusion one must draw if the fact that everything is functioning correctly is rendered invisible. The cows get tricky, they pretend they don't get it, they refuse to work in a rhythm that is imposed on them, they try to see what they can get away with—all for their own reasons, but all of which renders perceptible by contrast that they participate in work, and do so intentionally, in a certain way. I am reminded of a remark by Vicki Hearne, who asked why dogs often drop the stick they fetch a couple of feet in front of you. She suggested that it was a way for the dog to give to the human a sense of the limits to the authority that she is ready to concede, with an almost mathematical precision, reminding us that not everything goes without saying.

CALLING FOR RESPECT

What changes, for the cows, so that the active investment in working together is made visible? Concretely, and on the side of empirical relations, something changes, of course. As Porcher wrote in 2002, "Taking care of animals, seeing oneself as at their service, feeling a moral obligation in regard to them, all these are representations and feelings that give rise to confidence and make cooperation and collaboration possible in a context of work. Talking to animals, putting oneself in their shoes, so to speak, and learning patience in regard to them, respecting them as they are, implying that you know them and recognize them—all this belongs to communication, to being together engaged in work."[27] I remember hearing about a friend who came back from a training session with a dog named Baruch, who was told by a trainer, "Remember, you're not his master, you're his pupil." And that changed many things.

26. Isabelle Stengers and Bruno Latour have in their work insisted on the importance of studying the "recalcitrance" of certain objects of scientific study (Stengers, *L'invention des sciences modernes* (Paris: La Découverte, 1993); Latour, *Politics of Nature* (Cambridge: Harvard University Press, 2004).
27. Porcher, *Éleveurs et animaux*, 237.

Further, considering that breeders and cows share their working conditions relocates the manner in which the question is usually raised. We are required to think about people and animals as connected in a single experience, which they are living through together, and in which they jointly constitute their identities. This obliges us to consider the manner in which the two communicate with each other, the manner in which they keep faith with each other—not that they act based on shared assumptions, but that they respond to each other through the consequences of their actions, and their responses are part of the consequences.[28] If animals don't cooperate, work becomes impossible. Therefore it is not a matter of animals "reacting"; they only do that when we cease to see anything other than the functioning of a machine.

If we allow that shift of meaning, then the animal is not, strictly speaking, a victim, because being a victim implies passivity and all its consequences; saying that the animal is a victim is not a mode of being engaged in the question—and we should not forget that culpability is easier to tolerate than responsibility, if only because the latter prevents the question from being closed. Following this, and just as pragmatically, we know that a victim does not invite curiosity, and that curiosity is essential in relations in which two beings learn to look and to look back,[29] to respect in the etymological sense of the term, from the Latin *respicere*.

It is evident that Porcher's cows give rise to greater curiosity than if they had been portrayed as victims. They are more alive, more present; they invite more questions. They are interesting to us and they get the chance to become interesting to their owner. A cow who disobeys consciously is in a completely different relationship from the one who is disobeying because she is stupid or because she does not understand what is being done. A cow who does her job engages us in a totally different manner than an animal who is the victim of the authority of her breeder.

Even supposing that Porcher's research allows us to say that cows help in the breeder's work, is that the same as saying that they do work? Can we say, Porcher asks, "that they have a subjective interest

28. Haraway, *When Species Meet.*
29. See on this point the critique Haraway addresses to Derrida in *When Species Meet.*

in the work?" Does work increase their awareness, their intelligence, and their ability to improve and to achieve a life? This question requires us to distinguish between situations in which constraint makes work visible and situations in which animals make a contribution and thus make work invisible in the way we have mentioned. In order to construct this difference, and to take account of which of these descriptions characterizes situations in stock raising, where animals and humans work together, Porcher reconsiders the theories of the psychoanalyst Christophe Dejours and extends them in an original way.

JUDGING THE BONDS

According to Dejours, whose writings constitute a central reference for Porcher, work can be defined as follows: "In our view, from a clinical standpoint, work is what is implied, in human terms, by the fact of working: gestures, know-how, the involvement of the body and the intelligence, the ability to analyze, interpret and react to situations."[30] The power of work is threefold: it transforms the world, objectifies intelligence, and produces subjectivity. The subjective relation to work represents a fundamental relationship to life.[31] Dejours makes available a concept of work that allows escape from the regime of exploitation. He insists that working is not just something that has to do with economic rationality, but participates in other forms of rationality, in relation to identities, to other relations, and moral rationality. Marx proposed something like this, but he explicitly excluded animals from the domain of work. Work, as a means of reproduction, "must not be considered simply as being the reproduction of the physical existence of the individuals. Rather it is a definitive form of activity of these individuals, a definitive form of expressing their life, a definite *mode of life* on their part."[32] Working is a means

---

30. Dejours, *Subjectivity, Work and Action*, 72.

31. We can see that Dejours' conception of work is historically and disciplinarily situated. One may find in the writings of Denis Grélé, and especially in his analysis of Fontenelle's book "La République des philosophes ou Histoire des Ajaoiens" a very interesting history of the various conceptions of work, in particular in the relationship to God—oscillating between (among others) obligation and curse; obedience to Nature or mastering it; or, for the human-worker, assertion of its own existence. I thank Matthew Senior for his precious advice.

32. Marx, *The German Ideology*, 653.

of accomplishment and self-realization through the expression of the creative potential of each person.

If human work, as Dejours suggests, can be for us a source of pleasure and can participate in the construction of our identity, it is because it is a source of recognition. Dejours articulates this recognition in connection with the exercise of two types of judgment: a judgment about the "usefulness" of such work, a judgment rendered by beneficiaries, clients or users, and a judgment about the "beauty" of the work, which concerns something being well done, and relies upon the recognition of one's peers. Porcher suggests that we should consider and add a third kind of judgment: the judgments about the bond. This is the judgment that the breeders feel is rendered by the animals. It does not concern the work as accomplished, nor the results, but only the means of the work's doing. This judgment is the very core of the relation to the breeder. It is a reciprocal judgment, through which the breeder and his animals may recognize each other. And that is where a contrast can arise between situations, between work that causes death and destroys identities in stock-raising operations where everyone suffers, and places where humans and animals share things, achieve things together, accomplish themselves. The judgment of the bond, or the judgment about the conditions of a life lived together, makes the difference between work that alienates and work that builds up, even in situations that are radically asymmetrical, such as those between breeders and their animals. The judgment of the bond goes along with this proposition by Haraway, that "work" is a process that crafts identities and "response-abilities," capabilities to answer for, and above all to answer to.

And the possibility that work might be a process that involves beings also takes into account, for example, the testimony of the salaried worker at an industrial stock farm who said sadly, producing a new version of Wittgenstein's famous (and quite meaningless) observation, "If animals could speak we would get shouted at every day," showing in an exemplary and tragic manner that the judgment of the bond is at the center of all relations. This judgment of the bond, which gives meaning to living together on stock farms, finally takes account of the fact that "we work with animals in order to be able to live with them, not the other way round."[33]

33. Porcher, *Vivre avec les animaux*, 124.

TO BEGIN ANOTHER STORY . . .

It remains for us to write the story, to recreate a story that gives meaning to this present in order to offer it a future that is a little more viable. Not an idyllic story of a Golden Age long ago, but a story that whets our appetite for possibilities, that opens the imagination to the unforeseen and to surprises, a story that might make us wish for a sequel. A speculative fabulation, Haraway would say. This is what Porcher is getting at when she tells the story, in the last lines of her 2011 book, recounting something that happened back when she herself was raising goats: "The work was the locus of our unexpected encounter, the possibility of our communication, although we belong to different species, thought to have had little or nothing to do with one another before the Neolithic, or before Neanderthals."[34]

Everything is being said, and yet everything still remains to be said.

---

34. These words echo those of Cary Wolfe in his wonderful *Before the Law: Humans and Other Animals in a Biopolitical Frame* (Chicago: University of Chicago Press, 2013). What our times dramatically and urgently need, he says, is "another thought of the biopolitical in which human and nonhuman lives are deeply woven together de facto, even if, de jure, they 'politically' have nothing to do with each other" (48). As Wolfe addresses the difficult issue of why we afford some animals unprecedented levels of care and recognition while subjecting others to unparalleled forms of brutality and exploitation, this essay might be considered not so much as an answer, but as an attempt to reformulate (maybe optimistically) the problem.

DAVID L. CLARK

What Remains to Be Seen: Animal, Atrocity, Witness[1]

In memory of Ross Greig Woodman, mentor and friend.

What does it mean to fall under the gaze of a non-human animal and to be dispossessed in its singular presence? What does it feel like to be glimpsed by a creature whose eyes are not so much unmet as met without the consolation of recognition or comprehension? In *The Animal That Therefore I Am*, Jacques Derrida explores the significances of yielding to an animal's address. "The animal looks at us, and we are nude before it," he writes: "And thinking begins perhaps there."[2] The animal's gaze, which is not simply a matter of observation but of enduring the passion of that which "exhibits me as being-for-the-other,"[3] summons thinking and is the calve of thought. A scandalous proposition. Derrida's hesitancy about making it is telling: Perhaps there? Perhaps thinking? Perhaps beginning? An uncertainty that borders on derangement overtakes the philosopher who thinks in the company of animal others and who wagers that thought

1. I thank Jenny Fisher, Roshaya Rodness, and Tracy Wynne, with whom I first discussed the Liepaja footage. Danielle Martak, Rebecca Gagan and Jessica Carey helped prepare this essay for publication. Special thanks go to Jennifer Fay, Jacques Khalip, Anat Pick, and Sharon Sliwinski, whose thinking about photographic images has made my own work possible.
2. Jacques Derrida, *The Animal That Therefore I Am*, trans. David Wills (New York: Fordham University Press, 2008), 13.
3. In his prefatory note to Emmanuel Levinas's essay, "Truth of Disclosure, Truth of Testimony" (1972), Adriaan T. Peperzak argues that for Levinas the human subject is both constituted and undone by the necessity of exposure, i.e., that which "exhibits me as being-for-the-other." See Levinas, "Truth of Disclosure, Truth of Testimony," *Basic Philosophical Writings*, ed. Adriaan T. Peperzak, Simon Critchley, and Robert Bernasconi (Bloomington: Indiana University Press, 1986), 97. In *The Animal That Therefore I Am*, Derrida similarly speaks of "the involuntary exhibition of the self," as if "the self" were always already the scene of a bearing witness of itself, always an unthought testamental remnant of itself (p. 11). Such will be my working thesis here.

YFS 127, *"Animots": Postanimality in French Thought*, ed. Senior, Clark, and Freccero, © 2015 by Yale University.

is always already under their unfathomable watch. In the no man's land between thinking and not-thinking, animals are on the prowl, looking at us looking at them. But from where? Their reconnaissance emerges from a place that is elsewhere, forever in transit. Their indeterminate glances steal us from ourselves.

My focus in this essay is to pursue some of the implications of Derrida's inexhaustibly rich provocations regarding animals who regard us and whose attention unsettles the very idea of inhabiting single worlds of "us" and "not-us," human and non-human. But my aim is to shift the emphasis from the animal gaze to a somewhat different question: can a non-human animal be said to bear witness to atrocities committed against human beings? More specifically: in the wake of atrocities, can we think of animals acting as testamentary remnants, attesting to unregarded deaths and useless suffering? How does animal witnessing – if there is such a thing – make irrefutable demands on the present and on the future?

An animal looks at us. Mercilessly those who call themselves human harm others before it and in fact take pleasure in such violence. Does witnessing begin or end there? By way of responding to that query, I turn to rare archival film of Nazi executions of several groups of Jewish men in Latvia in the summer of 1941.[4] In this gruesome "trophy" footage, an animal, a small terrier, makes an unexpected and fleeting appearance, easy to miss, given the horrific murders that we are given to see. Why concern ourselves with a dog who leaps out of the margins of the frame when all that matters is that the Nazis are killing Jews in front of dozens of spectators, including a sailor with a home movie camera? But once glimpsed, the dog, *this* dog, proves as impossible to ignore as its testamentary role in the footage is difficult to understand. Cognizant of Anat Pick's trenchant observation that "in post-Holocaust rhetoric, . . . human and animal, humanity and inhumanity continue to circle one another in contagious proximity,"[5] let me wager an opening hypothesis: a distinction must be made be-

---

4. The footage is available in at least two places: the website of the United States Holocaust Memorial Museum (See "Massacre on the Beach," *Some Were Neighbors*, n.d., http://somewereneighbors.ushmm.org/#/exhibitions/neighbors/un1629); and Yad Vashem ("Mass Murder of Jews in Liepāja, Latvia, 1941, Archival footage of JUDENEXEKUTION IN LIBAU 1941," *The Untold Stories*, n.d., http://www.yadvashem.org/untoldstories/database/murderSite.asp?site_id=571).

5. Anat Pick, *Creaturely Poetics: Animality and Vulnerability in Literature and Film* (New York: Columbia University Press, 2011), 25.

tween a cat arriving at one's bathroom door, the wondrous image that Derrida bequeaths to us, and the advent of a dog on the scene of a filmed murder.

*   *   *

After a week of heavy fighting, the 291st Infantry Division of the *Wehrmacht* captured the seaport of Liepāja from Russian troops on 29 June 1941.[6] Elements of *SS-Brigadeführer* Walter Stahlecker's *Einsatzgruppe A* accompanied regular army forces into Latvia's second largest city and immediately began murdering Jews. As Edward Anders notes, "assisted by Navy personnel, the SD, and the Latvian police, the SS conducted daily executions within the city limits, near the lighthouse and the beach."[7] During the summer and autumn mostly Jewish men were killed. "Women and children were largely spared until the big *Aktion* of 14–17 December, 1941, when 2749 Jews were shot."[8] These murders "were watched by hundreds of German soldiers and their sweethearts."[9] Eventually the SS and its agents killed all but a handful of Liepāja's 5700 Jewish residents, mostly at the point of a gun: "Bullet by bullet by bullet," as David G. Marwell

6. See Andrew Ezergailis, *The Holocaust in Latvia: 1941–1944. The Missing Center* (Riga: The Historical Institute of Latvia, 1996), 271–95.

7. Edward Anders, "Liepāja," in *Encyclopaedia of Camps and Ghettos*, general ed. Geoffrey P. Megargee, vol. 2, *Ghettos in German-Occupied Eastern Europe*, volume ed., Martin Dean (Bloomington: Indiana University Press, 2012), 1012. The detachments of the *Einsatzgruppen* responsible for the executions in and around Liepāja were, as Ezergailis notes, "assisted by numerous groups, including the German SD detachment of Liepāja, the Ordnungspolizei of Liepāja, the Latvian SD Guard Platoon (Latvian SD Wachmannschaft), parts of the Latvian Liepāja Schutzmannschaften, and the Arajs commando, from Riga." "There is also more than a strong possibility that some German Wehrmacht and naval forces participated in the killings, especially in the beginning phase." See Ezergailis, *The Holocaust in Latvia*, 279. For what it is worth, in an interview conducted in 1981, Reinhard Wiener testified that he wasn't "sure if the execution squad" in his footage "was made up of SS men, but the supervising detail was made up of SS." "You can see that on the film," he notes, adding, the SS "had their summer uniforms on." The United States Holocaust Memorial Museum holds a copy of the transcript (and translation) of that interview, conducted by Ester Hagar. See "Mr. Wiener's Interview Re Libau," *United States Holocaust Memorial Museum*, n.d., http://data.ushmm.org/intermedia/film_video/spielberg_archive/transcript/RG60 _0346/ED8FF8C2-70E7-4990-BB1D-629F8C1F9846.pdf.

8. Anders, "Liepāja," 1012.

9. Ibid. Anders' work on the Holocaust in Latvia remains seminal. See, for example, Edward Anders, *Amidst Latvians During the Holocaust* (Riga: Occupation Museum Association of Latvia, 2010).

says.[10] On a single day in late July or early August, an off-duty German Navy sergeant named Reinhard Wiener recorded the shootings of several groups of Jewish men using an 8 mm Ciné-Kodak camera. About a minute and a half in length, his footage is the only motion picture recording of SS shootings known to have survived the Holocaust.[11]

The intensifying atrocities in formerly Soviet controlled territories proved irresistible to photographers, both official and amateur, in part because, initially, the murders were meant to be seen. Timothy Snyder points to the gruesome example of the shootings of thousands of Jews from Minsk in the autumn of 1941. "Even at the height of Stalin's Great Terror," he remarks, "the NKVD was always discreet, taking people by ones and twos in the dark of the night." By contrast, the "Germans were carrying out a mass action in the middle of the day, made for public consumption, ripe with meaning, suitable for propaganda film."[12] Several months after Wiener filmed the executions in Liepāja, *Reichsführer-SS* Heinrich Himmler officially prohibited the photography of killings, but as Georges Didi-Huberman notes, his interdiction hardly stopped pictures from continuing to be taken. Indeed, the scope of the surviving photographic archive betrays the operation of "an epidemic power" that is "as sovereign as that of an unconscious desire."[13] Joshua Hirsch suggests that Wiener's footage marks the inaugural moment of a uniquely complex relationship between the Holocaust and its cinematic representations, a relationship

10. David G. Marwell, in *Hitler's Hidden Holocaust*, a TV documentary by Peter Hankoff (Creative Differences and National Geographic, 2009). Ezergailis notes that before that war about 7,600 Jews lived in Liepāja and the surrounding towns, 25% of whom escaped, leaving about 5,700 "trapped by the Germans." "It is not likely that 300 of them survived the Holocaust." See Ezergailis, *The Holocaust in Latvia*, 273.
11. The singular rarity of the Liepāja footage is often noted. See, for example, Joshua Hirsch, *Afterimage: Film, Trauma and the Holocaust* (Philadelphia: Temple UP, 2004), 1; and Stuart Liebman, "Introduction," *Claude Lanzmann's* Shoah, ed. Stuart Liebman (New York: Oxford University Press, 2007), 14. Other SS atrocity footage appears to have existed, now lost, including film that Himmler's cameraman took of executions in Minsk. See Peter Longerich, *Heinrich Himmler* (New York: Oxford University Press, 2012), 552; and Timothy Snyder, *Bloodlands: Europe Between Hitler and Stalin* (New York: Basic Books, 2010), 230. Ezergailis notes that "soon after the first killings, pictures began to surface from the massacre sites." See Ezergailis, *The Holocaust in Latvia*, 223. Moreover, "[SS-Brigadeführer Walter] Stahlecker . . . ordered photographs of the killings to be made" (ibid., 237 n. 78).
12. Snyder, *Bloodlands*, 226.
13. Georges Didi-Huberman, *Images in Spite of All: Four Photographs from Auschwitz*, trans. Shane B. Lillis (Chicago: University of Chicago Press, 2008), 23.

that is still unfolding and the subject of considerable controversy.[14] The stakes could not be higher, which helps explain why thinking about Holocaust images so often leads to questions about the nature and limits of photography itself.

Claude Lanzmann's brief treatment of the footage is perhaps the most provocative. That Wiener's film is absent from his masterpiece, *Shoah*, goes without saying, given the director's refusal of all archival photographs in favor of immersing audiences in the voices of survivors and perpetrators as well as in images of the present-day settings in Poland where the exterminations took place. As Lanzmann says, Wiener's images "are not intended to say anything; in a certain sense, one sees such things every day. I call these 'images without imagination.' They are just images that have no power."[15] *Des images sans imagination* is in fact the phrase that Lanzmann will use to dismiss all photographs of the Holocaust.[16] Moving well beyond the *Bilderverboten* that governs the *mis en scène* of *Shoah*, he disavows the significance of documentary images in general because they constitute a grotesquely impoverished vision, reflecting only the SS's sight of the Jews: as disposable, unheard, unable to resist, and marked for death. Moreover, photographs of Nazi atrocities are empty because, in their now iconographic familiarity, they shun what matters most, namely, responding to the incalculable losses and the inconceivable suffering of the individual victims. They colonize the unimaginable with images, offering thoughtless and sometimes prurient onlookers "a refuge in visibility."[17] To stare at these pictures is to hazard collaborating with SS violence, not only because we see the Jews through the Nazi viewfinder, but also because passively consuming archival images takes the place of wrestling with the residuum of Nazi murderousness that haunts the complacencies of the present. Atrocity photographs engender a historicist impulse to locate the calamity of the Holocaust safely in the past, thereby indemnifying viewers against

14. See especially the first chapter of Hirsch, *Afterimage*, 1–28.

15. Claude Lanzmann, interview by Marc Chevrie and Hervé Le Roix, "Site and Speech: An Interview with Claude Lanzmann about *Shoah*," in *Claude Lanzmann's Shoah*, ed. Stuart Liebman, (New York: Oxford University Press, 2007), 40.

16. See, for example, Lanzmann, "La lieu et la parole," in *Au sujet de Shoah*, ed. Michel Duguy (Paris: Belin, 1985), 297; and Lanzmann "Parler pour les morts," *Le monde des débats*, May 2000, 15.

17. I borrow Akira Mizuta Lippit's phrase. See Akira Mizuta Lippit, *Atomic Light (Shadow Optics)* (Minneapolis: University of Minnesota Press, 2005), 14.

its still unfurling legacies. For Lanzmann, the inert powerlessness of photographic representations of the Holocaust lies in their capacity to refuse the victim's gaze.

There is very little, almost nothing, to protect the Liepāja footage from these dangers, since they are not accidents that befall photographs of Nazi atrocities but elemental both to the history of their reception and to their violating nature. How then to do justice to these images, which both record and impose a perverse law: routinized murder must not only be done, it must also be *seen* to be done. Yet Didi-Huberman invites us, contra Lanzmann, "not to eliminate but to *rethink the image*" of Nazi atrocities; he resists treating these photographs as so hermetically self-possessed and under-determined that they are left well enough alone.[18] As he argues, "[a]n image without imagination is quite simply an image we have not had the time to work on."[19]

We will hardly find sufficient time here. Yet Didi-Huberman's careful discussion of rare photographs of SS gassings at Auschwitz (images taken by an anonymous victim) helps us understand that the Liepāja footage (images taken by a known spectator-perpetrator) makes horror palpable–*not*, as Lanzmann fears, palatable–precisely because it forces the commonplace to bear the weight of the extraordinary, and commands the familiar to share the same visual space as the homicidal. The presence of the terrier, someone's pet dog, running about the execution site condenses that gruesome phenomenon into a single memorable image, and that is one of several contradictory reasons why the animal catches the eye and forms the punctum through which I will consider the footage. The dog is hardly the only detail to bring out the promiscuous mixing of worlds into which the Jewish men are thrown, but it is arguably the most unexpectedly affecting. In fact, the dog and the footage are intimately connected at this cinematic juncture: the film puts a household pet and another family accouterment, the portable movie camera, together at the scene of the executions, thereby demonstrating by example that these ordinarily disparate worlds are now somehow equivalent. The dog, who occupies the margins of the frame, and the camera, which is the blind spot occupying the center of the frame as the unseen apparatus of seeing, find each other and form a nexus of atrocity. Seeing the

18. Didi-Huberman, *Images in Spite of All*, 62.
19. Ibid., 58.

incredible and the credible mimic each other makes it hard to believe your eyes, there where nothing is forbidden and where everything is compelled to be visible. One searing question – "In the face of ultimate degradation, who could lift a camera?"[20] – blends into another: "Who could bring a dog to an execution?" Who but those possessing uncontested authority? Who but those for whom the outcry of the photographed victims – "I am going to be killed" – fails to "sound an emergency alarm"?[21] A German occupier carries his own camera to the murders because watching them isn't enough. A Latvian local brings a dog to the shootings because they resemble an outdoor social gathering. It is not the dog and the camera alone that are disturbing but the apparently *un*disturbed nature of those who use these props to make the absolutely inhumane and unrecognizable take on features of the humane and the recognizable. Far from contributing to the self-cancellation of the significance of the footage, the presence of the dog and the camera suture the repugnant into the homely, thereby putting an awful truth to us: the extermination of the Jews of Liepāja was "thought; it was therefore thinkable."[22]

Wiener's film both documents a moment in the history of Nazi violence and forms part of that history. But it is hardly containable *as* history, the first sign of which are the affects –including repugnance, sorrow, and disbelief – that it prompts in the viewer. The little dog acts as a kind of well in which those testamentary feelings gather and take shape. Its sudden appearance at the scene of the murders is tied to the horror that comes not from watching soldiers and SS men, Germans and Latvians, executioners and onlookers together doing what is impermissible but in the ordinariness of doing what is. Perpetrators kill Jews, but in a universe in which the "non-criminal putting to death"[23] of others is admittable and insolently unhidden.

20. Bernd Hüppauf, "Emptying the Gaze: Framing Violence through the View-finder," *New German Critique* 72 (Autumn, 1997): 33.

21. Ariella Azoulay, "The Execution Portrait," in *Picturing Atrocity: Photograph in Crisis*, ed. Geoffrey Batchen, Mick Ridley, Nancy K. Miller, and Jay Prosser (London: Reaction Books, 2012), 258.

22. Didi-Huberman, *Images in Spite of All*, 25. In this passage Didi-Huberman, citing the French historian Pierre Vidal-Naquet, notes that "'[The genocide] was thought, it was therefore thinkable.'"

23. Derrida, "Eating Well, or the Calculation of the Subject," in *Points: Interviews 1974–1994*, ed. Elisabeth Weber, trans. Peggy Kamuf (Stanford: Stanford University Press, 1995), 278. "Non-criminal putting to death" is Derrida's description of the sacrificial fate of non-human animals and animalized humans.

For Derrida, that is the bleakly mundane condition of exposure to both violence and visibility that animals of all species are differently compelled to endure at the hands of irrefutable power. Victims are tortured to death, but the violations they suffer occur in a setting in which the means to speak *as* the tortured has been eliminated and where the idea that torture constitutes a wrong goes unregarded because it has been dissolved into a quotidian of countenanced brutality. For Lyotard, the "animal" names the creature who most vividly embodies this violation in plain sight. As he argues, the "animal is deprived of the possibility of bearing witness according to the human rules for establishing damages, and as a consequence, every damage . . . turns it into a victim *ipso facto* . . . That is why the animal is the paradigm of the victim."[24]

That Lyotard makes this case for the animal in a book that is haunted by the unwitnessed deaths of Auschwitz is telling. Even to bring animal suffering and the victims of the Final Solution into proximity risks analogies between death-worlds of the sort that Heidegger notoriously made[25] and that Levinas condemned as "beyond commentary."[26] And yet against that over-determined background, Lyotard implies that injustice is irreducible to inhumanity. He proceeds under the assumption that ethical and political judgment after the Holocaust need not be governed by the hope of recovering or protecting humanity, a speciesism that is replete with terrible dangers, as Nazism precisely demonstrated, but instead by attending thoughtfully and compassionately to all creatures whose suffering has been denied address and appeal. Derrida too calls for "the most radical means of thinking the finitude that we share with animals, the mortality that belongs to the very finitude of life, to the experience of compassion, to the possibility of sharing the possibility of this non-power, the possibility of this impossibility, the anguish of this vulnerability and the vulnerability of this anguish."[27] Like Levinas be-

24. Jean-François Lyotard, *The Differend: Phrases in Dispute*, trans. Georges Van Den Abbeele (Minneapolis: University of Minnesota Press, 1988), 28.

25. In a series of lectures on technology that he gave in Bremen in 1949, Heidegger claimed that the "motorized food industry" was "in essence the same as the production of corpses in gas chambers and extermination camps." See Martin Heidegger, *Bremen and Freiburg Lectures: Insight Into That Which Is and Basic Principles of Thinking*, trans. Andrew J. Mitchell (Bloomington: Indiana University Press, 2012), 27.

26. Levinas, "As if Consenting to Horror," trans. Paula Wissing, *Critical Inquiry* 15 (Winter 1989): 487.

27. Derrida, *The Animal*, 28.

fore him, Derrida brings the question of violence against human and non-human animals into contiguity without saying that they are the same thing, which is what Heidegger loftily suggests.[28] The French philosopher tarries passionately with the fact of mortal exposure and the affects of torment. What is indubitable for him is that suffering is a summons and leaves its traces in the world, even if that call and those marks have not yet been thought and remain to be seen.

Looking at this cinematic animal, it helps provisionally to separate out the dog's surprise from its role as part of the image's Nazi *dispositif*. On the one hand, we must wrestle with the obscenity of watching neighbors of the murdered men bring their mutt to the execution site. On the other hand, the terrier's reaction to the sound of the executioners' guns demonstrates a corporeal faithfulness to the event, as if to bear living witness to the atrocities when no one else can or will. We are reminded of Derrida's insistence that the *act* of testifying must be distinguished from its content, and that any testimony is composed of "these two heterogeneous strata, even if they come together in a single occurrence that has become in some sense its own homonym."[29] Within months of the Liepāja footage, the SS will have murdered almost every Jewish person in the city.[30] The Nazi fantasy of eliminating all the witnesses is almost perfectly realized and Wiener is there to document a step towards that accomplishment – before Himmler grasps that photographic images of executions might have the uncanny effect of corroborating the crimes and of testifying to their inhumanity *as* crimes rather than pleasurably commemorating their non-existence. While Wiener watches the killings, his film produces and reproduces a terrible muteness and invisibility at the heart of the murder scene. His confidence that the Jewish men cannot meet his gaze ensures that his photographic images thrum with barbarous power. The fact that the footage is itself silent non-diegetically mimes the enforced inaudibility of the Jews. The images affirm their incapacity to refuse this violence, a disabling

28. For a discussion of Levinas, see David L. Clark, "On Being 'The Last Kantian in Nazi Germany:' Dwelling with Animals after Levinas," *Animal Acts: Configuring the Human in Western History*, ed. Jennifer Ham and Matthew Senior (New York: Routledge, 1997), 165–98. Derrida speaks of the Nazi genocide in the context of "animal genocides" in *The Animal*, 25–26.

29. Derrida and Maurice Blanchot, *The Instant of My Death / Demeure: Fiction and Testimony*, trans. Elizabeth Rottenberg (Stanford: Stanford University Press, 2000), 38.

30. See, for example, Snyder, *Bloodlands*, 193.

cruelty that Pick identifies as an elemental characteristic of the deprivations endured by animals[31] and that helps us grasp why Lyotard says that animals epitomize the victimhood that is unique to the state of exception. So it is uncanny when, in the midst of that muteness and indifference, a little dog leaps into view, breaking the silence by instantly translating the crack of the executioners' guns into a picture of movement. We must have our wits about us to pick up that indexical signal, broadcasted immemorially from the margins of the footage's field of view. The animal who, like the Jews, is presumed not to have a voice, finds a voice, after a fashion. In Lyotard's terms, the dog's startle, its involuntary exhibition of itself before the other, takes on the aura of *le differénd*, the remainder and reminder of injustice that slips through the spaces between the authorized phrase regimes that not only harm others but render those harms imperceptible. Lyotard compares the differend's unanticipated emergence to a *blow*, i.e., an experience that is felt before it is cognized, a delayed action that he compares, of all things, to the sound of a whistle whose tone is audible only to dogs.[32] Is the image of the terrier in the Liepāja footage a traduction of that sound? Are we those dogs?

*   *   *

In groups of four or five men, the Jews are forced out of the back of a small truck, hurried past a crowd of onlookers, and ordered to jump into a deep execution trench. Many spectators have turned out on this brightly lit summer day: the SS officers and German security police overseeing the killings, including a bored looking man who smokes a cigarette; the Latvian auxiliaries who keenly assist; German sailors, a few sitting in their bathing suits; assembled townsfolk, including children; and of course, Wiener, who claimed accidentally to have come across this scene, but whose film tells us that he consents to the horror.[33] We see what appear to be four separate groups of Jewish men brought to the site to be killed. With remorseless efficiency, the gunmen kill the men in exactly the same way. In one

31. Pick, *Creaturely Poetics*, 43.

32. Lyotard, *Heidegger and "the jews,"* trans. Andreas Michel and Mark Roberts (Minneapolis: University of Minnesota Press, 1990), 15.

33. See "Mr. Wiener's Interview Re Libau," *United States Holocaust Memorial Museum,* n.d., http://data.ushmm.org/intermedia/film_video/spielberg_archive/transcript/RG60_0346/ED8FF8C2-70E7-4990-BB1D-629F8C1F9846.pdf.

continuous motion, a line of marksmen steps up to the lip of the pit. They point their rifles downward toward the Jewish men and shoot. The murdered collapse into the floor of the trench. The spectators watch, mesmerized. Some crane their necks forward, hoping for a better look. Wiener films from several different spots, starting and stopping his hand-held camera, repositioning himself at least half a dozen times, seeking vantage points from which to record the victims, the killers, and the crowd whose eyes feast upon the deaths.

The managed orderliness of the footage is disrupted only once. What unexpectedly occurs takes up a few scant seconds during the first of the executions Wiener records, but the event is preserved indelibly in the footage, where it proves to be complexly affecting to consider. The irruption of the animal feels ambiguously in excess of the otherwise irrefutable authority that Wiener films and for which it is an agent. At the instant the marksmen fire their rifles, a small spotted terrier suddenly jumps excitedly in front of the camera. Startled by the retort of the rifles that we cannot hear and whose percussive blast we cannot feel, the dog translates those phenomena into the observable shape of its bounding body. For a moment, we are given to "see" the force of the salvos in impossibly different but viscerally connected ways: in the background, the collapsing bodies of the Jews, and in the foreground, the animal's unexpected leaps. Like a camera-less photograph or photogram, the terrier's movements register something of the violence of the executions, translating their force into a corporeal image *of* force. The terrier's moving body in effect "films" what otherwise goes unexpressed by the onlookers and perpetrators, who are remarkable not only for their indifference to the cruelty of attending the murders, but also for their strange physical impassivity at the sight of the killings when they take place. The spectators appear frozen, fixated on the murders, while the Jewish men crumple in death and the dog jumps to life. The animal's singular and autonomous faithfulness to the killers' fatal blow seems uncannily to fill a void at the execution site. But with what? So far as one can see, no one looks away, or covers their face, or otherwise reacts in horror in ways that, for example, Sharon Sliwinski discusses in her work on those who witnessed the attacks on the World Trade Center.[34] The bystanders stare while also remaining outwardly unmoved by the murders, a duplicity that seems uncannily mirrored in the dog, who attends the

34. See Sharon Sliwinski, "New York Transfixed: Notes on the Expression of Fear," *The Review of Education, Pedagogy, and Cultural Studies* 30 (2008): 332–52.

executions but who is presumed as an animal to be blithely unaware of their significance.

No one flinches, except for the terrier . . . and, surprisingly, Wiener, whose camera jolts momentarily, the only time it does so while he is taking his pictures. Throughout the filming his hand remains steady, even when, at a later point in the footage, he stands at the very edge of the execution pit. Nothing else shakes him: not the tasks associated with making his camera work, not the excitement of the gathered spectators, not the cries of the mortally wounded, not even the ear-splitting crack of the executioners' guns. Farther away from the murders, it is the *dog's* shock that seems to catch him off guard, as if fugitively to break his unblinking view of the torture and slaying of the Jewish men. He feels the sudden intrusion of the animal into his field of vision before he sees it, assuming he sees it at all. Wiener quickly recovers, but not before a strange and unstable circuit of autonomous reactions and indexicalities flash before our eyes. The dog's startle reflex triggers another startle reflex, the first leaving its bodily trace on the film, the second leaving its trace on the body of the filmmaker, whose trembling hand in turn blurs the image in whose margins the dog appears. In each case, non-human and human, the animal body forms a kind of sensitive recording surface that captures details that might otherwise go unnoticed or that happen so quickly as to escape conscious perception.

Although it occupies the same visual space, the blur *in* the image is not the same thing as the blurred image. The latter shakily reproduces the killings, from which Wiener's gaze never wavers, even amid his startle, while the former translates his corporeal reaction to the sudden appearance of the dog into a smudge. The blur viscerally embeds the camera into the scene of the shootings, but here the point of contact to the executions is mediated through the animal, and specifically through the dog's embodied fidelity to the force of the executioners' guns. A momentary loss in the image's clarity nonrepresentationally "photographs" Wiener's reaction to the dog whose sudden unruliness leaves him briefly beside himself. The tremor has the unexpected effect of opening up the footage, and of prying apart what the camera photographs *from* the irrefutable power that otherwise saturates the scene. Pointing to the event of the animal's stirring, and reminding us that Wiener cannot refuse its interference in the filming of the executions, the blur invites us to distinguish two aspects of the footage: on the one hand, the candor of the dog's self-showing, the involuntary spasm of its exhibition of itself as mortal and singular; on the other hand, the horrid significance of the terrier's appearance at the killing site, which demonstrates how, in the SS's state of exception, the routine and the bloodthirsty are mixed together. Another way of saying this is that the dog's reaction points not only to its proximate cause, the sound and force of the executioners' guns; like all deictic gestures, that animal utterance also refers to itself, demonstrating its capacity *to demonstrate*. The blur inadvertently points to the dog's indexicality, which notionally separates it from the horror to which its own startled body points and of which it also forms an unwitting part. Whether through the aperture of his Ciné-Kodak or through the becoming-aperture of his own trembling body, Wiener picks up signs of animal life, easily missed on this day so focused on death and on collaborating in the manufacture of the everydayness of death. We too might well miss the dog's appearance, even if Wiener's camera implacably records it, not once but twice, and in two qualitatively different ways: as blur and image. From their inception, as Baer notes, photographs have always been attractive because of their uncanny "ability to confront the viewer with a moment that had the potential to be experienced but perhaps was not."[35] Wiener's footage precisely demonstrates that strange revelatory quality, beginning with the little dog's surprise, through which is threaded foreground and background, death and life, the homely and the murderous, the irruptive and the administered, the seen and the unseen.

How to situate the dog in the midst of this ghastly photographic setting? Rather than averting our eyes from photographs of SS atrocities, as Lanzmann counsels, Didi-Huberman makes a case for working interrogatively with their minute particulars, including what appear to be the most nonessential elements. The dog is one of those details, moving not because it is mawkish (although this kind of response is always possible while looking at the antics of what Deleuze dismisses as "family pets, sentimentalized, Oedipal animals each with its own 'petty' history"[36]), but because it is an image that leaps out at us, demanding attention without our necessarily knowing what we are seeing, and because it affirms the piercing role that affective

35. Ulrich Baer, *Spectral Evidence: The Photography of Trauma* (Cambridge, Mass.: MIT Press, 2002), 8.

36. Gilles Deleuze and Felix Guattari, *A Thousand Plateaus: Capitalism and Schizophrenia*, trans. Brian Massumi (Minneapolis: University of Minnesota Press, 1987), 240.

life can have in responding to photographs of historical violence. Contextualizing photographs is important, Didi-Huberman argues, as long as doing so isn't at the expense of ensuring that we are answerable to their minutest details. "We must *tighten our point of view* of the images and omit nothing of all the 'imaging substance,' attending even to those features in which it appears that 'there's nothing to see.'"[37] For Lanzmann, the Liepāja footage in its entirety is an exemplary instance of the Nazi "nothing to see." But as Didi-Huberman notes, even those who attend critically to photographs of SS atrocities can too quickly screen out elements deemed to be "empty of informative value."[38] And the fact is that the Liepāja footage remains curiously under-discussed, notwithstanding its completely unique status in the archive of the Holocaust. It is often mentioned in scholarship on Holocaust photographs, to be sure, and it plays a role in Holocaust museums, exhibits, and documentaries, yet it still awaits a scrupulous frame-by-frame analysis.[39] The film is, as it were, mostly left to speak for itself, or functions as an icon of undifferentiated Nazi war crimes. About the terrier's appearance in the viewfinder, next to nothing is said. Perhaps the dog's familiarity renders it imperceptible and untroubling, a fate to which animals in the field of vision are generally relegated, as John Berger has well described.[40] The fine-grained summary of the footage's contents by the Fritz Bauer Institute ignores the creature, but not without noting other details: the dark color of the sedans parked nearby, for example.[41] Under what conditions does the color of a car have "informative value" in an atrocity photograph yet a dog does not? You start to wonder about the possibility of a kind of hysterical blindness among the archivists. The terrier is not simply deemed to be insignificant; nor is it "withdrawn" in Berger's sense of the term, i.e., replaced with something more anthropomorphically pleasurable. The image of the animal is instead blanked out altogether, plainly part of the footage's image substance but experienced symptomatically as invisible. The shade of the inanimate car

37. Didi-Huberman, *Images in Spite of All*, 41.

38. Ibid.

39. An account of the various ways in which the footage is misdescribed and underdescribed in the literature would take up a separate essay.

40. John Berger, "Why Look at Animals?" in *About Looking* (London: Bloomsbury, 1980), 3–28.

41. For the Fritz Bauer Institute's archive entry on the Liepāja footage, see "Executions of Jews in Libau in 1941," http://www.cine-holocaust.de/cgi-bin/gdq?dfw00fbw000799.gd

bears looking at and archiving but the moving image of the animated dog is more problematical, perhaps because in exhibiting itself before the other, the animal, *this* animal, looks upon us, returning a complicated gaze across the gulf of time at the moment when the human gazes of the victims are obliterated.

The notable exception to this disregard of the animal regard comes in the form of remarks that David G. Marwell, Director of New York's Museum of Jewish Heritage: A Living Memorial to the Holocaust, makes in a film by Peter Hankoff about SS killings in Eastern Europe.[42] In a brief but richly suggestive commentary on the Liepāja footage, Marwell raises questions about the errant creature that serve here as a lure to thought. "Who brought the dog there?" Marwell quietly asks, while the footage is slowed and the terrier's image is highlighted: "Did the dog go back home? What was the dog doing on this scene when people were being murdered?" Hankoff puts the terrier vividly before us at this moment in the documentary, but Marwell reminds us that, metaphorically speaking, it remains curiously hard to place. Where it arrives from or is en route to, what it is "doing" amid the murders, remains not only open to question but also *worthy* of questions and of remaining open *as* a question. "I don't know why that moves me," he concludes, "but it does."[43]

What is the *that* that works on or over Marwell, as it certainly does me, about which neither of us seems to know anything definitive? Something automatic and anonymous connects us to the footage. How to account for this response that feels more like a reaction, something unconsidered, unbidden, and perhaps "animalistic" welling up in the historian and important enough to be captured on film by the documentarist? The dog's vibrant body speaks, making an obscure but irrefutable claim on us. And it does so in the same place and

---

42. See David Marwell, in *Hitler's Hidden Holocaust* by Peter Hankoff. In an interview, Hankoff, who directs the documentary featuring Marwell's remarks, also acknowledges the presence of the dog. "What struck me in the film footage were little details like a dog running around in the middle of the shooting," he says: "The banality of it is even more chilling." See Gerald D. Swick, "Producer Peter Hankoff – Why Historical Documentaries Matter," *Armchair General*, August 11, 2009, http://www .armchairgeneral.com/producer-peter-hankoff-why-historical-documentaries-matter .htm. To my knowledge, the only other reference to the dog is indirect: "Dog" is one of the searchable key words for the film and photograph archive at the Steven Spielberg Film and Video Archive at the United States Holocaust Memorial Museum, the archive that includes a copy of the Liepāja footage. Searching "dog" brings up the Liepāja footage.

43. Marwell, in *Hitler's Hidden Holocaust* by Peter Hankoff.

moment that we bear witness to the murders. Focused on the torture and execution of the Jewish men, Wiener may well have missed seeing the other creature. But his footage records its appearance, making legible what might have gone unseen. From their inception, photographic images have held that uncanny power over viewers, the capacity to show us things that we did not or could not see with our own eyes.[44] But *how* and *why* the dog is present, the meaning of its *being-there*, remains more difficult to determine, as Marwell intuits. The historian asks questions of the footage for which he concedes there are no simple answers, reminding us of the importance of occupying interrogative relationships with photographs of Nazi atrocities rather than confidently knowing ones, for example, assuming that the image is fully accounted for by the SS, and thus empty, or that it is iconically illustrative of the Holocaust, and thus a photograph of what is already understood or imagined to be understood. Instead, we appear to be in the indeterminate region of the affective and the symptom, and what is admirable is the historian's willingness to let himself tarry with the advent of the dog, registering what it pulls into the frame at the same time as it gestures toward the unapprehended that lies beyond it.

Lyotard notes that "the authority of the SS comes out of a *we* from which the deportee is excepted once and for all."[45] Does that "we" unequivocally include the little dog? To whom does it belong? Did the dog accompany one of the Latvian men, women, or children who attend? The neighbors enjoy the prospect of the companionship of a pet dog and the hearth that that fellowship symbolizes, but these are pleasures that have been wrenched from the Jews. Or is the dog a stray, and so belonging to no one in particular, yet clearly not wild either, not entirely dispossessed of a relationship with human beings? Does the terrier belong only to the Nazi gaze? Or does the image of the dog belong finally to *us*, to viewers who are undone by the act of witnessing otherwise unregarded suffering, viewers—modeled by

44. Speaking of Eadweard Muybridge's experiments with the *zoopraxiscope* in the 1870s, Jennifer Ham notes: "For the first time in history, movements could be recorded, replayed, and slowed down, allowing the human eye to see what actually transpired. The camera rendered visible and conscious, movement that had previously been invisible and unconscious." See Jennifer Ham, *Elastizität: The Poetics of Space, Movement and Character in Frank Wedekind's Theater* (New York: Peter Lang, 2012), 106–7.

45. Lyotard, *The Differend*, 101.

Marwell—who are moved by the advent of the terrier and who follow its quivering life, as I do, here? The very concept of "belonging" starts to waver because, insofar as the dog makes an enigmatic claim on us, it is more accurate to say that we belong to it.

★   ★   ★

When we look at Wiener's footage we bear witness to what Didi-Huberman calls *"naked horror,* a horror that leaves us all the more devastated as it ceases to bear the hyperbolic mark of the 'unimaginable,' whether the sublime or the inhuman, bearing instead the marks of human banality at the service of the most radical evil."[46] The presence of the domestic animal, the human familiar, amid the monstrosity of the Nazi unfamiliar, blocks us from too quickly assimilating the footage to the unwatchable or inexpressible. The SS torture and humiliate the Jewish men by delivering them to the execution site in nothing more than the clothes they were wearing when they were chased down in the streets of the city they called home. The rumpled clothes in which they perish testify to the suddenness and irrevocability of their having been kidnapped and transported to this place. Seeing (and filming) *both* the commonplace of the victims and its gruesome violation is central to the spectacle of the malevolent infection of the prosaic. For the onlookers of Liepāja, the SS have conjured up a malignant paradox: although clearly treated as less than human, the Jewish men are also not so unfamiliar as to be unrecognizable to local townspeople. Far from it. We can assume that some of the spectators and some of the men who are murdered know each other or know of each other. As Marwell says of the bystanders: "they're not witnessing anonymous people being shot. They are witnessing their neighbors, their teachers, their pharmacists, their physicians, people with whom they grew up, whom they looked up to, perhaps." What the SS require to be watched is not the extermination of the wholly unfamiliar but extermination *amid* familiarity. What makes this film *maudit* is not the incomprehensibility of the executions but their unabashed and given-to-be-seen comprehensibility, the grotesque manner in which the visually recognizable must bear the weight of evil *and remain recognizable*. The excited dog, one

46. Didi-Huberman, *Images in Spite of All*, 81.

of the *d'hommestiques*, as Lacan might call him,[47] moves literally and symbolically between these worlds of murder and everyday life, his animated body connecting them in ways that are difficult to put into so many words, but as horrific to watch as they are impossible to ignore. The terrier, whose body starts in syncopation with the force of the executioners' guns, resolves that grotesquery, which otherwise saturates every detail of the atrocity footage, by, as it were, focusing it in one place. It forms the punctum of a deeply sobering knowledge: "You realize, almost as you never realized it before, that the Jews were murdered in a place on earth."[48]

*   *   *

There where there is a surfeit of onlookers and where spectators delight both in seeing murderous harm done to others and in being seen *seen* to take pleasure in that harm; there where the Jewish men are killed and where the very idea of the human is shown to be mortal and vulnerable, not a positive substance requiring protection squads but a precarious claim, a hominizing attestation that must be made and remade, especially in the face of its having been utterly unmade; there in this place that is bereft of responsible witnesses and where, in the days and months to follow, all the witnesses will be killed . . . there amid the sand dunes and the cruelty the terrier appears and leaves its indelible trace on Wiener's film. Almost despite itself, the footage admits the self-showing of the dog's flinching body, and, so to speak, lets the animal speak. Can we be certain about what it says? Or from where? Or to whom? To be sure, the terrier inhabits the death-world that the Nazis have created, and like the domesticating prop that it is compelled to be, the animal plays an unwitting role in making the homicidal a feature of the everyday. What is torture and humiliation to the Jewish men means something like a field day to Latvian neighbors who let their pet dog tag along. Yet the same Ciné-Kodak camera that collaborates in the creation of this scene of horror also exposes Wiener's film to a kind of parallel universe, fortuitously absorbing images of myriad phenomena, including animal

47. Jacques Lacan, "Television," trans. Denis Hollier, Rosalind Krauss, and Annette Michelson, *October* 40 (Spring 1987): 9.
48. I cite Leon Wieseltier, who is speaking of the deeply sobering effect of viewing the color images in Claude Lanzmann's *Shoah*. See "*Shoah*," in *Claude Lanzmann's Shoah: Key Essays*, ed. Stuart Liebman (New York: Oxford University Press, 2007), 90.

animacy, that might well go unnoticed or undetected while Wiener focuses on the spectacle of men killing other men. As Jennifer Fay suggests in an illuminating discussion of André Bazin's lifelong fascination with cinematic realism, although "the photographer must select the when, where, and what of the image, it is in the moment of aleatoric abandon after he presses the shutter that man recedes from the process and nature imprints itself both photochemically and phenomenologically."[49] These layered forms of mediation are not the antithesis of realism in Bazin's sense of the term, but constitutive of it; realism is the occasion of dynamic translations and displacements—apperceptive, chemical—vis- à-vis "nature" rather than a bare encounter with anything like an in-itself or "real." The intrusion of the agitated dog into the margins of the frame makes the camera's passive susceptibility to this accidental imprinting strangely legible because the film's inhuman exposure to the inhuman other apparitionally reproduces itself in the recoil of the terrier, whose sensitive body makes it into a kind of bio-camera or zoo-phonogram. Neither simply organic nor mechanical, the dog is a living index that sneaks the inaudible retort of the executioners' guns into the film's imaging substance. It is also a *mise-en-abyme* of the indiscriminate wildness of exposure that is elemental to the photographic image and a chief source of its uncanny power. In the sliver of time between the blast of the rifles and the play of reflected light on the surface of Wiener's film stock, the terrier is itself imprinted and imprints itself, phonochemically and photochemically, respectively. The image of the dog's reflex is a "photograph," as it were, of the cinematically realistic. The Liepāja footage is thus an example of realism not only in the sense that it is documentary in kind, but also because, at the moment of the terrier's response, we glimpse how it hews impersonally to the contingent, exposed to the carnal exposure that all living creatures share as the immanent condition of what Jean-Luc Nancy calls "singularly plural existence."[50] The footage corroborates this animal animacy by preserving its signs in the film, but it does more than that. It also *testifies*, insentiently, to what Pick names "creatureliness," hospitably framing a space for the animal other to exhibit its flinching

49. Jennifer Fay, "Seeing / Loving Animals: André Bazin's Posthumanism," *Journal of Visual Culture* 7/1 (2008): 51.

50. Jean-Luc Nancy, *Being Singular Plural*, trans. Robert D. Richardson and Anne E. O'Byrne (Stanford: Stanford University Press, 2000), 3.

vulnerability and thus, against the grain of the malicious design of Wiener's film, refusing to refuse the other's address.[51]

The perpetrators and collaborators are blind to the suffering of the victims at the precise moment they believe their Jewish difference to be perfectly discernable; yet amid that cruel willfulness the alterity and non-power of the animal's mortalizing fragility makes itself felt. The German sailor documents a radically administered world, yet he does so using an instrument whose "program," as Baer says of the camera that Genewein carried into the Łódź ghetto, "knows no politics, no morality, no intention."[52] If the photographic image *qua* photographic image is what the world looks like without human beings in it, as Stanley Cavell suggests,[53] then it offers fleeting and uncanny glimpses of an environment undominated by and indifferent to the needs, fears, designs, and histories of the *anthropos*. The photographic image's formal inhumanness, its availability to what Fay calls the "surplus of detail or a 'chance event' that the photographer could neither have anticipated nor orchestrated,"[54] unsettles the anthropomorphizing desire to recognize and affirm ourselves in "our" images. Here chance or randomness does not mean chaos but inhumanness, although it is telling that the latter often finds itself normatively erased and reconfigured by the former. That is why we are obscurely *taken* by the photographs that we take, falling under the indeterminate gaze of what isn't self-evidently human about them. As Lippit, argues, "looking at the photograph, one is looking into a place without subjectivity and, moreover . . . something like a nonsubject returns that look."[55] We begin to understand why human beings sharing the photographed field with unpredictable animals can be so disarming: the inhuman quality of the photographic image reso-

51. Pick, *Creaturely Poetics.*

52. Baer, *Spectral Evidence,* 169.

53. For example, Cavell argues that photographic images maintain "the presentness of the world by accepting our absence from it." See Stanley Cavell, *The World Viewed: Reflections on the Ontology of Film,* enlarged ed. (Cambridge, MA: Harvard UP, 1979), 23.

54. Fay, "Seeing / Loving Animals," 51. But lest we inadvertently attribute a kind of plenitude to the camera "eye," it is important also to emphasize that the human eye also always sees "more" or differently than the camera eye, and that human and—presumably—non-human perceptions of the executions in Liepāja registered myriad details that do not feature in the Liepāja footage.

55. Akira Mizuta Lippit, *Electric Animal: Toward a Rhetoric of Wildlife* (Minneapolis: University of Minnesota Press, 2000), 176.

nates with the inhuman quickness of the animal other, both human and non-human. As Fay says, "the photograph is like an animal," not negatively because both are haunted by absence but positively because each has the capacity to absent itself from the anthropocentric.[56] That eschewal unfurls a macrocosm, albeit one that is often difficult to discern under the atomic light cast by "man," which all but washes out visual traces of the advent and persistence of the non-human and of a universe that is unconcerned with the task of shoring up the primacy of the human. Discussing Bazin, Tom Gunning nonetheless notes that the "nearly inexhaustible visual richness" of the photograph, "combined with a sense of the photograph's lack of selection,"[57] means that the image "opens up a passageway to its subject, not as a signification but as a world, multiple and complex."[58]

Among the many reasons why the terrier in the Liepāja footage proves to be so affecting is that it also helps to unseal the film from its ferociously hominizing execution, disconnecting the viewer from a concentrationary realm where we are told we know in advance all that is shown. Instead of a world *sans imagination* we encounter something strangely indeterminate, irreducibly mediated and on the move, *there* where everything is also brutally pacified. Strictly speaking, even the most under-determined documentary footage conceivable—filmed images in which the viewfinder is indistinguishable from the gun sight—is always also the site of incalculable over-determinations to the degree that the camera's mechanical "program" remains both inhuman and erratically exposed to the inhuman, including the inhuman animal, the "animality" that is as indifferent to the hierarchical determination of species boundaries as it is to the mastering fantasy of the dissolution of species boundaries. But the contingent intercession of animal animacy makes the camera's hospitality especially palpable. Contemplating the terrier's image caught on camera, we find ourselves momentarily both at the center *and* to the side of the anthropocentric frenzy to separate the human from the non-human, of which Nazism is perhaps the limit-case but whose "immunologic of war" reverberates everywhere—wherever the avowal of the human demands the disavowal of life that is deemed to be less than human

56. Fay, "Seeing / Loving Animals," 62 n. 4.
57. Tom Gunning, "What's the Point of an Index? Or, Faking Photographs," *Nordicom Review* 25/1–2 (2004): 47.
58. Ibid, 46.

and unworthy of life.[59] Wiener's Ciné-Kodak incarnates the compulsion to render Jewish "difference" legible so that the Nazis can make a mirroring spectacle of their violent dis-identification with it. Not for nothing did Leica cameras become the prized objects of exchange for Jewish lives in Liepāja, so closely wedded is the "anthropological machine" to the photographically representational in the Nazi universe.[60] Yet as Pick suggests, images in which the accidents of non-human life occupy the same cinematic space as the *anthropos* mark "the absorption of the human within the leveled plain of the photographed world."[61] In the "cine-zoo" or "*cinema as a zoo,*" as she puts it, motion picture images become a "stage that transforms all living beings—including humans—into creatures,"[62] each of which is not a discrete living quanta but, as Nancy says, a moving part of a continuum of "being-with-others," circulating "in the *with* and as the *with* of this singularly plural coexistence."[63]

*   *   *

"No Jew ever returned alive from the executions in Liepāja," Anders remarks.[64] Looking at the shootings, we are accosted by an absence that historical memory cannot redeem or repair. Not a single man, woman, or child survived the shootings, and very few escaped the scourging of the city. Moreover, none of the men murdered in the footage has been identified, notwithstanding its unique archival significance as the only surviving film of SS executions. We see the images of their faces, imagine the lives from which they have been seized, observe their last moments, and watch their murders, yet we do not know the names that their respective families gave them, leav-

59. I borrow the phrase "immunologic of war" from Bishnupriya Ghosh, who uses it in her forthcoming book, *The Virus Touch: Living With Epidemics.*

60. See Kalman Linkimer, *19 Months in a Cellar . . . The Holocaust Diary of Kalman Linkimer 1941–1945*, 3rd ed., ed. Edward Anders, trans. Rebecca Margolis (Riga: Museum of Jews in Latvia, 2008), 33. Agamben's phrase, borrowed from Furio Jesi, is from *The Open: Man and Animal*, trans. Kevin Attell (Stanford: Stanford University Press, 2004), 27.

61. Pick, *Creaturely Poetics*, 106.

62. Ibid.

63. Nancy, *Being Singular Plural*, 3.

64. Anders, "Comments by the Editor," in Linkimer, *19 Months in a Cellar . . . The Holocaust Diary of Kalman Linkimer 1941–1945*, 43.

ing a ruinous void that cuts through everything that can be said and known about the killings and the images of them. The lives and the deaths of the men are extinguished in a disaster of useless suffering, there in the very place where one has to go on appealing in faith to the necessity of bearing witness. What is the nature of that attestation? Cary Wolfe is hardly alone in arguing that "what must be witnessed is not just what we can see but also what we cannot see—indeed, the fact that we cannot see. That too must be witnessed."[65] But as Sara Guyer cautions, such unqualified confidence in the capacity of witnessing to attest to its own finitude, and, indeed, in essence *to be* that traumatized appeal, makes "failure" into a "sublime knowledge" that grounds both witnessing and the witness.[66] Wolfe's choice of words here is telling; the "fact" to which he refers registers his wish for a moment of certainty and clarity amid the uncertainties of attestation, a desire to arrest the recessive chain of appeals and appeals to appeals that routes witnessing through the inhumanly figurative and groundless rather than through the humanly apperceptive and phenomenological. The "we" who bears witness to witnessing's finitude functions as an anthropomorphizing figure for attestation's outside and for a subject of testimony who is imagined to be free from this chain of claims, a doer who stands behind the witnessing deeds and heroically bears the burden of the unwitnessable and knows it as such. Witnessing, or a certain concept of witnessing, also forms part of the hominizing labor of the anthropological machine.

In the still unfolding wake of the exterminations of those who were "refused not only life but also the expression of the wrong done to them," however, Lyotard is more circumspect.[67] Amid the "silence" of the victims and among the "shades" who "continue to wander in their indeterminacy,"[68] Lyotard suggests, "something remains to be phrased which is not, something which is not determined."[69] "An enigma perhaps, a mystery, or a paradox," as he says, at a loss for words to describe a "feeling [that] does not arise from an experience

65. Cary Wolfe, *What is Posthumanism?* (Minneapolis: University of Minnesota Press, 2010), 167.

66. Sara Guyer, *Romanticism after Auschwitz* (Stanford: Stanford University Press, 2007), 24.

67. Lyotard, *The Differend*, 56.

68. Ibid.

69. Ibid, 57.

felt by a subject."[70] What seems clear is that we are no longer in the company of a witness in possession of the "fact" of its own finitude. The "something" that remains may not be human. As if to bear witness to that possibility, Lyotard's language slows thinking down; the hesitancy, the lateral movement of his adjacent figures and his redoubled "nots" function like an abeyance, preventing "something" from being too quickly assimilated to the minimal surety of the "not determined." An uncertain "not" [*ne l'est pas*] takes precedence over the "not determined" [*n'est pas déterminé*].[71] Yet *quelque chose* remains, a *milieu* of survival more than an object of thought or memory, residua left over from the hominizing work of coming to know the unknown and see the unseen. In other words, if there is a ruination to witnessing it is not simply the witness's to declare, possess or experience. In Guyer, too, "remains" is a figure for a non-subjective and inhuman desistance at the heart of witnessing, a leaving and a leaving off from determination and from the temptation to fall back on the reassurance that comes from claiming to bear witness to the limits of witnessing. Whatever survives the Nazi atrocities is in an altogether different register and calls for thinking attestation otherwise. Sensitive to the inhuman movements of hominizing figures, Guyer looks for traces of what she calls "a non-restorative, non-redemptive testimony."[72] She cites a fragment from Celan, drawn from his translation of Jean Caryol's text for Alain Resnais's *Nuit et brouillard*: "'And we, we alone strive to see what remains remain . . .'"[73] "Rather than merely stating its own failure,"[74] Guyer points out, the poet's text "*founders*:" "'What remains remain . . .' may "mean that it remains to be known, remains to be understood, remains to be seen, and so forth, but in the absence of knowledge, understanding, and vision, it remains *as* its remains, unrecovered, unredeemed—and thus it cannot recover us in the knowledge of our failure and finitude."[75] We begin to understand why the last lines of Celan's mysterious poem, *Aschenglorie*, remain so powerfully generative for Derrida: "*Niemand | zeugt für den | Zeugen* [No one | bears witness for the |

70. Ibid.

71. English lines quoted from Lyotard, *The Differend*, 57. French lines quoted from Lyotard, *Le différend* (Paris: Les Editions de Minuit, 1983), 91.

72. Guyer, *Romanticism after Auschwitz*, 22.

73. Ibid, 204.

74. Ibid.

75. Ibid, 205.

witness]."[76] What attracts Derrida to Celan's poem is how it attends and attests to the *quelque chose* without redeeming itself in the figure of the knowing witness. No one bears witness for the witness to the extent that there is "something" cinderous in witnessing that is *not* readily described as human and that in any case is *not* expressly *for* the human. Bearing witness takes place without reassurance or redemption, not only because it is always possible violently to be refused an auditor and a language with which to speak of suffering, but also because a lacuna or "refusal" already occupies the testamentary as the condition of its possibility. Bearing witness bears this burden without apprehending it, without making it either an object of knowledge or the subject of testimony. If the paradigmatic victim of being silenced and unheard is the animal, this is because something inhuman lurks at the heart of witnessing. "[W]hat remains remain": something that isn't determinately human or in whose name the human determines itself, something that survives as nothing more or less than remains.

If it is possible to speak of a "legacy" of the Holocaust, it lies in the incapacity either to come after it or to do anything but come after it. We follow it, inhabiting an unquiet condition of survival with which Derrida also associates falling under the gaze of the animal. Insofar as the shades of its victims make a claim on us, we are relegated to a future that is not yet present and perhaps will never be. Witnessing can always suffer its utter disappearance, meaning that there is no place in the world from which to observe the catastrophe from a position of complete safety, not while we remain the creatures we are, exhibiting our exposure and thus both appealing *in faith* to the other and being appealed-to by the other. Among the things to which we attest is being human. Nothing guarantees that that appeal can or will be heard or understood, and yet no appeal could be made without also assuming the risk of its erasure as its very form. What makes bearing witness possible is also what makes it impossible. As Derrida suggests, bearing witness carries the weight of this cataclysm within itself; to shift metaphors, it is the mortal horizon before which the testamentary entrusts itself and makes its claim. To witness is not only to attest but also recursively to attest to an attestation; where witnessing

76. See Derrida's reflection on Celan's words in Derrida, "Poetics and Politics of Witnessing," in *Sovereignties in Question: The Poetics of Paul Celan*, ed. Thomas Dutoit and Outi Pasanen (New York: Fordham University Press, 2005), 65–96.

takes place, if it does take place, if it can be said to have taken place, there is already a withdrawn remainder, an immemorial "past" or "not" to which witnessing also insentiently attends, unknowingly figuring something it cannot recall or make the object of thought. Without these remains *remaining* irrecuperably remains, witnessing would be merely corroborative, the programmatic transmission of information rather than wildly promissory, excessive, and inhuman. In other words, an unrecollectable recessiveness or unrevealed remains is the "secret" of the witness, as Derrida says so cryptically, "to which witnessing bears witness without knowing or meaning to do so." "We are witnesses of something we cannot testify to, we *attend* the catastrophe of memory."[77] In a certain way, all witnesses are what Derrida calls "strange witnesses," strange "because they are witnesses who do not know what they are witnessing. They keep a secret without knowing anything about it . . . They are witnesses to something they are not witness to."[78]

Is this another reason why the dog is so affecting and troublesome, because it is an example of a *strange witness* and of the strangeness of witnessing, there where there are no witnesses and where all the witnesses are killed? Among the many generative possibilities flowing from Derrida's exploration of the question of witnessing is that it appeals to forms of attestation that are irreducible to the psychic, intentional, conscious, or experiential. In his work we are invited to follow a "passage," as he says, "from traumatism to promise,"[79] *from* a psychic focus on what it means to be subjected to a violent event that "may occur as an absolute inability to know it,"[80] a disruption of apperception that is tacitly if not explicitly anthropocentric, *to* formal, and, as it were, material understandings of attestation and exhibition that may or may not be human. Where the dominant discourse about witnessing returns the testamentary to the agonistically psychological, another understanding casts light on the degree to which bearing witness is impersonal and routed through the inhuman. Derrida models what it would mean to think of witnessing otherwise in his reading of Celan's *Aschenglorie*, to whose testamentary powers he

77. Derrida, "Passages–from Traumatism to Promise," in *Points: Interviews 1974–1994*, ed. Elisabeth Weber, trans. Peggy Kamuf (Stanford: Stanford University Press, 1995), 392.

78. Ibid.

79. Derrida, "Traumatism to Promise."

80. Caruth, "Traumatic Awakenings," 208.

responds by divorcing the poem from authorial intention, autobiography, and indeed history. In the rustle of the *Aschenglorie*'s turns, ellipses, and polyphony, addressed to no one and emerging from an unidentifiable place, Derrida overhears an appeal to the other and the other's appeal: the text reproduces what it cannot cognize, not unlike the photographic image that Roland Barthes says "repeats mechanically what could never be repeated existentially," operating in ways that aren't easily integrated into perception and consciousness.[81] What was once exclusively the provenance of the human subject, the victim who was refused speech, shares something ambiguous, powerful, and uncanny with marks and markings that are speechless and yet address the other and leave traces of speech. Are we in a position to treat animals in an analogous fashion? Is there something non-human about witnessing? The dog's tremors move us, cause a stirring within the viewer who looks through Wiener's viewfinder but realizes that there is more to see than is shown.[82] What prompts a shudder in us is the disconcerting chance that witnessing is irreducible to the human. To bear witness is not to proffer evidence but an attestation that may not itself be sentient or discursive.

That which exhibits me as being-for-the-other is what Levinas calls the "truth of testimony."[83] In what language is that testament spoken? "We should not thus say, or believe," Derrida says, "that bearing witness is entirely discursive, through and through a matter of language."[84] A look, a gesture, a poem: these too can testify. And what of the dog's agitation, its flight response, which, let us insist, lest we summarily reduce the creature to a condition of dumb instinct, doesn't take place in a thoughtless vacuum but in the midst of a scene that thrums with human languages, ranging from excited murmurs to cruel commands to mortal cries? Who could do more than *claim* that the terrier is oblivious to the terror, sorrow, aggression, boredom, and even pleasure coursing through this macabre gathering or that its barking makes no claim on this *milieu* and leaves no mark?

81. Roland Barthes, *Camera Lucida*, trans. Richard Howard (New York: Vintage Books, 1993), 4.

82. I recall Sharon Sliwinski's phrase: ""What is seen in a . . . photograph is not all that is *shown*." See "Icarus Returned: The Falling Man and the Survival of Antiquity," in *Contemporary Art and Classical Myth*, ed. Isabelle Loring Wallace and Jennie Hirsh (Burlington, VT: Ashgate, 2011), 211.

83. Levinas, "Truth of Disclosure, Truth of Testimony," 97.

84. Derrida, "Poetics and Politics," 77.

Let us assume that much more than the sound of the executioners' guns makes an impression on this dog and inflects the involuntary exhibition of its body. After Derrida, Leonard Lawlor asks whether it is "possible to separate the pointing with the finger of man from the sign making of animals when they trace paths with their paws"?[85] To acknowledge an underlying collocation between these two gestures asks us to bring a kind of non-anthropomorphic camera eye to the question of language, which is to say a perspective that is indifferent to the hominizing insistence that human beings are graced with the capacity thoughtfully to respond, while animals are mostly relegated to the realm of instinctive reactions. The animal, it is sometimes said, *leaves* rather than *makes* marks. And yet both phenomena presuppose a generalized *marking* that is, as it were, older than the distinction between human and non-human communication, prior perhaps even to the distinction between sentience and insentience, life and non-life. Without collapsing the boundaries between animal reacting and human responding, Derrida points to the traces of living creatures that aren't easily described as belonging to either category because they form the remains of a matrix out of which marks of all kinds unceasingly and thoughtlessly emerge. Following possibilities submerged in Heidegger's notion of the *Zusage* (an elementary "acquiescence, affirmation, agreement, etc."), Derrida evokes an un-ascertainable and inhuman form of "engagement" or "showing" to which language belatedly testifies.[86] Everywhere Derrida looks there are attestations and pointings, and these include the myriad ways in which life exhibits and differentiates itself, leaving tracks to pick up and donating spoors that might include the traces written into an animal's body and into the animal body of film.[87] Is it possible, Derrida asks, that "the 'moment,' the instance and possibility of the *Zusage* belong to an 'experience' of language about which one could say, even if it is not in itself 'animal,' that it is not something that the 'animal' could be deprived of?" Insofar as the *Zusage* is the inhuman prom-

85. Leonard Lawlor, *This Is Not Sufficient: An Essay on Animality and Human Nature in Derrida* (New York: Columbia University Press, 2007), 50.

86. See, for example, Derrida, *Of Spirit: Heidegger and the Question*, trans. Geoffrey Bennington and Rachel Bowlby (Chicago: University of Chicago Press, 1989), 134–35. See also Derrida, *The Animal*, 166.

87. Nicole Shukin points to the basis of film stock in animal byproducts. "Cinema," she points out, "simultaneously encrypts a sympathetic and pathological relationship to animal life." See *Animal Capital: Rendering Life in Biopolitical Times* (Minneapolis: University of Minnesota Press, 2009), 108.

ise *of* language, we could nevertheless call it, after Levinas, "animal faith."[88] Derrida questions what the archaic origins of language are, and what "language" is "before" it is taken up by the impulse to attest to the humanity of human beings. His work is quickened by the possibility that language, like animal others, "might call upon and obligate me in ways that I cannot fully anticipate."[89] An analogous spirit activates Lyotard, who bears witness to the nonpower of the uncertain attestation. In this world, he asks, what of the "phrasings," markings and monstrations that are human and animal and finally neither human nor animal? There are always marks to be followed, or not, traces that recede into indistinguishability yet call upon me in ways and from places that I cannot predict and that remain to be seen: "A wink, a shrugging of the shoulder, a tapping of the foot, a fleeting blush . . . And the wagging of a dog's tail, the perked ears of a cat? – And a tiny speck to the West rising upon the horizon of the sea? A silence?"[90]

88. Levinas, "The Name of a Dog, or Natural Rights," in *Difficult Freedom: Essays on Judaism*, trans. Seàn Hand (Baltimore: Johns Hopkins University Press, 1990), 153.
89. Matthew Calarco, *Zoographies: The Question of the Animal from Heidegger to Derrida* (New York: Columbia University Press, 2008), 66.
90. Lyotard, *The Differend*, 70.

FLORENCE BURGAT

Facing the Animal in Sartre and Levinas

[The title given to this contribution exceeds its ambition. If these remarks concerning the concept of the animal as it appears in the work of Levinas are based on solid readings of cited texts, this is not the case for our Sartrian excursus.[1] In effect, here it is a matter of testing Sartre in three edifying moments. Such a presentation, however, cannot take the place of an in depth study of his thought concerning animals, in as much as it is possible to discover a complete doctrine on this subject. However, these moments forcibly illustrate Sartre's disinterest in animals *themselves* and his preference for a metaphorical usage of animals, or using them as a pretext to clarify a point of his thesis—in this instance, the question of freedom.]

FACED WITH ANIMALS, DOES SARTRE FEEL NAUSEA?

Eventually, but not always, nor only. Animals as such do not interest Sartre: Who are they? What are the moral issues concerning our treatment of them? All that does not interest the philosopher. But he appears indifferent rather than hostile, whereas Levinas, as we will see later, moves in a much more disturbing direction. The three moments, as we will call them, are as follows: (1) the "beasts" that populate *Nausea*; (2) bulls, this time very real animals in a bull-ring; and (3) the "humanized" dog in *The Family Idiot*.[2]

1. Both of the sections of this essay, on Sartre and Levinas, are slightly modified passages taken from Florence Burgat, *Une autre existence: La condition animale* (Paris: Albin Michel, 2012).
2. I am grateful to Enrique Utria for bringing this text to my attention.

YFS 127, *"Animots": Postanimality in French Thought*, ed. Senior, Clark, and Freccero, © 2015 by Yale University.

DO ANIMALS HAVE A PLACE IN THE DUALIST
ONTOLOGY OF *BEING AND NOTHINGNESS*?

Before identifying these three very distinct moments, we are curious to know whether animals appear in the dualist ontology of *Being and Nothingness*. Are they located on the side of nature, the in-itself [*en-soi*], or on the side of existence, the for-itself [*pour-soi*]? Does Sartre question the way in which animals *exist*? If we remain within the conceptualization of *Being and Nothingness*, without examining the problem of phenomenological ontology in this essay, it would seem legitimate to advance the hypothesis that animals belong implicitly to the in-itself, or nature (endowed with the distinctive criteria of the in-itself). Certainly, just as we should not confuse man and *Dasein*, we will not confuse man and the for-itself, if the for-itself is conscious-ness's movement of opposition, "that by which nothingness comes to things." However, it remains that *Dasein*, as well as the for-itself, are determinations that, for both Heidegger and Sartre, are only appli-cable to man. Faithful to Cartesian ontology, Sartre seems to include in one and the same group living creatures other than man and inert bodies on the side of the in-itself—the Sartrian *res extensa*. We must consider how life is conceptualized, knowing that it has no place in Cartesian dualism. The notion of life appears, though rarely, in *Being and Nothingness*, in the chapter devoted to "The Body-for-Others."³ Here, life means the unity of all of my actions, "the ensemble of mean-ings that are transcended toward objects that are not posited as *thises* on the ground of the world." Sartre adds that there is "no difference in nature between action and life conceived as a totality."⁴ I therefore grasp the other as life to the extent that her body does not appear to me in the form of distinct elements (arm, nose, eye . . .). This body appears to me as a "significant form" or a "synthetic totality."⁵ This is the rea-son why my perception of the body of the other differs fundamentally from my perception of things; if I focus my attention on a single organ, it makes sense "in terms of the totality of the *flesh* or *life*."⁶

Life, flesh, body: these notions are insufficiently distinguished to be able to rely on them. Besides, if the for-itself that designates

3. Jean-Paul Sartre, *Being and Nothingness*, trans. Hazel E. Barnes (New York: Philosophical Library, 1956), 339–59; 344.
4. Ibid., 345.
5. Ibid.
6. Ibid.

"human reality" is broadly defined—it is the ontological determinations of the for-itself that occupy the some seven hundred pages of *Being and Nothingness*—the in-itself is scarcely treated. Seemingly related to both the Parmenidian sphere and the Cartesian *res extensa*, the in-itself appears to be a simple counterpoint to the for-itself. *Being is in itself [L'être est en soi]*, meaning that it *is* this *itself*, completely. The in-itself is opaque, deprived of both within and without, without secret, massive. It is full positivity that knows neither relationship with itself nor alterity, and never presents itself as other. Absolute immanence, it *is* itself, indefinitely. Is it not in these terms that "nature" is defined, to which animal and vegetable life are indistinctly relegated, as well as "simple life," which is never anything but the tautology of itself, indefinitely?

THE BEASTS OF *NAUSEA*

If animals scarcely cross Sartre's thoughts, "beasts" haunt the imagination of *Nausea*; objects sometimes assume the terrifying aspect of "living beasts."[7]

> I see my hand spread out on the table. It lives—it is me. It opens, the fingers open and point. It is lying on its back. It shows me its fat belly. It looks like an animal turned upside down. The fingers are the paws. I amuse myself by moving them very rapidly, like the claws of a crab which has fallen on its back. The crab is dead: the claws draw up and close over the belly of my hand.[8]

After the hand, then the face:

> My gaze moves down, in boredom, over this face, these cheeks: it encounters nothing firm, it gets stuck. [. . .]. When I was little, my Aunt Bigeois told me: "If you look at yourself too long in the mirror, you'll see a monkey." I must have looked at myself even longer than that: what I see is well below the monkey, on the fringe of the vegetable world, at the level of jellyfish. It's alive, I can't say it isn't [. . .]. It is glassy, soft, blind, red-rimmed; it looks like fish scales. [. . .] I draw my face closer until it touches the mirror. The eyes, nose, and mouth disappear: nothing human is left. [. . .] You might say—yes, you might say, nature without men.[9]

7. Sartre, *Nausea*, trans. Lloyd Alexander (New York: New Directions, 1964), 10.
8. Ibid., 99.
9. Ibid., 16, 17–18.

Nature without men: isn't this enough to demonstrate that, for Sartre, animals are implicitly included in all that vacillates between the viscous, the vitreous, the "it's alive," and "nature" as determinism—an imposed order where everything is always already given? What is the function of these beasts? Metaphors? Nature's most disgusting objects? An imaginary, where they never occupy an infra-human place—they are too repugnant for that. They are, in their crude state, *living*, but already engaged in a process of rotting. Beasts are unclean flesh.

SARTRE AT THE BULLFIGHT

In a letter to Louise Vedrine (August 1939), Sartre reveals the line he draws between humans and animals in an account he gives of a bullfight he attended in the Arenas of Prado in Marseille.

> Over breakfast, I explained to Bost at great length all the marvels of the corrida. But it turned out to be a bad show and made him queasy. "I was sure he'd be indignant, that Protestant," said Beaver [Simone de Beauvoir]. Bad bulls, bad matadors. I can hear you say that speaking of "bad" bulls is as shameful as talking about "lazy natives," since they actually demand nothing of us, and it is we who seek them out. Agreed, and that's just what made Bost indignant. "You told me the bull played a part in the contest. But he's totally uninterested." And it is a fact that the ideal toro, with whom the torero "does as he pleases," is a sort of bull version of a military cadet: irascible, heroic, stupid, forever charging this way and that. But the ones they produced for us retreated at the first flash of a red rag, raking the dirt with their hooves and bellowing lamentably. There was even one they couldn't manage to kill: he just kept dodging. So they brought a calf with bells into the arena and the calf peacefully led the bleeding bull along behind him. The matadors made the correct passes but they killed badly. The beasts bled all they had, and it took four tries to kill them. The ineffectual sword stuck in the back of their necks was yanked out with a cane ("Why not with an umbrella"? said Bost, furious), and another was plunged in, and so forth, until they fell. And at that, the beasts still had to be polished off with a knife. [. . .] It bore no resemblance to the bullfights in Spain, yet it was fun for us because it reminded us of Spain.[10]

10. Sartre, *Witness to My Life: The Letters of Jean-Paul Sartre to Simone de Beauvoir, 1926–1939*, trans. Lee Fahnestock and Norman McAfee (New York: Charles Scribner, 1992), 208.

We will not dwell on the fascination that bullfighting holds for the "intellectual" world. If it is excessive to speak here of a fascination, Sartre's taste for bullfighting is strong and freely admitted, and it gives rise to a defense of "all the wonders of the bullfight." Nor will we dwell on Sartre's amused indifference to the slow massacre of the bulls, considering, like Simone de Beauvoir, its disapproval to be the prudishness of "the Protestant"! However, this indifference is disturbing: both in itself and in the blindness it betrays. There is, therefore, a lot to be said about this text. It could, paradoxically, be redirected and used as an indictment against bullfighting. Does it not provoke disgust for the sport, since all its "wonders" are exposed?

THE DOG AS FAMILY IDIOT

In a brief passage in *The Family Idiot*, Sartre refers to the strange state, a sort of ontological contradiction, to which domestic animals are subjected by their foray into the human world: outside of nature without being part of culture, they float in a pitiful in-between that exiles them twice over. It "seems clear," writes Sartre, that household animals, those that live in our homes, experience boredom: "Culture has penetrated them, destroying nature in them without replacing it." Dogs also resent the "frustration" of not being able to speak; "a disturbing privation" inhabits them living in a universe of speakers.[11]

Dogs are implicated in something that nevertheless escapes them. The function of language is apparent to them, but its usage impossible. When humans talk about dogs in their presence, they are aware of it. Language is there, insistent, it penetrates them. It is only when they return to their dog solitude, below, in their beds, that they can forget about it for a time, but verbal power encircles them.

Sartre describes the state of a dog who understands he is being talked about, because faces are turned toward him, but in a way that is neither an order nor a call, generally accompanied by an urgent look or a gesture. This certainty of knowing he is being spoken about, but in a more opaque way than other more familiar usages (such as orders or calls, which elicit actions), disturbs the dog, who is confronted with something almost recognizable.

---

11. Sartre, *The Family Idiot: Gustave Flaubert 1821–1827*, 5 vols., trans. Carol Cosman (Chicago: University of Chicago Press, 1981), vol. 1, 137.

I have seen fear and rage grow in a dog: we were talking about him, he knew it instantly [. . .] the sounds struck him with full force as if we were addressing him. Nevertheless we were speaking to *each other*. He felt it; our words seemed to designate him as our interlocutor and yet reached him *blocked*. He did not quite understand either the act itself or this exchange of speech, which concerned him far more than the usual hum of our voices.[12]

The humanization of such animals modifies their intelligence, extending it somehow beyond itself, "in the imbroglio of its presence and its impossibilities." From the world of nature to which it belongs, according to Sartre, the animal passes into culture. Culture, the simple environment in which the dog lives, becomes something quite different: it digs a sort of gap in the domestic animal, a "fission" that shifts the dog from the level of its ordinary comprehension, "raising him toward an impossible understanding even as his bewildered intelligence collapses into stupidity."[13] The dog's state of panic results from this sort of limitation that he would like to overcome: he understands that he does not understand what is being said, but that what is being said is being said about him. The dog then expresses his confusion by waking up (he was dozing on the rug), followed by an interrupted lurch, whining, agitation, then angry barking. "This dog passed from discomfort to rage, feeling at his expense the strange reciprocal mystification which is the relationship between man and animal."[14] This anger, Sartre continues, far from indicating a revolt, actually had a calming effect; the dog, by this display of anger, sought to "simplify his problems" and, in fact, left to go to sleep in another room and all was forgotten; he returned much later, continuing his interrupted "clowning."

In this strange state, immediate experience is "fractured," but the dog cannot make anything of this rift; he neither appropriates nor prevents it from happening. This is his new condition: floating in an in-between that no mediation can ever reconcile. A breakthrough seems to occur here in Sartre's text and invites us to review our initial hypothesis: "Peaceful immanence is changed into self-consciousness." Of course this mutation occurs because the human is implanted in

12. Ibid., 137.
13. Ibid., 138.
14. Ibid.

the dog, "as a denied possibility." The key to the particular boredom that besets domestic dogs resides for Sartre in this lurch toward something that seems near at hand, but is not, because it is produced by culture, the humanized world.

> Without culture, the animal would not be bored—he would live, that is all. Haunted by the sense of something missing, he lives out the impossibility of transcending himself by a forgetful relapse into animality; nature reveals itself through resignation. The boredom of living is a consequence of man's oppression of animals; it is nature grasping itself as the absurd end of a limiting process instead of realizing itself as biological spontaneity.[15]

What annoys the domestic dog therefore is not being able to be human, a failure constantly renewed by the "desire to transcend itself towards the human." In other words, for Sartre, the animal is simply a living thing immanent within nature, but animality is not a determinate state that the dog could absolutely not escape. This half-entry into the humanized world makes the animal lose, without compensation, the easy innocence of "simply living." If it is through the human and according to the measure of the human that Sartre thinks the animal condition, his analysis nevertheless diverges from the usual ways of attaching animals to nature. In these animals, partly separated from nature and from the sole sphere of needs, life is lived differently; a distance is established in their hearts; man has ruined the equilibrium proper to mere living organisms; he has jammed the machine. At the conclusion of this page, we could ask whether Sartre might not have gone further in discovering that boredom, or other states, may affect animals so that, precisely, they are not simply living, and "that's all."

THE FACE "IS NOT OF THE WORLD," OR EMMANUEL LEVINAS'S CONFUSION WHEN FACED WITH ANIMALS

That which invites violence and simultaneously restrains it. The ethics of the face—the "shimmer of the infinite"—coined by Levinas, has, for several years, been appropriated and repurposed.[16] Although

---

15. Ibid., 139.
16. Emmanuel Levinas, *Totality and Infinity: An Essay on Exteriority*, trans. Alphonso Lingis (Pittsburgh: Duquesne University Press, 1969), 207.

strictly limited to man, several philosophers consider this ethics to be the best way of extending our sense of responsibility to animals, since these philosophers are using Levinas's ethics for this purpose at the same time as developing a reflection in moral philosophy specifically devoted to animals, to our responsibility toward them, to their rights, to their moral standing, and so on. The ethical relationship as both asymmetric and non-reciprocal, the definition of the other as a vulnerability that makes demands on me, are themes central to Levinassian ethics. Are they so entirely lacking in the ethical reflection devoted to animals that we must go looking for them in the work of an author who has conspicuously excluded animals from his ethics?

Must this conceptualization be judged so rich a resource that it should be utilized *against* its author's thought, for not only did Levinas refuse to extend his ethics of the face to animals, he also categorized as "work" any killing that is not first directed toward a face. Killing for a purpose is work. Levinas asserts this at least twice: "Neither the destruction of things, nor hunting, nor the extermination of the living—are aimed at a face. They are still the result of work, they have a finality and respond to a need. [. . .] Some other person is the only one I might want to kill"; or again, "Violence only affects a being who is both perceptible and escaping from capture. Without the existence of this contradiction existing in the being experiencing violence, the deployment of violent force would be reduced to work."[17] If hunting clearly evokes animals, considered by Levinas outside the category of an otherness that makes demands, one might ask whether the other does not also fall under a similar menace, since the ethical status of that other depends on the gaze of the person who kills. This doubt is all the stronger since Levinas speaks of "the extermination of the living," without it being entirely clear that such extermination is necessarily targeted at animals. The project of extermination that would not seek to violate a face, but "simply" to delete from the map a group of living beings deemed undesirable, would thus be a an instance of work, of the banality of evil that does not see the face.

There would seem to be three categories to consider: 1) violence, defined by the perception *and* the transgression of the prohibition of killing coming from the face; 2) the work of killing that does not see the face and is, in this instance, merely a force that kills without committing murder; 3) the face that forbids me to kill, whose injunction

17. Ibid., 198, 223.

I perceive and that makes me, infinitely, the voluntary hostage of the other. What is exceptional, we are told, is that the order not to kill can be understood. The law of evil for Levinas is that of being, such that the appearance of the face makes a break in being, interrupts being in its perseverance in existing. Ethics breaks the egoistical line of being that persists in its essence.

BEING MORE LEVINASIAN THAN LEVINAS

Does this ethics contain elements capable of displacing humano-centrism, to which it is, however, fundamentally attached? The attempt by philosophers who, in some fashion, seek to complete Levinas's thought, by making it give birth to a truth that it harbors but that remained beyond the understanding of its author—this attempt is interpreted as a perversion of his thought by his faithful followers. Barbara J. Davy argues,[18] for example, that the Levinasian face contains its own overcoming, and if her analysis is unfaithful to the letter of the text, it is faithful to the spirit. If the face is capable of interrupting me in the pursuit of my being and makes demands on me, if it is an injunction to responsibility without consideration of the other's capacities, and if I must admit that I can experience strong ethical obligations in the face of entities other than humans, then I have seen a face, *since to see a face is not at first nor essentially a matter of perceiving a face or a man, but of encountering an obligation.* If the face is the call to responsibility, it does not matter who is calling me; I respond to that appeal *prior to all thematization* of this other. Here is a position that, while remaining faithful to Levinassian ethics, remains infinitely open to those beings who call. Levinas

18. Barbara J. Davy, "An Other Face of Ethics in Levinas," *Ethics and the Environment* 12 (2007), 39–65. Others have commented at length on this text in which Levinas "thinks of Bobby" (the dog who always recognizes the humanity of men whose humanity has been denied by other men) in order to express their disappointment in Levinas as he seems to approach, openly and frankly, an expanded definition of the other, only to close this opening more decisively: David L. Clark, "On Being the Last Kantian in Nazi Germany," in *Animal Acts: Configuring the Human in Western History*, ed. Jennifer Ham and Matthew Senior (New York: Routledge, 1997), 165–98; Alphonso Lingis, "Animal Body, Inhuman Face" in *Zoontologies: The Question of the Animal*, ed. Cary Wolfe (Minneapolis: University of Minnesota Press, 2003), 168–82; John Llewelyn "Am I obsessed by Bobby? Humanism of the Other Animal," in *Re-reading Levinas*, ed. Robert Bernasconi and Simon Critchley (London: Indiana University Press, 1991), 234–245; Christian Diehm, "Facing Nature: Levinas Beyond the Human," *Philosophy Today* 44 (2000): 51–59.

seems to have left the question open. Davy quotes "Name of a Dog or Natural Rights," where it is always a question of an open debt to the dog, and especially to Bobby, the pseudo hero of the text, the wandering dog who recognizes the humanity of men whose humanity is refused by other men.[19] It is Bobby, a dog, who broadens the community, but his fault in Levinas's eyes is that he does so spontaneously! This text, according to Davy, constitutes an "interruption" in Levinas's thought, the moment of doubt, an opening, yet quickly closed in the last lines of the text. No, Bobby is not the last Kantian of Nazi Germany, since he is incapable of universalizing his maxim! (But he does indeed universalize without a maxim!) Thus we find, here and there, mention of the "Kantian cyborg," in order to evoke, fundamentally, what this dog means for Levinas, whose role, however, was so essential. This animal with no brain, who seems unaware of what he does, recognizes any and every man as a member of humanity. Levinas, the great philosopher of responsibility to others, has not, any more than Kant, Heidegger, or Lacan, "taken into account, in any serious and decisive way, the fact that we hunt, kill, exterminate, eat and sacrifice animals, use them, make them work, or submit them to experiments that are forbidden to be carried out on men," so that we can ask ourselves, following the analysis of Jacques Derrida in this regard, whether there has been a real displacement of the subject in his philosophy.[20] For what does not change is the subject of enunciation, for none of these philosophers has considered the possibility of being looked at by the animal that they observed. The important point is not to restore to animals what has been taken from them conceptually, but to question ourselves more thoroughly about the axiom that allows giving to one what is denied to another, in this "mobile system of one discursive organization extended to several tentacles."[21]

Somewhat in the same vein as Barbara Davy, Matthew Calarco, who does not fail to recognize the position, in his words, "dogmatically anthropocentrist," of Levinas, considers that the underlying logic of his thought does not allow such anthropocentrism. Calarco goes on to show that he is more Levinasian than Levinas, by emphasizing that Bobby is a *wild, nomadic* dog, who is struggling to survive,

19. Levinas, "Name of a Dog or Natural Rights, in *Difficult Freedom: Essays on Jadaism*, trans. Seàn Hand (Baltimore: Johns Hopkins University Press, 1990): 151–53.
20. Jacques Derrida, *The Animal That Therefore I Am*, ed. Marie-Louise Mallet, trans. David Wills (New York: Fordham University Press, 2008), 89.
21. Ibid., 91.

without anything or anyone coming to his aid; he is welcome neither in the prison camp nor beyond. Thus Bobby goes beyond egotistical perseverance to welcome the prisoners in his own way and restore to them, in disinterested fashion, their stolen humanity; for Bobby does not come looking for food, which he doesn't find in the camp. He comes to *be with* the prisoners, offering them his vitality, his gaiety, his affection. Calarco questions whether Bobby is not therefore an example of something other than being, and whether we don't have the right to say that there is transcendence in the animal?[22] Calarco thus suggests "naturalizing" the transcendence . . . invoking examples of altruism in the animal world, formerly provided by Darwin and currently and notably by Franz de Waal. It is easy to imagine the extent to which Levinas would have shown his opposition to such a reading of his thought!

As for Peter Atterton, he puts Levinas's thought to the test in a face-to-face encounter with the animal conceived by Martin Buber.[23] Atterton refers to occurrences appearing in publications prior to *Totality and Infinity*. In "L'égo et la totalité" (1954), Levinas speaks of an "animal that is free, wild, faceless"; in "La philosophie et l'idée de l'infini" (1957), he writes, "a face [. . .] differs from the head of an animal in which a being, in its uncouth silence, is not yet in relation with itself." Atterton quotes yet another text written thirty years later, which we will consider later, "The Paradox of Morality," in which Levinas admits that one cannot completely deny a face to an animal. John Llewelyn has devoted several works to Levinas's thought. In "Am I Obsessed by Bobby?" he suggests opening a path to a "humanism of another being" in answer to the question asked: who is my neighbor?[24] In Levinas's profoundly Kantian world, Bobby barks, but does not say "hello." According to the distinction established by Levinas between saying *[dire]* (the force of a calling) and the said *[le dit]* (statements), the dog's calling is merely saying. However, this calling is not the same as saying, for the simple reason that it

22. Matthew Calarco, "Facing the Other Animal: Levinas," in *Zoographies: The Question of the Animal from Heidegger to Derrida* (New York: Columbia University Press, 2008), 55–77.

23. Peter Atterton, "Face-to-Face with the Other Animal," in *Levinas and Buber: Dialogue and Difference* (Pittsburg: Duquesne University Press, 2004), 262–81; see also Atterton, "The Name of a Dog, or Natural Rights: Ethical Cynicism," in *Animal Philosophy: Essential Readings in Continental Thought*, ed. Atterton and Matthew Calarco (London: Continuum, 2004), 47–61.

24. Llewelyn, "Am I obsessed by Bobby?" 234–45.

comes from an animal. Thus, the distinction between saying and the said—which Levinas takes pains to establish in order to give importance to saying (the force of a calling), and not the declaration of what is said—if it is limited to human forms of calling, no longer has a reason to exist: What does it actually contribute to metaphysical humanism? John Llewellyn does not see a difference between Levinasian "metaphysical ethics" and Kantian ethics, to the extent that, in each case, I only have direct responsibility for beings who can speak (formulate statements), that is, beings endowed with a rationality capable of universalization.

SEEING A FACE

What then is the force of this so-called rampart—the face—whose fragility we are well aware of, as well as its paradoxical character and non-phenomenal status? Prohibition is not impossibility; it "even presupposes the possibility of that which it specifically forbids,"[25] and this possibility is contained in the face, whose exposed character would seem "to invite an act of violence,"[26] and forbid it at the same time. The face would be the expression of "Thou shalt not kill," and its resistance has the resistance of that which has no resistance. The face "is not of the world": it is not given as a being.[27]

The inclusion of the notion of the face at the core of ethics can be seen as a missed opportunity for going beyond humanism; for, after all, if the face consists of a composition of eyes, nose, and mouth, in that expressive triangle that contains the gaze, it is difficult to see how the evidence of animal faces can be denied.[28] But the face is abstracted from the field of perception, so that its empirical character no longer exercises control over its concept. The face, in as much as it "is not of the world," can thus cover a smaller space than that of the set of all living bearers of a face of flesh, an inclusion that does not coincide with its extension, nor anything else. Since the word "face," in current language, refers to a part of the body, one cannot entirely ignore its existence as a visible, perceived object; Levinas

25. Levinas, *Totality and Infinity*, 232.
26. Levinas, *Ethics and Infinity: Conversations with Philippe Nemo*, trans. Richard Cohen (Pittsburgh: Duquesne University Press, 1985), 86.
27. Levinas, *Totality and Infinity*, 198.
28. Françoise Armengaud, "Le visage animal: bel et bien un visage," in *Du Visage*, ed. Marie-José Baudinet and Christian Schlatter (Lille : Presses universitaires de Lille, 1982), 103–116.

evokes moreover the bare skin of the face, always bare, and therefore more vulnerable than any other part of the body. Besides, the face is sometimes considered in a metonymic sense, as a part for the whole. But since this part is always already in excess of the whole, we must see in the face that (perceived) part that allows us to "facialize" [*visagéiser*] the other parts of this body that cries out to me. Thus the neck is given as an example of a part of the body that is not the face but reveals all the weakness borne by the face. It is because any individual has a face that she has a neck that speaks as her face would.

In response to the question of what "his phenomenology of the face" consists of, Emmanuel Levinas answers on several occasions that one cannot speak of a phenomenology of the face, to the extent that phenomenology describes what appears.[29] The face, as understood by Levinas, has a meaning prior to my conferral of meaning, and the meaning of the face is independent of my initiative and power. This face is not the perceived face. Its transcendence does not result from its expressivity. The face is what exceeds the idea of the Other in me, what exceeds the plastic image the Other leaves in me. The face is an appeal, an outstretched hand.

Shouldn't the more than secondary importance given to resemblances lead to an expansion of such a face to animals? Do they not address appeals to us? Are they not vulnerable given the fact they cannot speak? Are they not in a state of expectation before us without reciprocity? But this is not the case for two complementary reasons: On the one hand, if the fraternity uniting men owes nothing to their resemblance, it is, according to Levinas, in the sense that it owes everything to monotheism. On the other hand, the face is logocentric; Levinas states that the face and discourse are bound together, even if he distinguishes, as we have noted, the *said* (the field of statements) from the *saying* (the face's ability to speak to me and elicit a response). The face is disembodied; its odor of sanctity is not attached to a body, since it does not appear as a phenomenon and thus owes little to the fact of being perceived. However, it speaks or could speak. It is therefore necessarily perceived, but in a singular fashion; it breaks the calm and orderly web of perception; it summons me. We

29. Notably in two interviews: *Ethics and Infinity*, op. cit., 85–92; and "The Paradox of Morality: An Interview with Emmanuel Levinas, Tamra Wright, Peter Hughes, and Alison Ainley," trans. Andrew Benjamin and Tamra Wright, in *The Provocation of Levinas: Rethinking the Other*, ed. Robert Bernasconi and David Wood (London: Routledge, 1988), 168–80.

can understand a little better now how violence also becomes disembodied: if the murderer does not aim at this impalpable otherness, he
does not kill, he works. If it is possible to show that the power of the
Levinasian face comes from its abstract, non-phenomenological character, which owes nothing to its constitution, it could also be shown
that this is the source of its weakness.

The weakness of the face can therefore be linked to the fact that
it is not a phenomenon (the face is not that expressive bodily part
through which I encounter a singularity); on the other hand, however,
taken in its empirical sense, one can question the efficacy of the face
in protecting *all* men. Thus Elisabeth de Fontenay observes that every
face can one day be struck by deformity.[30] We must then ask ourselves
whether it is so easy to cross the barriers of deformity and ugliness,
whether it is not precisely by our focusing on the face, read according to more or less ethnocentric canons, that we are led to exclude
certain individuals from the rest of humanity. Does metaphysical
humanism—be it that of the other man—really need such a notion?
Certainly, for Levinas, it is a question of making a radical philosophical shift at the heart of a concept of being in favor of a concept of the
other, a matter of shattering a subjectivity occupied first with itself.
But doesn't the face present serious weak points, evident, on the one
hand, in the oblique uses it is put to (the neck), and, on the other,
in the ambiguity that haunts it (it is perceived without being a phenomenon)? The face's weakest point in our eyes is that it is "not of
the world," because one can see it wherever one wants to, where one
has already decided to see it. It is a weak point at least in the sense
that such a usage cannot, through the *encounter*, be extended to other
living beings thanks to an understanding that would render its reach
truly infinite. It must be said that the ethics of the face represents a
backward step with regard to the ethics of compassion that, intrinsi-
cally, is inscribed in the perspective of an infinite responsibility toward sentient beings in general. Why does the concept of the face
ultimately protect so little? Why is it so narrow, so humano-centric?

DO ANIMALS HAVE A FACE?

The question of knowing whether animals have a face was clearly
addressed to Levinas in an interview given to three students in 1988,

30. Élisabeth de Fontenay, *Le silence des bêtes: La philosophie à l'épreuve de
l'animalité* (Pars: Fayard, 1999), 683.

for which—and this is important—he had been sent the questions in advance.[31] "One cannot entirely refuse the face of an animal. It is via the face that one understands, for example, a dog."[32] But it is because we have first had access to a human face, Levinas states, that we can carry out such a transposition. The animal face is, itself, reduced to the rank of a "phenomenon," and this phenomenon "is not in its purest form in the dog," for we are given other characteristics at the same time, such as the vitality of the dog. Levinas is asked: "Is it necessary to have the potential for language in order to be a 'face' in the ethical sense?" He responds: "The beginning of language is in the face. In a certain way, in its silence, it calls you."[33] This call is one of responsibility toward another entity; it does not depend on difference but on transcendence, the most important element of which is vulnerability. Understandably, we might want to draw Levinas over to the side to which he seems quite close, notably on account of the importance he accords to the idea of vulnerability and thus to asymmetric relations.

Let us return to this discussion. It is strange that Levinas has not recognized that his questioners are trying to get him to specify the ethical status that he seems to give to animals. He dodges the problem, and the questions become ever more precise and insistent. "According to your analysis, the commandment 'Thou shalt not kill' is revealed by the human face; but isn't the commandment also expressed in the face of an animal? Can an animal be considered as the other that must be welcomed? Or is it necessary to possess the possibility of speech to be a 'face' in the ethical sense?"[34] Emmanuel Levinas admits his hesitation in determining the moment when one can speak of the face in the way he understands it. "I cannot say at what moment you have the right to be called 'face' [. . . .] I don't know if a snake has a face," but in any case Levinas reaffirms the absolute singularity and precedence of the human face.[35] The choice of the snake is no accident; it is the image of temptation or evil, and this makes it particularly difficult to attribute a face to a snake. But above all, this example allows Levinas to avoid other more troubling examples. We are reminded of Heidegger, in his seminar on animality (1929–1930),

31. Levinas, "The Paradox of Morality."
32. Ibid., 169.
33. Ibid.
34. Ibid.
35. Ibid., 172.

judging it prudent to "stop with the bee"! In regard to evolution, as is to be expected, Levinas takes up an anti-Darwinian position in radically separating man from the rest of living creatures, and, as we have seen, even from the happiness of enjoying life. The animal struggles for its life, whereas man struggles for the other's life to the detriment of his own. . . . Levinas admits, however, that "a more specific analysis is needed" to truly respond to the question of the animal face.[36]

USELESS SUFFERING

The admission of not knowing "at what moment you have the right to be called 'face,'" is considered by Derrida to be an extremely risky proposition, for it is nothing less than "confessing that one does not really know what a face is," so that Levinas, without considering the consequences, runs the risk of ruining his whole edifice, of "calling into question the whole legitimacy of the discourse and ethics of the 'face' of the other."[37] Levinas doesn't weigh the consequences, for how could such a danger come from what in his eyes, in his thought, is the most insignificant and indigent from an ontological point of view—an animal? However, his interviewers press him to clarify his position: "If animals do not have faces in an ethical sense, do we have obligations towards them? And if so, where do they come from?" "The ethical extends to all living beings," Levinas declares, which means, "we do not want to make an animal suffer *needlessly* (my emphasis)."[38] This "needlessly" is all the more remarkable considering that in a beautiful text entitled "Useless Suffering," Levinas insists on the fact that suffering, in its essence, is useless.[39] No theodicy justifies suffering. And Levinas writes this crucial sentence that makes all suffering unjustifiable, that makes the criterion of "useful suffering" a monstrosity and a scandal: "For an ethical sensibility [. . .] the justification of a neighbor's grief is undoubtedly the source of all immorality."[40] Who is my neighbor? As soon as any statement whatsoever is made that justifies suffering, we should be seized by the greatest anxiety. Who is this other who is sacrificed for me and who I dare not call my

36. Ibid.
37. Derrida, *The Animal That Therefore I Am*, 109.
38. Levinas, "The Paradox of Morality," 172.
39. Levinas, "Useless Suffering," trans. Rcihard Cohen, in *The Povocation of Levinas: Rethinking the Other*, ed. Robert Bernasconi and David Wood (London: Routledge, 1988), 156–67.
40. Ibid., 163.

neighbor? Is the reason for this precisely because I have decided *in advance* not to call him my neighbor, in order for him to endure this suffering that I don't want? What I want are the benefits his suffering brings me. At first Levinas does not consider suffering a given of consciousness, but rather a lived sensation. This is a fundamental point. It breaks with the long tradition that establishes a fallacious distinction between physical pain and moral suffering, thereby upholding the distinction between "animal pain" and "human suffering." We might ask ourselves whether Levinas is not very close to seeing the suffering of animals when he finally evokes the "pure suffering of psychically disinherited beings," who cannot distance their suffering, who cannot deal with it as an object of reflection, nor name it in speaking. Let us consider this passage in its entirety. These mentally disinherited beings are still called

> backward, handicapped in their relational life and their relationships to the Other, relationships where suffering, without losing anything of its savage malignancy, no longer covers up the totality of the mental and comes across novel lights within new horizons. These horizons, none the less remain closed to the mentally deficient, except that in their "pure pain," they are projected into them to expose them *to me*, raising the fundamental ethical problem posed by suffering "for nothing."[41]

When I say that Levinas is closest here to seeing and understanding animal suffering, it is not because I consider animals to be psychically disinherited beings, but rather because their situation, in regard to suffering, is comparable, as far as we can judge, and to the extent that we can judge any suffering that is not our own, to that of humans who cannot speak of their suffering. This analogy rests on the impossibility of distancing or objectifying suffering, of taking it on—as a result of which it becomes *"pure* suffering," suffering "for nothing," which the subject can't do anything about, except endure it, because "its savage malignancy" makes it untamable. We can go even further concerning Levinas's closeness to what he has nevertheless distanced himself from; for in the following text, it is a question of an opening that allows for "a moan, a cry, a groan or a sigh, an original appeal for help."[42] How can we both limit the domain of the neighbor to the human while seeing in this *saying* without *the said*, in the moan, the

41. Ibid., 158; slightly modified.
42. Ibid.

groan or the cry (!) the original call of a humano-centric ethics? This ethics—is this the right word?—of useful suffering, good for animals, and for which one measures all the distance that separates it from that which I owe to the other man, is, Levinas argues in this discussion, an extension of the prototype that constitutes human ethics. Thus vegetarianism is also, according to Levinas, based on the transfer to animals of our idea of suffering.

Thus Levinas never considered in his philosophy the possibility of including animals in his ethics; he never saw that the relationship with animals offers the perfect prototype of a asymmetric relationship at whose heart the other is at my mercy, nor did he ever see that the animal is in an extreme state of vulnerability that calls to me all the more because it is deprived of language. We would conclude by saying that an ethics limited to an invitation to "not cause useless suffering to animals," is not an ethics, but a rule of "good practices," prescribed rules, that workers whose job consists in killing domestic animals (workers in slaughter houses and laboratory technicians) are asked to observe.

—Translated by Yvonne Freccero

ÉLISABETH DE FONTENAY

The Slaughterhouse or a
Common Fate

Alfred Döblin, a socialist and a neurologist who went into exile in 1933, wrote one of the rawest and most sentimental novels of the period between the wars: *Berlin Alexanderplatz*. In this book, which recounts the tribulations of a recently released prisoner in Berlin, two chapters describe animal butchery in minute detail: their titles read, respectively: "For it happens alike with Man and Beast; as the Beast dies, so Man dies too"; "And they all have the same Breath, and Men have no more than Beasts."[1] Reading Döblin's pages is almost unbearable, owing to the exactitude of their staging: in the description of the treatment inflicted on cattle and of the way the animals die, the clinical precision of the doctor rivals the pathetic rigor of the narrator, and then there are the minutiae of an accounting system worthy of the great capital city, a system that does not fail to penetrate the so-called meat market as well. "Supply at the cattle-market"[2]—not the market where cattle are sold, as in the provinces, but the stock market, where prices rise and fall. And we can readily imagine the commotion and the trampling that preside over these stockyards traversed by death.

"1399 steer, 2700 calves, 4654 sheep, 18,864 hogs. Market conditions: prime steers firm, otherwise quiet. Calves firm, sheep quiet, hogs opening firm, closing weak, overweights lagging."[3] Döblin is the only writer who denounced, in animal murders, the violence of the market economy, the one that treats living beings (human and animal) as things, no longer just consumer products, but henceforth

1. Alfred Döblin, *Berlin Alexanderplatz: The Story of Franz Biberkopf*, trans. Eugene Jolas (New York: Continuum, 1993), 172 and 188.
2. Ibid., 179.
3. Ibid.

YFS 127, *"Animots": Postanimality in French Thought*, ed. Senior, Clark, and Freccero, © 2015 by Yale University.

abstract objects of speculation. With him, a new line of writers takes shape: those who pass casually from animals to humans and from humans to animals.

"The horror of the slaughterhouse on which everything is based," writes Elias Canetti[4] in a principial proposition whose exorbitant character is also revealed by Isaac Bashevis Singer. In his autobiographical text, *A Young Man in Search of Love*, whose opening volume is titled *A Little Boy in Search of God*, Singer meditates on the evil, willed (and not simply allowed) by God, evil that is manifested by the war of all against all, men and beasts alike. His adolescence was marked by his reading of Darwin and—especially—Malthus. He understood once and for all that there was nothing on earth in sufficient quantity and that, with or without free will, men had to destroy one another. "Malthus's contentions denied all the claims of the Scriptures that God despised bloodshed. Actually He had so constructed the world that blood should spill, that children should starve to death, that beasts should devour each other."[5] The adolescent even observes that the Scriptures indirectly confirm Malthus's theories. His reading of the Kabbala reinforces a pessimism nourished by Schopenhauer: the world, Singer says in his turn, is nothing but "one huge slaughterhouse."[6] Hence his profound sadness in the face of reality as it is, of the ceaseless cycle of cruelty and suffering that is manifested—produced by unique inexplicable principles—in the history of nature as well as in the history of humankind. "The cause of my gloom was often the same—unbearable pity for those who were suffering and who had suffered in all the generations."[7]

But the scandal of human suffering was experienced by Singer from the outset in a shared communal fate, in a relation of blood kinship (*consanguinité*) with animals. Mice being tortured, chickens with their throats cut, lambs being devoured all enter the catalog of eternal martyrs. The little boy looking for God demands an accounting for the fly whose wings are pulled off by mischievous urchins as well as for the pogroms inflicted on the Jews of Bilgoray: a series of cruelties unfolding in an endless chain.

4. Elias Canetti, *The Human Province*, trans. Joachim Neugroschel (New York: Seabury Press, 1978), 156.

5. Isaac Bashevis Singer, *A Little Boy in Search of God* (Garden City, N.J.: Doubleday, 1976), 53.

6. Ibid., 49.

7. Ibid.

I once heard the scream of a mouse that a cat had caught, and this cry haunts me still. Do the chickens slaughtered in Yanash's Market have a choice? Do they have to suffer because of *our* choice? Well, and those children that died of scarlet fever, diphtheria, whooping cough, and other diseases—how were they guilty? I had read and heard that the souls of the dead were resurrected in cattle and fowl and that when the slaughterer killed them with a kosher knife and said the blessing with fervor, this served to purify these souls. What about those cows and hens that fell into the hands of gentile butchers?[8]

Suddenly, at the heart of this philosophical autobiography, Singer exclaims: "The real innocent martyrs on this earth are the animals, particularly the herbivorous."[9]

This obsession calls for close attention, from the moment someone seeks to denounce the heavy rhetoric—humanistic and progressive, amnesiac or ignorant—that leans on the extermination of the Jews during the Second World War the better to repeat the sophism according to which attention paid to animals is incompatible with devotion toward human beings. For Singer proclaims the mysterious concordance of suffering with a legitimacy that would seem provocative if one did not feel his work anchored in the initial shock of childhood. Thus the hero of his novel *Enemies*, Herman Broder, a survivor of the extermination camps, tortured by his memories, has retained from that period of his life an inability to bear animal suffering, as if that suffering alone had the power to bring back his own and that of his loved ones. When his companion Masha serves him stewed meat and groats, he reproaches her for cooking meat after he had made her promise to give it up. "'I promised myself, too,'" she replies, "'but without meat there's nothing to cook. God eats meat—human flesh. There are no vegetarians—none. If you had seen what I have seen, you would know that God approves of slaughter.'"[10] And when a mousetrap was set up in his room, "the sound of the trapped creatures in agony was too much for Herman. He would get up in the middle of the night and set them free."[11] When he is on vacation, in marvelous country where nature shows itself "as if it were the morning after creation," he thinks he hears "the screech of a chicken or a duck. Somewhere on this lovely summer morning, fowl were being slaugh-

8. Ibid., 57.
9. Ibid., 137.
10. Singer, *Enemies, a Love Story* (New York: Farrar, Straus and Giroux, 1972), 33.
11. Ibid., 41.

tered; Treblinka was everywhere."[12] And Herman repeated to anyone who would listen that "what the Nazis had done to the Jews, man was doing to animals."[13]

Armed with the same subversive analogy, the hero of Singer's *Certificate* stopped in front of a kosher sausage shop and silently addressed the sausages:

> "You were once alive, you suffered, but you're beyond your sorrows now. There's no trace of your writhing or suffering anywhere. Is there a memorial tablet somewhere in the cosmos on which it is written that a cow named Kvyatule allowed herself to be milked for eleven years? Then in the twelfth year, when her udder had shrunk, she was led to a slaughterhouse, where a blessing was recited over her and her throat was cut?" . . . Is there a paradise for the slaughtered cattle and chickens and pigs, for frogs that have been trodden underfoot, for fish that have been hooked and pulled from the sea, for the Jews whom Petlyura tortured,[14] whom the Bolsheviks shot, for the sixty thousand soldiers who shed their blood at Verdun?[15]

These are not just isolated remarks, a few inconsequential outbursts: they are part of a carefully-argued thesis based on dread, a terrible lesson from experience. On Yom Kippur, the same Herman Broder persists in his lamentation: "How could a fowl be used to redeem the sins of a human being? Why should a compassionate God accept such a sacrifice?"[16] His companion, Masha, reluctantly spins a fowl overhead, pronounces the ritual formulas, but stubbornly refuses to take the fowl to the sacrifice. "The two hens, one white, one brown, lay on the floor, their feet bound, their golden eyes looking sideways."[17]

Singer's frequent evocations of the eyes of suffering animals seem drawn from the same source as some of Chagall's paintings. And yet there is also a proximity to Chaïm Soutine. This can perhaps be explained by the artists' similar origins in Jewish villages of Poland and Lithuania. Soutine (whose first name, Chaïm, means "lives") experienced a sort of primal scene, in his youth; one does not have to be

12. Ibid., 112.

13. Ibid., 145.

14. Symon Petliura headed the Ukrainian military forces that carried out terrible pogroms in 1918.

15. Singer, *The Certificate*, trans. Leonard Wolf (New York: Farrar, Straus and Giroux, 1992), 227.

16. Singer, *Enemies*, 145.

17. Singer, Ibid.

an expert in the unconscious to suppose that the incident marked his inspiration, his obsessions as a painter. He had made several portraits of the village rabbi, and had thus defied the prohibition on representing the human face; to punish him for this profanation, the rabbi's nephew (who was a ritual butcher) dragged him back among the hanging carcasses and beat him to a pulp. So if Soutine's work is so constantly haunted by dead fowl and skinned cattle, it is not only owing to his admiration for the way Rembrandt and Chardin treated the same still-life subjects; it is also because the existence in the village of those Russian Jews, so powerfully structured by the letter of the Law, allowed them to perceive not as a lowly task but as a ritual act the moment of giving death, the palpitations of an animal whose blood (the soul) was draining away little by little. Thus there seems to have been an element of life and of thought common to Singer and Soutine: a refusal, above and beyond the organizing of violence by rules governing food, to be blind to the putting-to-death of animals. And even if their fixation on slaughter for the purpose of food does not seem to cover the modern and post-modern dimension (that is, less and less sacrificial) of the animal question, even if the ritual character of the immolation appears completely archaic today when compared to the common practices of the agro-food industry and the multiple sacrifices made in "experiments," the fact remains that the eyes of these scandalized children enriched works that recite or incite a *lamento* for mute suffering. In the societies of the Book, only mystics and artists have been given permission, or rather have extracted the right, to pray for animals.

In *Life and Fate*, Vasily Grossman in turn devotes an entire page to the death of a hen, to the point of making it the primal scene of what one doesn't quite dare call a "formation," when it is only the riddle of cruelty and death revealed to a child. The story begins with the purchase of a hen in the market where little David goes with his grandmother one day. He notices that the beloved old woman is carrying the hen upside down, holding it brutally by its feet:

> David was walking beside her. He wanted to reach out and help the hen lift up its powerless head; he wondered how his grandmother could be so inhumanly cruel. . . .
>
> They went into a yard; an old man in a skull-cap came out to meet them. His grandmother said something in Yiddish. The old man picked up the hen in his hands and began mumbling; the hen cack-

led unsuspectingly. Then the old man did something very quick—
something barely perceptible but obviously terrible—and threw the
hen over his shoulder. It ran off, feebly flapping its wings. David saw
that it had no head. The body was running all by itself. The old man
had killed it. After a few steps it fell to the earth, scratching with its
young, powerful claws, and died.

That night, David felt as though the damp smell of dead cows and
their slaughtered children had even got into his room.

Death, who had once lived in a fairy-tale forest where a fairy-tale
wolf was creeping up on a fairy-tale goat, was no longer confined to
the pages of a book. For the first time David felt very clearly that he
himself was mortal, not just in a fairy-tale way, but in actual fact.

He understood that one day his mother would die.[18]

Here again, before the violent and pathetic death of this poor barn-
yard animal, a death administered in the most total indifference, the
solitary and secret experience of the kinship of suffering submerges
the child, shapes the sensibility of a writer who will bear witness to
the greatest abominations of history.

It is in fact in *Life and Fate*, that great novel about Stalinism and
Nazism, that the solidarity of human and animal destiny seems to
impose itself with the most painful self-evidence.

Twice David went to the goods-yard and watched bulls, rams and pigs
being loaded into the cattle-wagons. He heard one of the bulls bellow-
ing loudly—complaining or asking for pity. The boy's soul was filled
with horror, but the tired railway-workers in their torn, dirty jackets
didn't so much as look around.[19]

And again:

Before slaughtering infected cattle, various preparatory measures have
to be carried out: pits and trenches must be dug; the cattle must be
transported to where they are to be slaughtered; instructions must be
issued to qualified workers.

If the local population helps the authorities to convey the infected
cattle to the slaughtering points and to catch beasts that have run
away, they do this not out of hatred of cows and calves, but out of an
instinct for self-preservation.

18. Vasily Grossman, *Life and Fate: A Novel*, trans. Robert Chandler (New York:
Harper and Row, 1985), 209.
19. Ibid., 211.

Similarly, when people are to be slaughtered en masse, the local population is not immediately gripped by a bloodthirsty hatred of the old men, women, and children who are to be destroyed. It is necessary to prepare the population by means of a special campaign. And in this case it is not enough to rely merely on the instinct for self-preservation; it is necessary to stir up feelings of real hatred and revulsion.[20]

In a book recounting his travels in Armenia, Grossman evokes the profile of a ewe. "There was something human about her—something Jewish, Armenian, mysterious, indifferent, unintelligent."[21] And he adds:

> Shepherds have been looking at sheep for thousands of years. And sheep, for their part, have been looking at shepherds. And so shepherds and sheep have become similar. A sheep's eyes look at a human being in a particular way; they are glassy and alienated. . . . The inhabitants of a Jewish ghetto would probably have looked at their Gestapo jailers with the same alienated disgust if the ghetto had existed for millennia, if day after day for five thousand years the Gestapo had been taking old women and children away to be destroyed in gas chambers.
>
> Oh God, how desperately mankind needs to atone, to beg for forgiveness. How long mankind needs to beg the sheep for forgiveness, to beg sheep not to go on looking at them with that glassy gaze. What meek and proud contempt that gaze contains. What godlike superiority—the superiority of an innocent herbivore over a murderer who writes books and creates computing machines![22]

The recollection of Nazism and the mention of industrial society in its most advanced form, cybernetics, are articulated here in a way that some will see as not very progressive, and yet it opens onto a humanism that finally measures up to the horrors of our times. Primo Levi himself did not fail to meet the disconcerting obligation to compare what is purportedly incomparable. In one chapter of *The Drowned and the Saved*, he describes the "scientifically useless tortures"[23]

---

20. Ibid., 213.

21. Grossman, *An Armenian Sketchbook*, trans. Robert and Elizabeth Chandler (New York: New York Review Books, 2013), 37.

22. Ibid.

23. Primo Levi, *The Drowned and the Saved*, trans. Raymond Rosenthal (New York: Vintage Books, 1989), 123.

that were inflicted—among others—on prisoners in Dachau for the Luftwaffe: "It seems significant to me," he writes, "to recall these abominations at a time when, for good reason, there are discussions as to within what limits it is permissible to perform painful scientific experiments on laboratory animals."[24]

Do we need still more examples of this obsession that has the power to overturn common preconceptions? If I were to be asked about the meaning of this accumulation, I would respond that it is the philosophical climate of the times that impels such a pathetic inventory. Indeed, reading these texts, one wonders, with a nostalgia of which one might be ashamed, where these writers got their inconceivable legitimacy—even more, where did they come by their certainty that they were speaking the truth about an evil reality, the authority that let them speak about animals and humans with all their sufferings conflated. Such freedom, not curbed by any moralism or humanism, probably stems first of all, in these writers, from an experience of the unspeakable strangeness that human language can disgorge. We know that the vast majority of those who got off the trains and found themselves on the path to extermination camps spoke no German, understood nothing from the words that were not addressed to them as human speech but that pelted down on them in angry screams. Now, to be subjected to a language that is no longer made of words but only of cries of hatred and that expresses nothing but the infinite power of terror, the paroxysm of murderous unintelligibility: is this not precisely the fate reserved for innumerable animals?[25] The fact that the terror of certain men could have been unintelligible to others, and that it could have increased in a context of widespread apathy—it turns out that writers have found no way to express this fact, to understand it and to make it understandable, except to evoke the anguish of animals in the face of indifferent human cruelty.

These associations, however transgressive they may be, are the end result of an awareness of disaster so intimate that they would have had to upset, definitively, the convenient sophistry, the hackneyed syllogisms, and even the old reflex: "We weren't animals, after all!" The ultimate and pathetic recourse that writers have found

24. Ibid., 124.
25. See Béatrice Berlowitz, "Comme des moutons à l'abattoir," in *Le messager européen* 4 (1990): 219–28.

to make the incomprehensible understandable ought at least to intimidate and to provide food for thought. To be sure, it was Schopenhauer who, after certain Greeks, gave the impetus (and the first metaphysical credits) to the theme of the unity in suffering of all living creatures. But the unrepresentable turn that history took has reshuffled the cards, and these authors of the second half of the twentieth century, through their belated meditations, have conferred on this common fate the veritably historical dimension of its pessimism. What had to happen for a philosopher to reach the point of saying: "Every animal suggests some crushing misfortune that took place in primeval times"?[26] After all, there was a time when people spoke of how carefree and pleasant it was to be an animal, about the play, expenditure, coincidence, jubilation of life unspoiled by the *pour-soi.* Authors such as Jules Renard and Colette in particular evoked, with gay knowledge, the misfortunes and the happiness of animals. Yes, no doubt, and it can be said that Canetti, Singer, Grossman and the others exclusively describe animals whose ills are manmade. And if the same holds true for Adorno and Horkheimer, it is because their pages, written with "blood of the beasts,"[27] remain marked by the anguish and melancholia of the days of exile, during which these authors found themselves living like uprooted animals, depressed, condemned to a foreign life during which they felt paradoxical elective affinities with Schopenhauer.

Yes, these pages resound painfully because those who wrote them were suddenly discovering the vast and polymorphous scope of the drama of which man is the protagonist, and because they were experiencing their originary kinship with beasts, hunted down and exterminated from age to age and more mercilessly than ever in the industrial age. Reflecting on the fate of animals led them to think through the fate of the majority of humans, equally subject to man-made ills. I don't know if it is fair to go so far as to look back through the ages in search of an origin for the abject death-dealing practices of the Nazis, and for human indifference in the face of mass executions. This is nevertheless what Adorno does, in a chapter of *Negative Dialectics,* when he asks whether it is possible to "think after Auschwitz," since

26. Theodor Adorno, in Theodor Adorno and Max Horkheimer, *Dialectic of Enlightenment,* trans. John Cumming (New York: Herder and Herder, 1972), 247.
27. This is the title of Georges Franju's first film (1948).

the belief in reconciliation of the dialectical sort has definitively lapsed. "A child, fond of an innkeeper named Adam, watched him club the rats pouring out of holes in the courtyard; it was in his image that the child made its own image of the first man."[28]

—Translated by Catherine Porter

ÉLISABETH DE FONTENAY

Return to Sacrifice

In the interview with Jacques Derrida published under the title "'Eating Well,' or the Calculation of the Subject,"[1] Jean-Luc Nancy raises a question about Heidegger and his 1929 course[2] that slightly displaces Derrida's reading of that text. Doesn't being "poor in world" appear to be a fragile and even contradictory concept as soon as Heidegger attributes to animals "a *sadness*, a sadness linked to their lack of world"? Nancy asks how sadness could be "simply nonhuman," and whether it does not attest in spite of everything to a relation to the world[3]: a question that is not without echoes of the Romantic melancholy inherent in all creatures.[4]

In his response, Derrida recalls in a first phase that the specific mode of this deprivation precludes its interpretation as a form of indigence, as "the *lack* of a world that would be human."[5] Then he adds:

> perhaps the animal is sad, perhaps it appears sad, because it indeed has a world, in the sense in which Heidegger speaks of a world as world of spirit, and because there is an openness of this world for it, but an openness without openness, a having (world) without having it. Whence the impression of sadness—for man or in relation to man, in

1. "'Eating Well,' or the Calculation of the Subject," in Jacques Derrida, *Points . . . : Interviews, 1974–1994*, trans. Peter Connor and Avital Ronell, ed. Élisabeth Weber (Stanford, Calif.: Stanford University Press, 1995), 255–87.
2. Martin Heidegger, *Kant und das Problem der Metaphysik*, trans. as *Kant and the Problem of Metaphysics*, by Richard Taft (Bloomington: Indiana University Press, 1997).
3. Derrida, "'Eating Well,'" 277.
4. Michael Haar, *The Song of the Earth: Heidegger and the Grounds of the History of Being*, trans. Reginald Lilly (Bloomington: See Michel Indiana University Press, 1993), 28, and 161, note 16: ". . . to all life there is attached an indestructible melancholy" [Schelling].
5. Derrida, "'Eating Well," 277.

YFS 127, *"Animots": Postanimality in French Thought*, ed. Senior, Clark, and Freccero, © 2015 by Yale University.

200

the society of man. . . . [A]s if the animal remained a man enshrouded, suffering, deprived on account of having access neither to the world of man that he nonetheless senses, nor to truth, speech, death, or the Being of the being as such.[6]

Derrida's way of taking Heidegger to the extreme limit of his concept of "privation" authorizes him in turn to accumulate questions that are pressing and perilous for the construction of the 1929 course: "Does the animal hear the call that originates responsibility? Does it question? . . . Is there an advent of the animal? . . . Do we have a responsibility toward the living in general?"[7] Beyond Heidegger's text, which becomes for him here just one moment in the metaphysical tradition, Derrida suggests that questions like these are posed in such a way that the answer can only be "no," and that this holds for "the whole canonized or hegemonic discourse of Western metaphysics or religions."[8]

Starting from this observation, Derrida risks the hypothesis of a sacrificial structure, even though he says that he is not sure that his designation is accurate.

> In any case, it is a matter of discerning a place left open, in the very structure of these discourses (which are also "cultures") for a non-criminal putting to death. Such are the executions of ingestion, incorporation, or introjection of the corpse. An operation as real as it is symbolic when the corpse is "animal" (and who can be made to believe that our cultures are carnivorous because animal proteins are irreplaceable?), a symbolic operation when the corpse is "human."[9]

This hypothesis, which allies deconstruction to a questioning that is psychoanalytical in style and vocabulary, along the lines of Freud's *Totem and Taboo* and his *Moses*, allows Derrida to affirm that despite the disruptions the philosophies of Heidegger and Levinas produce in traditional humanism, and despite the differences that separate them, both "remain profound humanisms *to the extent that they do not sacrifice sacrifice.*"[10] There is no general proscription on the taking of life; the prohibition pertains only to human life, to the lives of the neighbor or the other, to *Dasein*. For Heidegger, what is lacking in animals—

6. Ibid.
7. Ibid., 278.
8. Ibid.
9. Ibid.
10. Ibid., 279.

even if he does not say this in so many words—is above all the "being-with," the *Mitsein*, the *Gewissen*, the origins of moral conscience.

Derrida then articulates with this "sacrificial structure" the "humanist" critique of philosophies of life, their refusal to take life into consideration in the structure of the *Dasein*. He discerns in these philosophies a carno-phallogocentrist figure of subjectivity: that of the masculine subject, speaking and carnivorous. In our cultures, the master and active possessor of nature, the dominant figure, he explains, is the one who "accepts sacrifice and eats flesh."[11] If the borderlines, the opposition between the living and the nonliving and the one that would separate humans from animals, seem so uncertain, it is because this real or symbolic experience of eating is not separated from the experience of speaking and of internalizing: modes of appropriation-assimilation of the other. Here, Derrida seems close to the positions of the anthropological structuralism of Claude Lévi-Strauss, for whom the exchange of words, women, and services—as well as of food, of course—function in a homologous way. He even says that our cultures are anthropophagic in spite of themselves, given the extent to which assimilation of the other and assimilation by the other constitute the origin of our exchange behaviors, and the extent to which this circulation passes by way of the various orifices, orality being only the most obvious opening of what is proper to us. "The moral question is thus not, nor has it ever been: should one eat or not eat, eat this and not that, the living or the nonliving, man or animal, but since *one must* eat in any case . . . , *how* for goodness' sake should one *eat well [bien manger]*?"[12] The *bien* of this *il faut bien manger* is overdetermined, owing to the ambiguity of the French adverb, which signifies here both the obligation to nourish oneself appropriately, with others and according to the rules of hospitality or quite simply of civility, and the vital necessity to nourish oneself with flesh. Now, we recall that in the Western Judaic tradition, it was only after the Flood that permission was given to kill in order to eat, because from that point on it was necessary to do so, but we also recall that the authorization was not granted without restrictions and the unprecedented complications of which we are aware.[13]

11. Ibid., 281.
12. Ibid., 282.
13. See Élisabeth de Fontenay, *Le silence des bêtes: la philosophie à l'épreuve de l'animalité* (Paris: Fayard, 1998), part VII, chapter 3, "Les narines du Dieu unique," 227–38.

Returning to the nodal point of his analysis, Derrida calls the authorization and justification given to the killing of animals "denegation" of murder, and he can say: "I would link this denegation to the violent institution of the 'who' as subject."[14] Moreover, he does not fail to point out that the question of "the living 'who'" is at the heart of the questioning induced by contemporary medicine and by what is called bioethics. This is to say how vertiginous his remark appears, if we limit ourselves strictly to the viewpoint of alimentary murder and sacrifice. I shall take it back to the point of departure: eating flesh, sacrifice, the subject. It seems to me in fact that the extrapolation, generalization, and radicalization of this sacrificial structure, noticed by him, end up obliterating animals and their murder, and take on a dimension that is more anthropological than deconstructive. Not that this extension to the totality of the symbolic strikes me as abusive—for, if the symbolic comes into play, all features of thought and culture have to constitute a system—but the subtle metonymy that is constantly at work there surely threatens to confuse the issue.

Thought about sacrifice is certainly not lacking in Derrida, were it only in the interview "Ick bünn all hier," where, with reference to Heidegger, he evokes sacrifice in two passages.[15] Nevertheless, do we not find in these pages what, in order to distinguish himself from Mauss and Cassirer, Marcel Detienne called a spiritualization of sacrifice, a consequence of the symbolization and generalization authorized by the psychoanalytic approach, to be sure, and one that of course is not spiritualist in the slightest? For, if we stay with sacrifice itself, alimentary sacrifice, at least, and if we consequently refuse to blend together in a single analysis the immolation of victims on an altar, or even their killing by butchers respecting the ritual laws of slaughter, with the practice of eating flesh secularized by Christianity, we are bound to recognize that there is no longer a single Christian Westerner who is immersed in a civilization of sacrifice. And it is even by virtue of this generalization—internalization of a bloody sacrifice, henceforth obsolete or prohibited—that the sacrificial drive, which is confused with the capacity to be structured symbolically, comes to take on all sorts of distorted and no doubt efficacious forms. But the most obvious consequence of this "progress" of sacrifice is

14. Derrida, "'Eating Well,'" 283.
15. "Istrice 2: Ick bünn all hier," trans. Peggy Kamuf, in Derrida, Points . . . , 306, 308.

that "we" eat anything at all in any way we like, we give life to animals, we make them live and die in the process of a "rational" technicity that is not unrelated to the technologies of concentration, if not of extermination, that marked the twentieth century with the seal of the unrepresentable. A "great feast" ("*La grande bouffe*"[16]) and a "great massacre" ("*le grand massacre*"[17]) without scruples: such is the modernity of a fate that is common—unbeknownst to the ones and to most of the others—to animals and man. Because I do not separate the reading of "'Eating Well,'" or the Calculation of the Subject" from that of "Che cos'è la poesia?"[18] I would fear that what, with regard to the death of the Derridean hedgehog, I shall call the historiality of life, that is, the body of thought about the modern condition—the thought of a life form so profane that it cannot be further desecrated—will dissolve into an unthought of the symbolic. Not—it must be said again—that in some irresponsible burst of nostalgia I would have "us" go back to sacrifices. But I only wonder what manner of being together—among men, among men and women, among the sick and the well, among the dead and the living, among children and adults, among the insane and the sane, among humans and animals, among animals themselves—could help re-inscribe animals within a symbolic chain that no longer cheapens their lives.

—Translated by Catherine Porter

16. The title of a film by Marco Ferreri, 1973.

17. The title of a memorable book by Michel Damien, Alfred Kastler, and Jean-Claude Nouet (Paris: Fayard, 1981).

18. Trans. Peggy Kamuf, in Derrida, *Points . . .* , 288–99.

ANAT PICK

Reflexive Realism in René Clément's *Forbidden Games*

> What happened to me that night, what moved me to tears at the time, was *both like a thought and like a proof* that there is no supremacy, neither of humans nor of beasts, that there are only passages, fleeting sovereignties, occasions, escapes, encounters.
>
> —Jean-Christophe Bailly[1]

I. THOUGHT AND PROOF

This essay examines figural and physical incursions into fictional space-time in René Clément's neorealist film *Forbidden Games/ Jeux interdits* (1952) by the figures and bodies of animals, in particular the body of one little dog, Jock. These incursions extend to the film's other frames: that of genre, narrative point-of-view, as well as to the film's historical and ethical frameworks. Beginning with a German air raid on a civilian convoy fleeing Paris in June 1940, *Jeux interdits* centers on the newly orphaned Paulette (Brigitte Fossey). Carrying her dead dog Jock, Paulette meets the farmer's son Michel Dollé (Georges Poujouly) and the two proceed to spend their time building an animal cemetery, which they furnish with creatures big and small and stolen crosses. When their deeds are exposed, the Dollés hand Paulette over to the Red Cross in the film's closing scenes.

Paulette's "dead dog will command a far greater portion of the little girl's sorrow than the corpses of her parents, which she must leave behind at the side of the road."[2] If the dying dog (who remains uncredited) in the film's memorable opening scene of the Luftwaffe attack affects us more vividly and more deeply than the deaths of humans, this is because, as Vivian Sobchack has argued, we know that

---

1. Jean-Christophe Bailly, *The Animal Side*, trans. Catherine Porter (New York: Fordham University Press, 2011), 2.

2. André Bazin, "Jeux interdits," in *Bazin at Work: Major Essays & Reviews From the Forties & Fifties*, ed. Bert Cardullo, trans. Alain Piette and Bert Cardullo (New York: Routledge, 1997), 129–136, 135.

YFS 127, *"Animots": Postanimality in French Thought*, ed. Senior, Clark, and Freccero, © 2015 by Yale University.

the dog is not playing dead, and this unsettles the boundaries of the fictional world of the film. Being so moved, our response mirrors that of the five-year old Paulette, though our reasons are different.[3] The erosion of boundaries between the staged but real spectacle of animal vulnerability, and other staged but unreal profilmic events helps to think through the peculiarity of cinematic animals, which, as Jonathan Burt claimed, mark an "extreme collapse between the figural and the real."[4]

This doubling of the animal, as indexical imprint and symbol, recurs in Jean-Christophe Bailly's extended essay on animals, *Le versant animal* (2007), published in English as *The Animal Side* (2011), in the dual form of "thought" and "proof." Animals are immanence and flesh, but living flesh itself is an articulation and a working out, and so, in fact, is thought: "the suspicion arises that *an animal itself is or might be something like a thought.*"[5] Here Bailly may have in mind Claude Lévi-Strauss's assertion that "animals are good to think."[6] But animals do not merely inspire human thought, or awaken human subjectivity. If animals are "something like a thought," then life itself is the fleshing out or the extrapolation of "mind," each life its own conjugation of being. Bailly pursues the parallelism of being and thought in the work of Rilke, Jakob von Uexküll, and Heidegger, as well as in that of Bataille and Deleuze, in order to return to animals the richness (and dignity) that Heidegger deemed their lives lacked.

The ontological mode of animal life-thought is "pensivity." Animal pensivity (*la pensivité des animaux*[7]) is neither self-reflection and reason, nor their absence. If animals are proof and thought, evidentiary and reflective, and if the animals in *Jeux interdits*, too, are "something like a thought," what sort of thought are they? Moreover, how might pensivity as a modality of being and thinking help to illuminate the film, whose protagonists are children whose own lives revolve around their encounters with animals, living and dead?

---

3. To the fictional character Paulette, the death of her parents and the death of her dog are equally real, though unequally traumatizing. The five year-old actress, Brigitte Fossey, on the other hand, is placed in a similar position to viewers: she would have known that no humans actually died, but would have realized that the puppy was not simply "acting."

4. Jonathan Burt, *Animals in Film* (London: Reaktion, 2002), 44.

5. Bailly, *The Animal Side*, 13 (my emphasis).

6. See Claude Lévi-Strauss, *Totemism*, trans. Rodney Needham (London: Merlin Press, 1964).

7. Bailly, *Le versant animal*, 15.

For Bailly, the overlaying of proof and thought is crystallized in the animal encounter that challenges human exceptionalism. Animals both demonstrate and make possible the knowledge that there is "no supremacy, neither of humans nor of beasts, that there are only passages, fleeting sovereignties, occasions, escapes, encounters." To follow Bailly is not, therefore, to offer a reading of Clément's representations of animals, representations that are ultimately banal, or to interpret the film through its animal figures. What follows is occasioned by, rather than integral to, the straightforward meaning of animals in *Jeux interdits*. To the extent that the film's animals are visually prominent, it is difficult to write about them. Animal life disappears as soon as it is put to use in the service of the film's chief preoccupations: the relations between adult reality—specifically war—and the world of children, and the superficially antithetical genres of the war film and the children's film. To retrieve from the film's doubly instrumental attitude to animals (as symbols in the film-world, and as pawns of the production itself) a different resonance, what Bailly calls "some small discrepancy"[8] of the animal encounter, it is necessary to read beyond, even counter to, the film's explicit logic of displacement, by which mourned animals stand in for the mourning of humans under the intolerable shadow of war.

II. ETIQUETTES OF THE REAL

Proof and thought graph neatly onto the cinematic axes of documentary and fiction that collide (or collapse) at the point where questions of reality and realism emerge. In *Carnal Thoughts*, Vivian Sobchack discusses the different codes that govern the representation of death in moving images. The sequence of rabbit shooting in Jean Renoir's *The Rules of the Game/ La règle du jeu* (1938) interrupts fictional space by introducing the actuality of animal death: "it is a real rabbit we see die in the service of the narrative and *for* the fiction. The human character who dies, however, does so only *in* the fiction."[9] "For me," Sobchack writes,

> the rabbit's onscreen death was—and still is—a good deal *more* shocking and disturbing than the death of the human character. And this, I would maintain, is because the rabbit's death ruptures the

8. Bailly, *The Animal Side*, 1.
9. Vivian Sobchack, *Carnal Thoughts: Embodiment and Moving Image Culture* (Berkeley: University of California Press, 2004), 245.

Figure 1. Paulette and the dead Jock on the bridge after the bombing. *Forbidden Games*, René Clément, 1952.

autonomous and homogenous space of the fiction through which it briefly scampered. Indeed, its *quivering death leap* transformed fictional into documentary space, symbolic into indexical representation, *my affective investment in the irreal and fictional into a documentary consciousness charged with a sense of the world*, existence, bodily mortification and mortality, and all the rest of the real that is in excess of fiction.[10]

Although information on the fate of the real Jock is vague, Clément, like Renoir, manipulates animal bodies in the midst of the fiction in the service of realism.[11] As Paulette cuddles Jock in her arms, the dog's legs quiver and twitch, and we know he has died [See Figure 1].

Whether or not the scene depicts the actual death of the dog is not my immediate concern. I am interested instead in one type of onscreen movement, which for Sobchack is particularly charged: the

10. Sobchack, *Carnal Thoughts*, 269 (my emphasis).
11. There is scant information on the shooting of the scenes of Jock's death. Anecdotal reports suggest that Clément attached electrodes to the dog's belly to induce the visible leg spasms, and that a fake dog was later thrown into the river. Online discussions of the film return again and again to the issue of the reality or unreality of the dog's death.

"quivering" leap in the scene from Renoir that transforms fictional space. Clément repeats the motion in Jock's leg spasms as he dies in Paulette's arms. The reflexive jerking at the indeterminate moment of death palpably breaches the actuality-fiction divide. It is a gesture that, like Sobchack, many viewers of *Jeux interdits* find uniquely *moving*. I will later return to the importance of these animal motion reflexes: the spontaneous twitching and flinching that unsettle the frame and constitute something like a "reflex arc" of film, in juxtaposition to Giorgio Agamben's humanistic cinema of gesture. Before doing so, it is important to think through the transformation from fiction to documentary that Sobchack describes.

Whereas for Sobchack animal death finally transcends fiction by investing it with "a sense of the world, existence . . . and all the rest of the real that is in excess of fiction," onscreen animal violence frequently functions in the opposite way, securing the fictional realm as the hallmark of human expression and thus maintaining a stable human-animal divide.

The respective ethics of documentary and fiction are chiastic: in wildlife filmmaking, for example, the real must not be (seen to be) staged or directed, and violence—associated with the raw state of "nature"—takes place without human intervention. In the wildlife or natural history film, it is the inherent violence of nature that upholds the hierarchical distinction between humans and animals. In the fiction film, conversely, the reality of art—associated with the exceptional reality of "man"—demands intervention and dramatic direction. What constitutes the real in one mode cancels it out in the other: the validity of fiction as an expression of human freedom is confirmed through the actual killing of animals, not least when this killing is used to critique violence (against humans). In the violent act, hierarchical distinctions between humans and animals are reinforced.[12] The reality of staged animal violence or death confers on film the seriousness and integrity of its artistic intentions. The real violence visited on animals in *Jeux interdits* is therefore highly

12. This is the case in quite a few European art films that do not seek the official approval of the American Humane Association (AHA). The "no animals were harmed in the making of this film" label has been the subject of ongoing controversy and suggests that what counts as animal cruelty is largely a matter codification, or etiquette. On the uses of animal death in art cinema, see my critique of the films of Michael Haneke in *Creaturely Poetics: Animality and Vulnerability in Literature and Film* (New York: Columbia University Press, 2011).

contrived; as staged and real, its role is not to transcend but to enhance the fiction, to lend it validity *as unreal*—as art.

Documentary and fiction, then, accrue their "reality value" in inverse ways. We are not dealing here with the presence or absence of reality, but with opposing *etiquettes of the real*. In the absence of an ontological divide between documentary and fiction, each filmic mode seeks to contract, construct, and honor the world of its making as a matter of etiquette.

III. UNFLINCHING

Clément's early training as a documentarian is evident in his first feature *The Battle of the Rails/ La bataille du rail* (1946), on the sabotaging of the German war effort by French Resistance railway workers. The neorealism of *Jeux interdits* borrows as freely from Eisensteinian montage (referenced in the first bombing sequence) as it does from French farce. The film's oblique treatment of World War II sets it apart from the conventional war film. In its focus on marginal beings (children, peasants, and animals) and fleeting events (Paulette's stay with the Dollé family is short lived; in the final scene at a Red Cross refugee center, Paulette disappears from view calling out for Michel), *Jeux interdits* may in fact tell us more about war than its generic counterparts.

What do dogs know of war? Does Jock's death contribute something to our understanding and critique of war? A similar question arises in the nonfictional context of the so-called "Liepaja film," less than two minutes of footage shot by German Navy officer Reinhard Wiener in July 1941 at the scene of a mass execution of Latvian Jews by the *Einsatzgruppen*. In the Wiener film, a small dog suddenly appears in the frame: "[f]or a fleeting instant, the dog's body registers the shock of the gunfire, while the crowd that has come to watch—or at least be present—at [sic] the execution stands mostly motionless, stilled by their spectatorial fascination with and moral unconcern for what has just happened."[13] If the twitching of Clément's dog punctures the fictional frame of *Jeux interdits*, the startled gesture of the Liepaja dog imbues the documentary footage with an uncertain, spec-

---

13. David L. Clark, "Towards a Prehistory of the Postanimal," 55. http://www.humanities.mcmaster.ca/~dclark/publications.html, accessed August 24, 2013. The final version of this paper appears in this volume as "What Remains To Be Seen: Animal, Atrocity, Witness."

ulative quality. The dog's presence and behavior raise questions about the "crisis of witnessing"[14] made palpable by the Liepaja film.

It is not the similarity between the two dogs that is striking (they could both be Jack Russell terriers, with light fur and dark patches), or the films' strange mirroring of one another—Clément's dog is present in a dramatization of human mass killing; the Liepaja dog is on the scene of an actual massacre. It is not even the shared elements of performance, staging, and shooting, or the necessity of an audience (the bystanders in Liepaja, and us, the cinema viewers, in Clément). What is remarkable is that in both films, the colossal event of war is haunted by the negligible presence of a dog, whose very marginality allows for a different contemplation of war.

In "Towards a Prehistory of the Postanimal," David L. Clark notes that, unique among scholars of the Liepaja film, the historian David Marwell sees the dog: "what catches Marwell's discerning eye is the uncanny arrival of an animal, a little dog, who darts excitedly across the foreground of the field of view at the moment that the executioners' guns go off."[15] Clark asks whether we could consider the dog as a witness, and if so, "what burden does the apparition of this animal bear?"[16] "Can an animal witness atrocity?"[17] Clark's answer is that to deny the dog the possibility of witnessing not only rehearses the old philosophic disavowals that define animals as lacking in capacities (of thought, agency, morality, language, and so on), but also misconceives the nature of testimony as a form of *being-for-the-other* which does not trade in facts, information, or evidence. Thus Clark, with Bailly and Derrida, wants to salvage nonhuman being from the impoverished ontologies that European philosophy, and, one ought to add, European politics tainted by genocide, has forced upon animals. "A thoughtlessness, an 'animal' witlessness, let us say, in honor of the dog who flinches—without reflection and without needing to reflect—at the sudden sound of the gunfire, and whose flinching proves to be otherwise than a privation."[18] Read beyond privation and lack, the dog's response makes possible nonhuman witnessing as that

14. Clark, Ibid., 54.
15. Ibid., 54.
16. Ibid., 61.
17. Ibid., 64.
18. Clark, "'Not ours, this death, to take into our bones': The Postanimal after the Posthuman," *World Picture* 7 (Autumn 2012), 10. http://www.worldpicture journal.com/WP_7/Clark.html, accessed May 16, 2014.

which is "known" without being articulated, understood with one's body without being fully thought; beyond the taxonomies of perpetrators, victims, and bystanders, the dog speaks—speaks to and for us—the unspeakable.

Like Jock in *Jeux interdits*, the Liepaja dog "has the potential to interrupt" established ways of seeing and thinking.[19] For Clark, the dog may be the "accidental witness" par excellence, embodying not just the precarity of the lives that are violently extinguished but of the event of witnessing itself that may be lost or go unheeded. On the one hand, Clark explains, the "creature's *reflex reaction* expresses or seems to express a lack of consciousness, which in turn is available as a figure for a lack of conscience,"[20] making the presence of a domestic pet at the site of the murders nothing more than the cruelest of jokes. On the other hand, "the dog reacts viscerally where no one seems willing or able to respond morally."[21]

There are a number of ways of thinking through the testamentary force of the animal moment in the Liepaja film. For me, in the context of this piece, the dog's reflexive response disrupts the supplementary chain of human exceptions that sets, and resets, "us"—highly contingent in the purview of genocide—apart from the beasts. Like language, or reason, moral judgment or tool use, "witnessing" can piously shore up human exceptionalism, when, ironically, what witnessing bears witness to in this case is the genocidal logic that singles out the "human" in the first place; a bearing witness to the human as a false universal. The dog-as-witness undoes human exceptionalism in the anticipation of a different ethos, a different community. "Perhaps it takes a nonhuman animal, *this* animal," Clark writes, "darting about this blood-soaked sand-dune on the outskirts of Liepaja, to throw into relief the limitless violence of that 'anthropocentric conceit,' and the limitless interdependencies that await us in a more frankly ethical (post)human world."[22]

A second undoing, as Derrida's "The Animal That Therefore I Am," is quick to remind us, is of the distinction between *reaction* (mechanical and mindless, that is, animal) and *response* (self-conscious and mindful, so human): "[t]he said question of the said animal in its entirety comes down to knowing not whether the animal speaks but

19. Clark, "Postanimal," 56.
20. Ibid., 63 (my emphasis).
21. Ibid.
22. Clark, "'Not ours, this death," 10–11.

whether one can know what *respond* means. And how to distinguish a response from a reaction."[23] At the moment of animal flinching, something in us realizes that the distinction between the thoughtful and unthinking on which is erected the entire ethico-political edifice of human civilization and nonhuman barbarism, as well as the distinction between human life (*bios*) and bare animal life (*zoē*), fails to account for the atrocities we are watching. For it is precisely the infinitesimal difference between *reflex* and *reflection* to which the dog of Liepaja testifies, which is why the dog's image, if we choose to acknowledge it, cannot fail to affect us.

The dogs in Clément and in the Liepaja film do not belong. In Clément, as already discussed, the dog displaces and sublimates (Paulette's true loss of her parents), and functions as a guarantor of cinematic merit (for us, consumers of the serious art film). In Liepaja, the dog must remain, to borrow Judith Butler's terminology, "unframed" and unseen, his/her presence ascribed to chance and quickly dispatched. But the involuntary responses of nonhuman animals in both films—and the equally involuntary human responses to those responses—pertain to the medium's grounding in movement and gesture over representation. In their treatment of World War II, furthermore, the films call attention to the dissolution, or destruction, of gesture at the moment of a catastrophic breakdown of modern European civilization.

In "Notes on Gesture," Agamben proposes a philosophy of film, influenced by Deleuze, that reconfigures cinema as gestural rather than imagistic.[24] The image is frozen and fixed, while the gesture is movement and action. But, even as action, "[w]hat characterizes the gesture is that in it nothing is being produced or acted, but rather something is being endured and supported. The gesture, in other words, opens the sphere of *ethos* as the more proper sphere of that which is human."[25] The gesture is not directed toward any particular end by representing purposive activity. It gestures the gestural as pure

23. Jacques Derrida, "The Animal That Therefore I Am (More to Follow)," trans. David Wills, *Critical Inquiry*, 28/2 (Winter 2002): 369–418, 377.

24. On Agamben's relation to Deleuze, see Benjamin Noys, "Gestural Cinema? Giorgio Agamben on Film," *Film-Philosophy* 8/22 (July 2004), http://www.film-philosophy.com/vol8–2004/n22noys, accessed November 18, 2013.

25. Giorgio Agamben, "Notes on Gesture," in *Means Without Ends: Notes on Politics*, trans. Vincenzo Binetti and Cesare Casarino (Minneapolis: University of Minnesota Press, 2000), 49–60, 57.

medium, as a mode of communicability without content (resembling Levinasian *saying*), and so is inherently ethical and political, that is intersubjective and communal: "the gesture is . . . communication of a communicability. It has precisely nothing to say because what it shows is the being-in-language of human being as pure mediality."[26] Because being-in-language exceeds any specific linguistic formation, "the gesture is essentially always a gesture of not being able to figure something out in language."[27] The relation between gesture and witnessing as modes of communicability on the threshold of verbal expression is clear enough. The gesture "allows the emergence of the being-in-medium *of human beings*, and thus opens the ethical dimension *for them*"; "what is relayed *to human beings* in gestures is not the sphere of an end in itself but rather the sphere of pure and endless mediality."[28] Yet what is it about the fundamental vital expressiveness of gesture that limits it to human beings? The epithet "human" in this essay gives the impression of an uneasy insertion, an add-on that brackets off gesture from a more general mediality in order to secure human chosenness. The problem with the designation "human" in "Notes on Gesture" is that it fails to gesture in precisely the way Agamben intends: it operates as a means to an end of human exclusivity, and so betrays pure mediality.

By reserving gesture as exclusively human, Agamben forecloses (flinches in the face of) the possibility of a more-than-human *ethos* that communicates and communes within and across species. An anthropocentric reading of gesture ignores the fundamental mediality of *all* life, from rudimentary biological systems based on the transmission of biochemical signals, to the complex sentient life forms privileged by humans, and even to so-called nonliving systems where data is distributed across information interfaces. A truly gestural cinema would fall short if it refused to account for the fundamental gestural structure of organic (and inorganic) life as such.

The involuntary reflexes in Clément and the Liepaja film push gestural film toward a broader expressivity of the living. Beyond anthropocentrism, as *ciné-malité*, film is not only gestural but reflexive; its mediality is not restricted to human being-in-language, but opens onto expression and communicability beyond the human.

---

26. Agamben, "Notes on Gesture," 59.
27. Ibid.
28. Ibid., 57, 58 (my emphasis).

IV. PENSIVITY, CHILDHOOD, AND FILM

> And in these moments of nakedness, under the gaze of the animal, everything can happen to me, I am like a child ready for the apocalypse.
>
> —Jacques Derrida[29]

"I would like to have a video camera set up," says Bailly in the opening "shot"—this is a text that begins like a movie—of *The Animal Side*:

> one that could position itself on this narrow uphill road (a camera that would know what to do, that would film a car speeding off into the night) and follow me. This is one of those moments of relationships—between consciousness and the countryside, between the speed of a point in motion and the space around it . . . the road becomes an estuary in which one is moving upstream. . . . Even if one is not speeding, there is a pure cinematic sensation of irreversible thrust, headlong flight forward, gliding.[30]

One is initially tempted to list the films in which a car snakes up the road in the dark, only to realize that the sequence does not belong in this film or that but is quintessentially cinematic. For Bailly, in the following passage, cinema becomes a three-way meeting between the inhuman mechanics of surveillance, the central consciousness of a human subject (cocooned in the carapace of the moving automobile), and the sudden disruption of an animal: "someone emerges—a phantom, a beast, for only a beast can burst forth in this way. A deer has come out of the undergrowth; frightened, it runs up the road, trapped between the hedgerows. . . . It rushes ahead, just as it is, just as it has to be—fear and beauty, *quivering grace*, lightness."[31] Again, the reflexive quiver marks the encounter that allows the worlds of humans and animals to be momentarily glimpsed and touched, "yes, touched with my eyes, despite the impossibility."[32]

The impossible is not merely the synesthetic tactility of sight—touching with one's eyes—but the abyss that Bailly (like Derrida) posits between humans and animals, which is never fully crossed. In place of a breaching of boundaries at which human and animal

29. Derrida, "The Animal That Therefore I Am," 381.
30. Bailly, *The Animal Side*, 1.
31. Ibid., 1 (my emphasis).
32. Ibid., 2.

become co-present; there is tentative, timid "contact, always singular and always consisting of touch, that is the ordinary mode of the bond between them and us—something scarcely formed, always nascent."[33] Indeed, one aspect of contact-as-touch involves the partiality and unreliability of feeling one's way in the dark. The touching described by Bailly departs from the tradition Derrida critiques, in his book on Jean-Luc Nancy, as "haptology," since it does not seek to make readily present the one who is touched.[34] As Laura McMahon explores in her work on the "cinema of contact," Nancy advances a new form of cinematic realism via the figure of touch. Nancy also redefines the notion of cinematic "evidence"—not unlike the meaning of "proof" that I have been tracing here in Bailly—as the simultaneity of revelation and occlusion. Touch, then, is not a form of verification but a mode of relation that avoids immediacy and totalization; it, too, is something between thought and proof.[35]

The abyss between humans and animals echoes Derrida's second hypothesis in "The Animal That Therefore I Am" concerning the "limit as rupture or abyss between those who say 'we men,' 'I, a man,' and what this man among men who say 'we,' what he calls the animal or animals."[36] Derrida's argument is directed both against Heideggerian humanism (where the abyss that separates human from animal is absolute and essential), and biological continuism, of the kind that inflects some "new materialist" relational ontologies that treat all bodies and objects as networked together in more or less horizontal arrangements of comingling matter. The abyss for Bailly and Derrida is not a border but an enumeration of borders. As Derrida puts it:

> The discussion becomes interesting once, instead of asking whether or not there is a discontinuous limit, one attempts to think what a limit becomes once it is abyssal, once the frontier no longer forms a single indivisible line but more than one internally divided line, once, as a result, it can no longer be traced, objectified, or counted as single and indivisible.[37]

---

33. Bailly, Ibid., 5.

34. See Derrida, *On Touching—Jean-Luc Nancy*, trans. Christine Irizarry (Stanford: Stanford University Press, 2005).

35. See Laura McMahon, "Post-deconstructive realism? Nancy's Cinema of Contact," *New Review of Film and Television Studies* 8/1 (2010): 73–93, and *The Cinema of Contact* (Oxford: Legenda, 2011).

36. Derrida, "The Animal That Therefore I Am," 398.

37. Ibid., 399.

The Animal Side is precisely such a reflection on "what a limit becomes once it is abyssal." Cinema recurs in this text as a way of seeing and thinking—evidentiary and reflective—that affirms the melancholy bond between humans and animals, a bond which Bailly describes, after Bataille, as "lost intimacy."[38] As a capturing and enframing device, cinema is both a revealer and creator of worlds. This "worlding" function, to use Donna Haraway's term in another context, allows cinema to actively make (or make up) multiple worlds that for Bailly come into being at the point of liminal difference between human and nonhuman being, where an opening is present at the very point of hermetic enclosure.

In its melancholy configuration, Bailly's ontology of the animal as "the great other, the first companion"[39] strikes me as still anthropocentric, even as it seeks to return to animals what has been stolen from them by a strident humanism that denies animals their place in the world, if only in the form of disappearance and loss. But I am less interested here in critiquing Bailly's residual humanism than in the seismic force Bailly associates with animals to alter "minded" topographies and set thinking off-course, a capacity that is closely linked to image-making. Such a shifting of the terrains of the mind is conveyed by the French word "versant": the sloping or tilting of thought brought about by the animal encounter.

The tilting of thought is pictured by Bailly as an opening onto the interim space of pensivity. Pensivity is neither abstract reasoning with which humans are allegedly uniquely endowed nor the stupor usually attributed to animals. Animals mark a *"pensive* path"[40] [la voie *pensive*] that links what is thought of as thought (self-reflection) in humans, construed as lack (dimness and dumbness) in animals, and as a gift (spontaneity and immediacy) in children, namely their innocence.

Pensivity describes Paulette's being-in-the-world of *Jeux interdits* that is neither mindless nor innocent, but childlike. Moreover, how can pensivity, characteristic of this strange film as a whole, help explain its awkward place in the history of French cinema? The film's oddities, from its generic misalliance, to its auteurist indistinction, its moral and historical ambiguities, or its initial dismissal by the

38. Bailly, *The Animal Side*, 10.
39. Ibid., 9.
40. Ibid., 15.

proponents of the *nouvelle vague*, suggest something offbeat and lop-sided, and a concern with marginality, most obviously the children's, but also of the poor, abject peasants, whose relation to the war is tenuous.[41]

The demarcations of genre are equally tenuous: *Jeux interdits* is not a children's film, a war film, or an animal film. Clément surveys the conventions of genre as an animal gazes out into Rilke's *open*. The film's generic overtures are tentative and misleading. The opening sequence of the German bombardment seems to promise convention, but by the end of the scene the drama has shifted from the realm of history (and the war movie), to the realm of the child. The self-proclaimed global dimensions of a "World War" are recalibrated to those of a child's universe. The direction, too, is scaled down and tight: "the film's terse suggestiveness," writes Peter Matthews, is like a short story, "slight" in the best possible way: "*Forbidden Games* is a distinctly slender work. Which is to say that it's exactly scaled to the intimate, laconic universe of children."[42] From this point on, the rest of the film will be a little bit skewed, made to fit, not a child's point of view but the coordinates of a child's world. Instead of inhabiting the child's world, the omniscient camera confirms that this world of the child exists. This is a world apart from the film's other worlds of the feuding peasants, and most importantly, of the war that announces the film's false start, then gradually fades from view.

Far from essentializing childhood as either innocent or as casually cruel, the film adjusts its dimensions to the world of children. This rescaling takes place primarily through the five-year old Paulette. Michel is ten, and his world, though still intersecting with hers, is already drifting toward adolescence. Animals are central to the world of the children, from the old barn owl (called the Mayor), to the chickens and bees who end up in Paulette and Michel's cemetery. The film's preoccupation with marginal beings—children and animals—without recourse to the conventional children or animal film—makes possible the modifications of worldhood.

---

41. On Clément's peculiar standing within French cinema and his authorial effacement, see Noël Herpe's "René Clément: L'auteur sans visage," *Positif* (May 1996): 78–79.

42. Peter Matthews, "Forbidden Games: Death and the Maiden," http://www .criterion.com/current/posts/408-forbidden-games-death-and-the-maiden, accessed November 18, 2013.

In his essay on *Jeux interdits*, Bazin compares the film to two archetypes of the children's film. Nikolai Ekk's *Road to Life* (1932) and *Emil and the Detectives* (1931) conform to a "traditional ethical mythology,"[43] in which in "a Manichaeistic universe, the child represents the forces of good."[44] Both films illustrate "a certain belief in the 'original innocence' of children. Evil in a child's world (whether moral or physical, and especially when the child becomes a martyr to his misdeeds) is the supreme moral scandal. Hence there is no 'guilty' or 'bad' child, only a 'delinquent,' 'misguided,' or 'unhappy' one."[45] Clément's film, on the other hand, eschews such moral mythology:

> [It] wants to have these two children occupy a place, in a story whose protagonists they happen to be, that is essentially identical to the one adult characters might have occupied. Their actions, their manner, what we can grasp of their thought, are not at all the reflections of an a priori idea about childhood. Michel and Paulette are neither good nor bad children: their behavior, which is by no means absurd, has to do only with psychology, and not in the slightest with morality. It is the adults, to whom the logic of Michel and Paulette's games is foreign, who project upon them a moral significance.[46]

What looks like morality or immorality (goodness or badness) is an adult imposition that perceives childhood only in hindsight. This is illustrated in *Jeux interdits*' anti-clericalism and the film's well-nigh misanthropic exposure of the phony, and petty, morality of priest and congregation alike. Looking back as adults, we tend to idealize, condemn, or see childhood teleologically as "just a phase." Bazin's emphasis in the passage on place and placing suggests that Paulette and Michel inhabit a world of their own whose measures and meanings are free from prefabricated adult definitions.[47] "The so-called pessimism for which Clément has so often been reproached . . . is in reality nothing more than the director's refusal to insert his child characters

43. Bazin, "Jeux interdits," 132.
44. Ibid., 133.
45. Ibid., 132.
46. Ibid., 133–34.
47. Something similar happens in Harmony Korine's 2012 film, *Spring Breakers*, which constructs an insular world of youth. There too, "forbidden games" are forbidden only if we insist on judging youth as a not-yet-realized adulthood. What the war allows Clément to do in *Jeux interdits*, spring break allows Korine to do in *Spring Breakers*.

into the moral framework by which we would like to define them. There is only one realism: the equal rejection of moral pessimism *and* optimism."[48]

"As near as possible, Clément maintains the integrity of childhood—its aloofness, its impenetrability, its silence, which, beheld from the outside, can appear sinister."[49] Clément shoots childhood from the outside, as it were, so that its contours become visible. The periphery reveals the truth of the center. Childhood in this film is not simply a victim of war, as would be the case in the conventional war and children's film. Instead, childhood offers a perspective adjacent to and competing with war. But in grounding the film in the alternative world of the children, another world—the world of the animals— remains hidden. The ambiguous enterprise of the animal cemetery— we suspect, along with Paulette, that Michel produces animal corpses in order to bury them—already rehearses the instrumentality that mars the use of animals in the adult world of farming, and in the world of film, including this film. The spectacle of animal vulnerability in the opening scene confirms the film's ambivalent commitment to the real in the staging of actual harm. What remains, I have tried to suggest, is the nervous twitch of the dog—and the film's own nervousness—a testimonial spasm, or reflex, that calls into question Clément's own forbidden games.

48. Bazin, "Jeux interdits," 134.
49. Matthews, "*Forbidden Games*: Death and the Maiden."

Contributors

Jean-Christophe Bailly teaches at l'École nationale supérieure de la nature et du paysage in Blois and is Professor of Philosophy at the European Graduate School in Saas-Fee, Switzerland. He is the author of *Le versant animal* (2007) as well as numerous books on art history, geography, and critical theory, including *Le dépaysement: Voyages en France* (2011), *La véridiction sur Philippe Lacoue-Labarthe* (2011), and *Description d'Olonne* (2010).

Bénédicte Boisseron is Associate Professor of French at the University of Montana. She is the co-editor of *Voix du monde: Nouvelles francophones* (2011) and the author of *Creole Renegades: Rhetoric of Betrayal and Guilt* (2014). She has published articles on, among others, Georges Bataille, Guillaume Dustan, Maryse Condé, and Dany Laferrière. Her current book project investigates the animal question within the context of the Black Diaspora of the Americas.

Florence Burgat is Director of Research in Philosophy at the French National Institute for Agricultural Research (INRA) and a member of the Archives Husserl de Paris (UMR 8547). She is the author of, among other works, *Animal, mon prochain* (1997), *Liberté et inquiétude de la vie animale* (2006), and *Une autre existence: La condition animale* (2012).

David L. Clark is Professor of English and Cultural Studies and Associate Member of the Health Studies Program at McMaster University. He has written extensively on contemporary theory, German idealism, post-Enlightenment philosophy, and British Romanticism. He is the author of *Bodies and Pleasures in Late Kant* (forthcoming) and edited a special issue of *The New Centennial Review* entitled "Animals . . . In Theory."

YFS 127, *"Animots": Postanimality in French Thought,* ed. Senior, Clark, and Freccero, © 2015 by Yale University.

VINCIANE DESPRET is Professor of Philosophy at the Université de Liège. She is the author of *Que diraient les animaux si on leur posait les bonnes questions?* (2012), *Penser comme un rat* (2009), *Bêtes et hommes* (2007), *Quand le loup habitera avec l'agneau* (2002), and *Naissance d'une théorie éthologique: La danse du cratérope écaillé* (1996).

ÉLISABETH DE FONTENAY is Professor of Philosophy Emerita at the Université de Paris I Panthéon-Sorbonne. She is the author of *Sans offenser le genre humain: Réflexions sur la cause animale* (2008), *Des hommes et des bêtes* (2000), *Le silence des bêtes : La philosophie à l'épreuve de l'animalité* (1998), *Diderot ou le matérialisme enchanté* (1981), and *Les figures juives de Marx: Marx dans l'idéologie allemande,* (1973).

CARLA FRECCERO is Chair and Professor of Literature and History of Consciousness, and Professor of Feminist Studies at the University of California, Santa Cruz. She is the author of *Queer/Early/Modern* (2006), *Popular Culture: An Introduction* (1999), *Father Figures: Genealogy and Narrative Structure in Rabelais* (1991); she is also the co-editor of *American Quarterly* 65/3 (2013), a special issue on *Species/Race/Sex*, and co-editor of *Premodern Sexualities* (1996).

YVONNE FRECCERO was born and raised in England, worked throughout Europe and the Middle East for the British Passport Control department before coming to the United States. She is the author of numerous translations, including René Girard's *Deceit, Desire, and the Novel* (1965), *The Scapegoat* (1986), and *Job: The Victim of His People* (1987) from French; and Gianpaolo Biasin's *The Smile of the Gods* from Italian. Her most recent translations include journal articles and the memoir of a Palestinian woman, *The Wind in My Hair.*

JEAN-LUC GUICHET is Professor of Philosophy at the Université de Picardie Jules Verne. He is the author of *La question sexuelle: Interrogations de la sexualité dans l'œuvre et la pensée de Rousseau* (2012), *Problématiques animales: Théorie de la connaissance, anthropologie, éthique et droit* (2011), *De l'animal-machine à l'âme des machines* (2010), *L'animal des Lumières* (a special edition of *Dix-huitième siècle,* 2010), *Douleur animale, douleur humaine* (2010), *Usages politiques de l'animalité* (2008), and *Rousseau, l'animal et l'homme: L'animalité dans l'horizon anthropologique des Lumières* (2006). He is also the author of a commentary on Condillac's *Traité des animaux* (2004).

SARAH KAY is Professor of French at New York University. She is the author of numerous works exploring the connections between medieval French and Occitan literature and antique and modern thought. Her most recent monographs are *Parrots and Nightingales: Troubadour Quotations and the Development of European Poetry* (2013) and *The Place of Thought: The Complexity of One in Medieval French Didactic Poetry* (2007). Her current work on medieval French and Latin bestiaries is supported by a Guggenheim Foundation Fellowship.

DONALD NICHOLSON-SMITH has translated many academic and literary texts from French, including work by Piaget, Wallon, Derrida, Lefebvre, Debord, Apollinaire, and Artaud. In 1972 he publised *The Language of Psychanalysis*, a translation of Laplanche and Pontalis's authoritative *Vocabulaire de la psychanalyse*. Recently he returned to both these authors by offering Pontalis's *Brother of the Above* (2012) and Laplanche's *The Temptation of Biology* (forthcoming in 2015). Born in Manchester, England, Nicholson-Smith is a longtime resident of Brooklyn, New York.

CATHERINE PORTER, 2009 President of the Modern Language Association, is Visiting Professor, Society for the Humanities, Cornell University, and Professor of French Emerita, State University of New York, Cortland. A free-lance translator in the humanities and the social sciences, she has translated numerous essays and more than three dozen books from the French, most recently Luc Boltanski, *The Foetal Condition*, and Anne Berger, *The Queer Turn in Feminism*. She received her doctorate in French literature from Yale University in 1972.

ANAT PICK is Senior Lecturer in Film at Queen Mary, University of London. She is the author of *Creaturely Poetics: Animality and Vulnerability in Literature and Film* (2011), and co-editor of *Screening Nature: Cinema Beyond the Human* (2013). In 2013–14, Pick co-curated a series of screenings on the relationship between flora, fauna, and artists' film at London's Whitechapel Gallery, Tate Modern, and the Goethe-Institute. She works at the intersection of continental philosophy and visual culture, and has published articles on Simone Weil, Giorgio Agamben, and ethical veganism.

MATTHEW SENIOR is Ruberta T. McCandless Professor of French at Oberlin College. He is the editor of *A Cultural History of Animals in the Age of Enlightenment* (2007), the co-editor of *Animal Acts: Configuring the Human in Western History* (1997), and the author of *In the Grip of Minos: Confessional Discourse in Dante, Corneille, and Racine* (1994).

Yᴜᴇ Zʜᴜᴏ is Assistant Professor of French at Yale University. She has published articles and book chapters on Georges Bataille, Maurice Blanchot, Roland Barthes, René Girard, and Pascal Quignard. She is currently finalizing a book manuscript entitled *La force du négatif: Georges Bataille et la question du sacré.*

Yale French Studies is the oldest English-language journal in the United States devoted to French and Francophone literature and culture. Each volume is conceived and organized by a guest editor or editors around a particular theme or author. Interdisciplinary approaches are particularly welcome, as are contributions from scholars and writers from around the world. Recent volumes have been devoted to a wide variety of subjects, among them: Levinas; Perec; Paulhan; Haiti; Belgium; Crime Fiction; Surrealism; Material Culture in Medieval and Renaissance France; and French Education.

Yale French Studies is published twice yearly by Yale University Press (yalebooks.com) and may be accessed on JSTOR (jstor.org).

For information on how to submit a proposal for a volume of *Yale French Studies*, visit yale.edu/french and click "Yale French Studies."